IN A WARRIOR'S QUIVER

REVISED EDITION
BOOK TWO

D. L. CRAGER

In a Warrior's Quiver

Trilogy Christian Publishers A Wholly Owned Subsidiary of Trinity Broadcasting Network

2442 Michelle Drive Tustin, CA 92780

Copyright © 2023 by D. L. Crager

No part of this book may be reproduced, stored in a retrieval system, or transmitted by any means without written permission from the author. All rights reserved. Printed in the USA.

Rights Department, 2442 Michelle Drive, Tustin, CA 92780.

Trilogy Christian Publishing/TBN and colophon are trademarks of Trinity Broadcasting Network.

Cover design by: Trilogy

For information about special discounts for bulk purchases, please contact Trilogy Christian Publishing.

10 9 8 7 6 5 4 3 2 1

Library of Congress Cataloging-in-Publication Data is available.

ISBN: 979-8-89041-228-7

E-ISBN: 979-8-89041-229-4

CHAPTER 1

Quickly walking through the palace to his final meeting before leaving Jerusalem, Shuriah's mind steadily went through the armory of resources for the extraordinary but highly secret mission ahead of him.

His personal and loyal guards, one on each side, who kept in military motion behind him, followed him to King Solomon's upper balcony. When they arrived at the entrance, two proud and stout guards were at attention, grasping long and strong gold-plated spears out to their sides. Their armor from head to toe was artistically gold-plated, having an angelic appearance (part of heaven's army itself), and was what all interior palace guards wore.

Shuriah stopped momentarily, staring at them as they stared back. All eyes were silently telling each other many things, and then the two guards simultaneously lowered their heads as they obediently knelt to the general of the Israel army and long-time personal bodyguard of their king.

Shuriah stated in a calm tone, proudly admiring his younger warriors, "Rise, mighty warriors. When I depart today, expectations will be lifted to new heights for you, the other mighty warriors, and the army of Israel I leave behind in my absence.

For you will have the responsibility to protect our king and the nation of Israel."

Shuriah lifted his hand, making a powerful fist, and beat his chest. "May the Lord of heaven's armies and His kingdom be held tightly to our hearts, and may His chosen people continue to reign with no other nation in sight."

The two guards stood tall, looking proudly at Israel's mighty general. They, too, pounded their chest armor twice. Their forearms were fitted all the way around with gold-plated, protective shielding that made strong, metallic sounds that echoed down the marble hallway from which the three warriors came. One guard stated boastfully, "We will always love, serve, and fight for our king and nation as we honor the Lord of heaven's armies with respect, obedience, and by His almighty strength.

"Shadowing the mightiest of all warriors, I present General Shuriah, who has demonstrated these things to all of the mighty warriors without an equal."

Shuriah, in a firm expression, gave a slight spark of a smile as he slowly nodded his head in gratitude for the comment. The guards stepped aside, allowing the three to enter the upper balcony room where King Solomon and other guards were waiting for their arrival and final meeting.

The men walked up to their king as he stood with his back to them on the outer section of the balcony looking out onto Jerusalem. Moving his head to one side where he had a direct and unobscured view of the great temple, where the presence of God was in the Ark of the Covenant, he heard their approach without looking back. "I will never stop being amazed at the fingerprints of God. His power and grandeur are as endless as His vision is limitless."

Solomon's mind and heart functioned with such depth that

everyone always needed a few moments to process what was spoken to understand him. Turning around to face the men, the sun was at such an angle, the reflection of his snow-white attire caused Shuriah and the other two mighty warriors to squint briefly. The golden crown adorned on the king's head had rubies and emeralds evenly patterned around the headpiece, but what caught everyone's attention was the detailed symbol of his mark. Centered at the forward-facing part of the crown that went up higher to a point was exquisite craftsmanship of a roaring lion with a large mane. But what was truly the focal point was the carved human eye held within the lion's teeth, appearing to be coming out with a large diamond in the place of the round center part of the eye.

With the sun shining brightly, the large diamond reflected intense rainbow-colored rays of light all over the place, looking as though the king's forehead was radiating holy knowledge to the men.

Shuriah and the two guards instantly dropped to their knees while lowering their heads and saying in unison, "We give praise to the Lord of heaven's armies and submit to the king of Israel."

Slowly and peacefully, the king instructed, "Rise, Shuriah. We have much to discuss."

The men stood, and the two younger warriors at his side kept their heads lowered as they walked respectfully backward from King Solomon and Shuriah to give them privacy. Once they were far enough away, Solomon began talking. "Shuriah, the mightiest of all warriors of Israel"—he paused to change his tone—"excluding my father, of course." Solomon smiled, giving out a quiet but confident laugh to lighten the atmosphere, and looked into his older friend's eyes.

Shuriah responded calmly with his aged smile, saying with a faint bow, to acknowledge King David, who had taught and trained the original mighty warriors of Israel, "Of course, my king, without question."

Solomon turned as they began to stroll around the outer part of the balcony looking over the city, and said, "I assume all is ready for your voyage?"

"Yes, twenty-five of our ships are being filled heavily with all the supplies we discussed for the unknown days of this journey as well as 10,000 soldiers. Twenty of King Hiram's strongest cargo ships will be filled with supplies, but we're leaving plenty of room to carry the load needed for the exchange of the precious cargo. Five thousand of his best workers will be ready by the time we arrive in Tyre in twelve days."

"Do you believe that is enough of our men?"

Answering proudly through his grand beard woven with colors of black, gray, and white that matched his full head of hair, Shuriah replied, "Along with the regular army, I will have two mighty warriors and their warrior sons on each ship...*including King Hiram's,* totaling ninety warriors, which means we can eliminate at least 27,000 that dare to cross our path."

Solomon wondered why Shuriah had changed his tone toward the other king. As he continued walking, he asked, "You do not trust King Hiram of Tyre?"

Shuriah answered, "Man is always tempted and weak. Dedication to conquer what is right takes the power of a strong heart and a submissive soul, which is strength beyond what man naturally strives for—fulfillment of the flesh and a pouch full of gold."

Solomon laughed softly, saying, "Spoken like a true warrior for the Lord of heaven's armies. You are definitely the right man for this quest." Stopping and turning to one another, the king put his hand on Shuriah's shoulder, adding, "I am going to miss these talks, my old friend. Before I was conceived in my mother's womb, you were protecting our kingdom and fighting for the Lord of heaven's armies alongside my father in your youth. Those must have been glorious days for you as a warrior's son—training under Uriah?"

Flashes of his childhood came to Shuriah when Uriah, one of the original thirty-seven mighty warriors under the command of a young King David, took him in as his own when he was nine, orphaned and scraggly, living on the outskirts of the city of Shechem.

Every mighty warrior was given special instructions for the future planning of military growth, strength, and longevity once they accomplished a highly-prized feat: killing three hundred or more enemies in one battle. They must adopt an older, Hebrew, orphaned child who was struggling and disconnected and then raise and mentor them as their own until they become of age to earn the title of "mighty warrior" themselves.

These boys would learn and train through the years to be respectful and honorable men after God's own heart. They would experience firsthand every battle at the side of his fathering mighty warrior, demonstrating in detail what it takes to fight and serve successfully under King David for Israel. As the process repeated itself over and over, it would grow a grand army of mighty warriors.

Shuriah answered, "My Lord, a day does not go by that I am not reminded of God's blessing when Uriah pulled me out of the shadows of the streets, starving with no one to call family, bringing me into his home to become who I am today—all because of your father and his excellence in military affairs and his relationship with the Lord of heaven's armies."

Responding confidently, Solomon said, "As I said when you walked in, God's vision is limitless. Submission to God is the beginning of our closed eyes opening to see the heavenly vision of his path for us. Until then, we are only blind, unable to see His eternal glory, which gives us the Lord's strength and power for him to conquer all giants in our own worldly plans and paths."

Shuriah gave him a friendly grin, pausing to absorb the wise words, and replied, "I, too, will miss these talks." Instead of disrespectfully putting his hand on the king's shoulder, he again bowed slightly his head, adding, "You always have a way of keeping me balanced and in my place with your words of wisdom. What will I do not having you there to keep me grounded and growing as an old man?"

Trying to sound serious, Solomon answered, "Your wife, Talia, and her servants have already had that talk with me as they join you on this journey."

Shuriah, amused at his quick wit, laughed loudly as his armor and older body (still strong and muscular) jostled up and down.

Solomon smiled back, glad his friend was entertained, and then gazed past him to a servant who had been waiting in the shaded part of the balcony. He was holding a silk, square pillow with fancy trim dangling all around it. Seeing the king's eyes, the servant walked up to the side of the men, bowing low while holding the fancy pillow high with something small but heavy, creating a depression in the center.

King Solomon picked up the solid, gold object, holding it between his forefinger and thumb, facing Shuriah. Once the servant left and was a good distance away with the others in the far room, he said, "The true answer is this."

Seeing what was held out to him, the only thing Shuriah could do was shake his head in bewilderment. Moving his eyes up to the kings, he adorned an appreciative expression, saying, "It is no wonder why the nations of the world open their treasures, freely pouring them out to you. You have the answers and solutions to all things before they are thought of or asked for. Obviously, your heavenly eyes are wide open."

"I am pleased our hearts beat in rhythm as friends with leadership and faith in the Lord of heaven's armies. It is a rare commodity, General Shuriah, mighty warrior of Israel." He paused, looking at what he was holding, and then requested, "Your hand."

Raising his hand up, Solomon slid on a large, golden ring on his ring finger. The crown of the ring was round and wide, covering the ring finger and half of both fingers on either side. Shuriah brought it close to see the distinct and honored, raised design on top as a feeling of weakness, very rarely felt in him, began to flow through his strong, confident, and experienced body; he stared at the intimidating symbol. Before he completed his thought, his friend and king said, "I *own* the weight and responsibility of everything the symbol on that ring represents and stands for—*not* you, Shuriah! You only have to carry the weight of the gold the ring is made of."

Shuriah looked up, grateful for the encouraging words, as the foreign sensation quickly dissipated. Peering back down at the face of the ring, he saw the raised formation of a roaring lion with a human eye coming out of its mouth between its jaws. It was exactly what was on Solomon's crown, minus the diamond in the eye.

The lion represented Solomon, the most powerful king the world had ever known. The eye represented Solomon's wisdom, the wisest man the world had ever known; he was able to see all things clearly. Combined, there was no equal in all humanity that could come close to his earthly greatness.

With confidence, Solomon stated, "The one that wears this ring will always have my power and authority with them—through time and throughout the world until God is ready to deliver the knowledge you found over a year ago, which He has hidden for so long in our great ancestors' ark.

"It was not by accident you found it, for God always directs our paths even when we are shipwrecked and chased by our enemies." They both found humor in the statement because a year earlier, Shuriah was shipwrecked off the coast of the Hittite kingdom in a storm on the Mediterranean Sea. Then he was chased for weeks by the Hittite army, which resulted in the hardest battle Shuriah was ever confronted with. He chose wisely to keep running from this enemy because he was way undermanned, and most of their weapons were lost in the shipwreck. A profound voice in his head was constantly telling him to run. This went against all laws of his fierce warrior nature.

Solomon continued as Shuriah listened patiently. "The path God is leading us on is one with no map. I trust you more than anyone on earth, Shuriah. With full confidence, I know you will be obedient to the Lord of heaven's armies in securing and establishing a new secret home for Noah's Ark far away—for now and into the unknown future.

"I foresee that we may never see each other again for the journey you are about to embark"—Solomon hesitated and nodded, knowing the grand difficulty ahead of his general—"is one of epic proportions with no equal. Only with God-sized strength, knowledge, and blessings will we be able to accomplish that which He alone has instructed us to do.

"Live passionately with every breath you take, Shuriah, as if it is your last. Give your all now so the Lord can bless you through eternity." Changing his tone and matching his focused facial expression, he added, "Whatever you need to do to keep this mission and Noah's Ark a secret, preserving it for the timing of the Lord our God, my authority and power will always be with you as long as you wear my signature ring. Do what you must to protect the knowledge within the ark and the ark itself, which I know"—again, he nodded for understanding—"will be difficult, especially if situations arise within our own people. But"—Solomon eyed Shuriah intently to get a nonverbal point across—"what must be done...must be done!"

Shuriah grasped tightly to the handle of the battle knife on his belt, completely understanding what his king was telling him, and replied with a hardened smile, "Until my death, I will obey these orders, passing them on to the next guardian if that time ever comes."

Solomon said, "Israel and its king are bountifully blessed because of who you are and what you have done for us, especially now as you become"—he emphasized the next couple of words—"the Guardian of the world's greatest secrets." He took a deep breath, knowing he needed to cover many things in this short and vital meeting while balancing their emotions and thought process. "Remember what I have always said, 'God does not need our help in protecting and growing His kingdom but enjoys our company as we join Him on His path.'"

Solomon paused, adoring the thought as a chuckle came out and said, "I am convinced our Lord has a deep sense of humor. I see him laughing as only an Abba can at His children fumbling along this path of His."

Shuriah always appreciated his king for having a way to soften the atmosphere to encourage everyone. Appearing as though he wanted to speak, Solomon nodded for him to talk so Shuriah responded, "My Lord, I have been blessed to have had two kings in my life—your father and you. Two men of the same bloodline, yet two men completely different. One having conquered by his fearless courage and strength, the other by his unfathomable wisdom and diplomacy. Yet both did so walking with Abba on His path. With that said, I have learned and experienced that everyone is on a different path with the Lord of heaven's armies. And we must stay on God's chosen path even when we stumble or else..." He shrugged his shoulders with a final statement-ending grin.

Waiting for the finishing comment, Solomon cocked his head and repeated, "Or else?"

The older man looked at his king, realizing he had stumped him. He tiptoed with his next words so as not to disgrace him and answered with a friendly smile, "Or else, you might as well be a Gentile."

Solomon was quick to laugh at the joke as he first thought Shuriah was going to have a deep, theological, and inspiring explanation. Having walked to the far side of the large balcony, they arrived at the outside lounging area. Servants were waiting, holding long and broad wicker fans that provided shade and a cool breeze. The two most powerful men of Israel and all the surrounding nations sat down comfortably among a large assortment of pillows surrounding a short marble table. As they lay down resting on their sides across from each other, servants arrived, bringing bowls of fruit and other delicacies along with gold-plated, wine-filled goblets decorated with precious stones.

Taking up a handful of dates, Solomon put one in his mouth, chewed for a moment, and continued with the purpose of the meeting at hand. "As you know, the Queen of Sheba has sworn an oath to me that she and her people will assist in this impossible task that God has presented to His chosen people. He has blessed us with this special relationship with the queen from the south, knowing in advance she would be of much use to us. The timing of her appearance to me is of heavenly preparation."

The king adjusted his position, taking a drink of wine, and then added, "She believes there is a place in her kingdom she has heard about that could hide this massive secret that God has unexpectedly put in our care." He paused, making a transition in thought, and asked, "Moving it will be a challenge; would you agree?"

Shuriah reflected back again to over a year ago when he first realized what he and a handful of his men, barely escaping from a large Hittite army, found within snow and ice up on a steep and high mountain in the far, northern region of Hatti. Over the ages, Noah's Ark had been buried, mummified, and perfectly preserved, showing very little signs of aging. Seeing the massive, wooden structure in his mind buried in the cold elements on a mountain that man had no reason for which to be, he answered, "As I have said before, by only the strength of God working through us will this undertaking come to completion."

Solomon said, "I do agree, but what I anticipate being the most difficult thing in this whole quest is time."

Shuriah pondered what the king said, thinking it through as Solomon finished his thought. "You said in our last meeting that you expect it to take approximately two years to take apart Noah's ship and assemble the decoy of one of Hiram's large cargo ships in its place. You accounted for the time to transport both ships in pieces, carried across the land of the Hittites once we conquer them if needed."

"Yes," Shuriah answered assertively.

"Queen of Sheba has stated this same time frame of two years for her scouts to find this perfectly isolated destination deep in the southwestern part of her kingdom and for her army to travel north, passing through Israel to inform me of this secret location. At that point, I will send them on their way to you with fresh supplies on our ships in Hatti with the instructions of where you will go with the new cargo.

"From the queen's limited knowledge, she believes this part

of her kingdom where her scouts are going fits my criteria for a permanent, secret home for the ark. We will then be able to live with it, protecting it for as long as God needs us to. She is told the vegetation is very thick and heavily forested, which means it will be extremely difficult to travel through."

Shuriah added, "During our meetings with the queen, she did say her advisors know that very few people live in this 'special area.' And the ones that do are dark-skinned and often unusually short—the size of children." He lifted his hand up to the height of his chest.

The king's facial expression went stone-cold, looking deeply concerned, and said, "Yes, she did say that, and this troubles me. I am afraid that our mighty warriors will have difficulty if we have to go to war with them."

Completely taken aback by the gravity of Solomon's demeanor, Shuriah hesitated to comment. It made no sense, but he knew Solomon's wisdom went deeper and broader than anyone's. He thought maybe Solomon saw something he did not. Then the king could not hold it in any longer as he broke a smile saying, "You should see your face, General."

Shuriah shook his head, surprised that such a grand king could have such a great sense of humor, and replied with a grin, "I am not sure if your father would be angry, saddened, concerned, jealous, or proud of you toiling with creative humor from the throne all the time, especially in moments as serious as this." Reaching out to grasp his goblet of wine, he held it high, giving the king a kind salute. "Thank you for continuously softening my armored mind and heart. Again, I will miss this."

Taking a quick drink and then setting down the goblet, the general said, "But to correct myself, I *do* know how your father would comment if he was here with us now. He would wrap up these emotions in one sentence that he frequently repeated to help himself more times than not: 'There is no other time than 'in the moment' to express what your heart feels. For tomorrow, you may have a sword through it, screaming out in pain as you die.'"

They both laughed. Solomon rose his goblet, which he so rarely did to anyone, and said, "Old friend, you make it easy to express my heart, for you are my consistent reminder of where I came from and who I am beyond the crown: just a normal man that has made as many mistakes as his own father."

For a spilt second, the comment struck Shuriah painfully to his very core, but he did not admit it bothered him. For Solomon's father, King David, had made a severe mistake, which forever scarred Shuriah deeply when he was fifteen years old. He had masterfully covered up the pain, hiding it within his soul where no one would know it ever existed—especially since that very day, he became the youngest mighty warrior Israel had ever known, continuing to faithfully serve the very king until his death.

Then to have become King Solomon's personal bodyguard, eventually the general of all Israel's army, never did he allow the embedded pain to surface and affect him mentally, emotionally, or physically with any relationships, duties, or obedience to God or the kings of Israel.

Acknowledging the compliment with a nod of his head but keeping buried what was hidden inside of him, Shuriah replied, "Getting back to these child-sized people, at first I thought she was making things up."

Solomon concurred, "It did sound peculiar, but I could see her heart clearly. She was telling the truth."

Shuriah answered, chuckling, "It is so appropriately centered in your signature symbol: the all-seeing eye." He glanced up to the king's crown, gave a stout smile, and added, "It gives me great peace and confidence that the leader of our kingdom has such a gift."

Remaining humble, Solomon went on, "She anticipates it will take the same amount of time. Two years for her scouts to find this perfect, secret place, to figure out a safe traveling route to get there, and then to travel back to her with the exact location. After that, the queen will send a small army dedicating their allegiance to Israel to meet me here. Then I will send them to you at the southern shores of Hatti with the vital instructions."

Shuriah finished chewing a few grapes and replied, "So much has to happen in a timely manner; everyone involved is traveling great distances. You are accurate when you say time will be an issue."

"Yes, that too, but I am not talking about the timing of the immediate part of this epic journey. The time I am talking about is the period in which we or the generations after us will wait upon the Lord after the traveling is all done and Noah's Ark is secure in its new home. Will it be only a few years, fifty, or hundreds of years after the two years of toil moving the ancient ship?"

Shuriah took a drink of wine and then set it down on the short table. He rested back, intrigued again with the king's thoughts, and Solomon continued, "The first years of labor, toil, sailing, and possibly engaging in battles here and there are years with a plan we can envision and understand. It is the time after these years I am talking about. Years of unknown waiting upon the Lord of heaven's armies for new plans that man cannot anticipate or foresee.

"I have pondered, my friend, on what to do, expecting that the wait could be years past our grandchildren's grandchildren when you and I are long dead. Like when Israel waited upon the Lord in the past—sometimes it has taken up to four hundred years as it was with Moses when he finally brought our people out of Egypt. With that type of timeframe in mind, I want to be wise in how we serve the Lord to the best of our abilities."

Solomon sat up straight, lifting his hand to get all the servants' attention. Then he waved them away. Once they were gone, the two men sat alone now in the sunlight on the balcony in the late morning hours. Shuriah understood the king was getting serious, so he sat up as well, giving him his undivided attention. Solomon paused in thought and then spoke quietly but directly. "Shuriah, you personally experienced what my father went through with his children attempting to take his throne. This misfortune, I am afraid, is not as uncommon as one might think. I, too, see signs of self-indulgent tendencies among my own children, and I foresee them not harming me in their attempts for power, but what they will do to the kingdom of Israel once one of them takes the throne after my passing…

"The Lord, as you know, has blessed me with a gift known throughout the nations. This precious gift has filled Israel's treasuries beyond one's imagination. You even touched on this subject moments ago. And it keeps growing daily exponentially with no end in sight until my demise. Yet I am only a mortal man, and many times I have fallen short of God's glory with my own sins." Pausing to simplify his thoughts, he continued, "But with the knowledge and wisdom I have concerning power, control, and most of all the wealth I have acquired, I am afraid no man who had what I have could keep himself focused on God while keeping his sanity and not destroying this nation.

"So, I have decided once you have settled Noah's Ark into this new, secret place far, far from here that no one will know about…" Solomon tilted his head down, giving him a determined look through firm eyes. "You and I will make sure of that! After such a time, I will secretly send you portions of my treasury to hide until it is the size of what a normal kingdom should have. This will keep the colossal abundance out of the hands of my weak sons who will take my place for they could do extreme damage and great injustice to other nations and even our own people without the phenomenal gift of wisdom God has given me."

Shuriah's head strained back as his face flushed at such a thought. Then his eyes went blank with many unfavorable visions coming to mind. Appearing for a moment to be panic-stricken, Solomon said, "Shuriah, mighty warrior of Israel, reach into your pocket for what I know you carry with you at all times that my father gave you."

Taking a couple of breaths to refocus, the older, burly man reached into a pocket of his armor made specifically for the object the king was talking about and pulled it out.

"Lift it up and tell me what it represents."

Looking at what he was holding (a plain, smooth, round stone the length of a small finger), Shuriah blinked, pushing back the painful memory of when he acquired it. He looked to King Solomon and replied, "This stone that your father killed Goliath with represents the power of God—small enough for a man to carry in the palm of his hand but powerful enough to conquer any giant this world offers…man, mountain, or circumstance."

Solomon nodded in agreement and said, "This 'giant' I know you can see. Having the responsibility of much of the world's wealth is something *God* can handle. Lift up your other hand."

Shuriah lifted his other hand with the large, gold signature ring on it.

"As I stated earlier, the power I have will be with you now and through time, no matter who is wearing the ring. This has been prophesied to me by God. Your responsibility is to be faithful to these powers, not to the magnificent items hidden away.

As long as this is maintained obediently, there will be no end to the success of this journey you and the others accompanying you will be on."

Switching back to a relaxed position and drinking a little more wine, Solomon added, "Noah's Ark is and will always be the reason for and priority of this undisclosed mission. However, let my treasures be the focus while the ark fades away out of sight and memory to the point that no one knows of its existence."

Having lowered both weathered, battle-scarred hands, Shuriah looked down at the stone and ring. After taking a moment, he looked up at the king.

"You stated *do what I must to protect the knowledge within the ark and the ark itself.* I shall protect your treasury equally even though at times it will be difficult, especially if situations arise within our own people, as you stated." This time, Shuriah was the one to bow his head with a stern, almost devilish look and say while grasping the handle of his battle knife again, "What must be done…must be done! Am I right, my king?"

Slowly grinning and giving Shuriah complete authority to do what he needed to do to conquer all the giants before him, he said confidently, "The ark and my treasury are definitely in good hands. I cannot wait to hear the news of your journey's end, my friend."

Days later, Shuriah arrived at Joppa, the seaport for Israel on the Mediterranean Sea. Ten thousand handpicked soldiers and ninety mighty warriors awaited his arrival, and twenty-five ships were stocked with seemingly endless supplies of food, tools, building supplies, gold and silver for trading, and a massive armory.

At the high point of the seaport city, looking out onto the bay securely holding the ships, Shuriah, the captains of each ship, and the ninety mighty warriors stood peering not only at their transportation but what would also be their homes for an undisclosed amount of time.

Shuriah was standing in the middle of everyone, facing the same direction towards the calm bay of blue water. The water reflected a soothing, cloudless, blue sky that gave the ships the appearance of being able to endlessly float on both the water and the sky at the same time.

The morning sun was at their backs as the men stood silently with anticipation and wonder about an adventure that no one completely understood. Only Shuriah knew its mission, destination, and when they were to return to their homeland, if ever.

He stepped out in front of everyone, turned around, and raised his left hand high in such a way that the men could see King Solomon's signature ring on his finger. Instantly, the warriors and captains kneeled on one knee.

He paused as everyone's heads slowly raised, waiting for him to say something, but he stood motionless. Then, to everyone's surprise, he kneeled to their level while he kept his hand held high, shouting out, "We all kneel to our king equally. I am his servant to my death as you are my servants to your death. I claim no equality to our king even though I wear his signature ring. The weight of his power and authority no other man can bear to carry. Even I am not worthy and do not have the human strength to be obedient with the power our king gave me while I wear it. Only for the weight of its gold do I have the strength to carry."

He paused while rising to his feet, not giving the signal for the others to rise yet. He lifted his closed right hand high as he lowered his left, ring-bearing hand. The men looked up curiously as he opened it, exposing what he was holding.

Shuriah contemplated every face, and after a few moments, he continued, "The only way I, a mere man, will be able to control myself to never abuse the authority and power the king's signature ring holds is by focusing all my attention and faith in what this small and simple stone represents.

"Many of my warriors know I carry this with me at all times. For those who do not know about this special but ordinary-looking stone—" He paused, bringing his hand down, and holding the stone out between his fingers so everyone could see. "It is the stone young David used to kill Goliath, the Philistine giant."

Heads turned to one another as murmuring rippled through the crowd at such a small but powerful weapon that had changed history.

Holding it out to them as they continued kneeling, Shuriah said, "This is made by the hands of God. It is harmless in nature just like a child. But when we honor God fearlessly and our faith is fully given to Him to fight our battles, even a child can kill giants with only a simple, smooth stone. God moves in majestic and mysterious ways, and it's through our faith in God and obedience to Him that we can boldly move forward without fear. This is when God's limitless strength and power appears in our lives."

Shuriah grasped his sword strapped to his back over his shoulder and held it up, saying, "This sword is made by man for the purpose of killing. Its power and abilities are only as strong as the man who trains to use it. When a man dies, so does his strength, rendering the weapon useless. So, tell me" He paused to make sure the men were clearly understanding what he was telling them and asked, "What are the limits of this as a man holds it?"

An eager captain who stood without being given permission believed he had the simple answer and boldly stated, "The sword is always limited to how well the man sharpens it and how strong the man is."

Before he took his next breath, the captain suddenly found himself flat on his back with the air knocked out of him. Gasping for air with eyes blinking rapidly, he looked around to see what had happened.

A mighty warrior (still kneeling obediently) had stretched his head over to him, inches from his face, with a menacing look. The highly trained killer had swiped the captain's feet out from under him because of his ignorance and disobedience. The warrior paused, letting everyone hear the captain moan in pain, and then respectfully asked without moving a muscle, "General?"

Proudly, Shuriah acknowledged, "Proceed, warrior."

Keeping his tone to a low shout and staying focused on the man's eyes, he stated, "Always be aware. You were not given permission to stand. Always be wise. Your answer was that of a dead man's heart—useless."

The warrior hesitated as everyone, especially all the other captains, listened intently. Then he slowly rotated his body, still kneeling to Shuriah, as he withdrew his knife that had been pressed to the captain's throat—something no one had seen until he slid it back into his belt.

The general, staring deeply and firmly into the captains' scared eyes, shouted out for the correct answer, "Mighty warriors!"

In unison, they shouted back, intimidating all the ship captains, knowing the prized answer imprinted deep within them. "Man has no limits of his mind or might when his heart and soul are filled with heavenly expectations and the glory of God!"

The captain who wrongfully spoke gradually recovered, getting back up to his knees but, embarrassed, did not raise his head or eyes.

Shuriah, having been influenced by Solomon's lead, used the king's wisdom on communication and human relations to build and rebuild a man. He promptly said to the other captains, "This captain has done you all a favor, so be grateful to him; do not scorn him. With his quick and unwise tongue, he may have saved our lives.

"He has brought awareness"—Shuriah nodded with gratitude to the disciplinary warrior who had put the captain in his place before looking back to the others—"to you for how we honor and respect those above us. Not only for me and our king but ultimately, the Lord of heaven's armies.

"He has also shared his human ignorance about wisdom for which"—his aggression built with every word as he shifted his demeanor—"no Israelite has an excuse!

"I will not allow one thought or breath of man's weakness to accompany me on this journey of all journeys! Only God's glory and the mindset on heavenly expectations will be on the tongues and hearts of every man and woman as we serve the Lord of heaven's armies!"

The mighty warriors again belted in unison, but this time with encouraging battle cries as, one by one, the ship captains fearfully followed suit.

The large group of leaders soon filtered their way down to their ships after Shuriah gave his inspirational and directive speech. His ship led the way into the open sea as many crew members blew long and loud blasts from rams' horns as the other twenty-four seafaring ships joined in the boastful commencement of a journey with no end in sight.

CHAPTER 2

Heading northward on the Mediterranean Sea following the coastline, Shuriah's fleet was joined days later by King Hiram's twenty stout ships built more for carrying large loads than for speed or warfare like the ones the Israelites were sailing. Shuriah anchored momentarily at a port in Tyre, a city in Lebanon, to have a cordial conversation and deliver a sizeable load of treasure, a gift for King Hiram's efforts and loyalty to its ally Israel and King Solomon. In addition, he paid in full for the twenty ships and the 5,000 ship builders, laborers, and sailors who were never expecting to return.

King Hiram attempted again (as he had many times before) to draw out information about why his ships and men were on this voyage. For all other voyages, he knew the exact whereabouts of both his ships and his men. But again, Shuriah's answer was, "This time, you must trust King Solomon and have full faith in the God of Israel. We are on an epic mission that must remain anonymous until the Lord of heaven's armies is ready to show the world."

Still, King Hiram persisted, "General Shuriah, I will learn to be satisfied not knowing anything about your venture, but tell me this: why did you have us make an extraordinarily large ship but not assemble it and load all the pieces onto my, or I should say *your*, ships as cargo?"

Shuriah only looked at him, shaking his head.

The king smiled, hoping he had not offended Shuriah, and replied, "You cannot blame me for asking. It is by far the strangest request your king has asked of me since he took over for his father, King David."

Shuriah nodded, acknowledging the apology, and said, "For now, King Hiram, be content that the God of Israel is pleased with you and your people, for He has chosen you, above anyone else, to accompany Israel on a journey no man has ever attempted since the beginning of time."

With the sun low on the horizon, the forty-five ships spread out on the Mediterranean Sea, heading north-northwest in what appeared to be a formation resembling a soaring eagle gliding on the dark, blue water. The sea was fairly calm, accompanied by a steady breeze that filled the sails of every ship as though the breath of God was giving its blessing to the voyage.

Shuriah's ship was centered within the fleet, while the rest of Israel's ships took the outer perimeter, surrounding the acquired fleet from Tyre. They were ready and prepared for any military action that may present itself.

Standing at the front of his ship, Shuriah watched the grand charge of boats pressing forward and slicing through the sea, sending showers of water outward from their pointed bows. His mind began to drift to his conversation with King Solomon: the words "epic journey" the king had used to describe this quest kept repeating themselves over and over. Then, he thought about the "unforeseen amount of time" Solomon had mentioned when explaining the four hundred years God took before He had Moses bring the Israelites out of slavery in Egypt.

Taking a deep breath, trying not to allow his mind to wander or his emotions to get involved, he reached into his special pocket, where he kept David's stone. Pulling it out, he slowly rubbed the sides, feeling its texture as he often did. Out of character, he looked down at it and talked quietly to it, saying, "It only took a little rock like you, thrown by a shepherd boy with a sling, to bring down a giant and the whole Philistine army."

Pondering the thought, he looked up to the sky, whispering into the distance,

"Lord of heaven's armies, I cringe inside every time I see the man's face in my head who was once an innocent boy that picked this rock up and slayed Goliath. Forgive me, Lord, for I know…David was an anointed king whom you chose. I am asking, please, anoint me right now, for I believe you have chosen me for this epic journey. Help me to be like the boy David, innocent and childlike in mind and at heart—without concern for his own safety or self-fulfillment but fully trusting the power of God to be his strength and shield through all trials and battles.

"I am a warrior trained to fight and kill. You had Uriah choose me to be a mighty warrior for Israel. Now I am assigned to be a prophet, priest, judge, counsel official, ship builder, carpenter, farmer, sailor, and explorer, with the king's authority having to perform these all at once throughout this epic journey. Direct my path as I walk within yours. Strengthen my wisdom and might so I do not fail you or my King."

Later that evening, when the moon rose, glimmering off the water and casting shadows from ship to ship, Shuriah went to his private sleeping quarters with his wife and fell fast asleep. He was restless at first as many things slithered though his dreams, not making any sense. Then, it went still as he suddenly saw himself as a young boy.

In his mind's eye, he was a dirty, skinny boy, about nine years old, wearing torn, ragged clothes and sandals. He lived homeless outside a city called Shechem at the base of two mountains: Mt. Gerizim and Mt. Ebal, north of Jerusalem, where no one cared for him.

His mother had purposely abandoned him there in the marketplace years earlier. It was a far distance from their small, poor town, and she was hoping someone would feel sorry for him and take him in as their own.

His father had gotten sick and died when he was about two. After that, his mother could barely feed them both. Any close family members helped as much as they could, but it wasn't enough since they were all poor themselves, barely surviving. Hearing from God to go to a distant, larger city where no one knew them, his mother left him alone in the busy marketplace, praying someone would take him in as their own son.

Here and there, he was taken into homes with hopes of being part of a family, only to be abused as an enslaved child. Forced to work and do other things far beyond his abilities at his young age, this always led him to run away and hide on the outskirts of the city, realizing he could not trust anyone but himself.

He stayed alive, avoiding harm and living alone on the mountainsides, watching out for any danger below during the day. He learned he could sneak into the city in the shadows of the night to steal food, clothing, and other things to survive.

One evening, as the sun was beginning to hide itself on the other side of the world, the boy watched a group of about forty extraordinary soldiers walking in unison down the dirt road at the foot of the mountains toward Shechem. A few rode horses in the front, but the majority walked behind them, with a couple of carts pulled by horses bringing up the rear. They all wore splendid but very battle-worn armor and carried different weapons: swords, long spears, and/or bows with arrows in quivers strapped over their strong but tired shoulders. Some of the men were bandaged from injuries on their arms, legs, head, abdomen…all over.

Hidden and watching with curiosity from above, the boy had never seen such a strong and intimidating force move along in silence, completely aware and unafraid of their surroundings. Looking closer, something odd caught the homeless boy's attention among the brawny group of warriors.

Between each soldier, there was a short, miniature-looking soldier who looked like his predecessor's shadow, imitating his every move.

Soon the boy was overwhelmed with curiosity, not by what he was seeing but by what he was feeling as he watched the group head to the city from which he stole or found food on a nightly basis. There was no fear emanating from them as they marched, flowing like one massive body. They were all pressing forward in confidence he had never seen before; even the wounded and the "shadows" were not showing signs of pain or holding up their fellow warriors.

As they walked past formidably, getting closer to the entrance of the large town, the destitute boy was drawn to follow them. Though faint rays of evening sunlight reached out onto the landscape, grasping to keep the day alive, he took the chance of being exposed.

Upon seeing the impressive armor and weapons they had with them, the boy's interest was piqued by what filled their carts. His stomach longed for it to be food, thinking he should be able to get his hands on something if they set up camp near or within the city for the night.

Keeping his distance while peering from behind rocks and

bushes as he sidled from one to another, excitement rose once they went in the city and the soldiers began setting up tents in the streets. Fires started here and there, bringing a glow between buildings as townspeople began coming out into the late evening to see what was going on—only to leave quickly and come back, supplying the tired warriors with food and drink. He couldn't help thinking to himself, *Why won't they treat me that way? I live in caves with nothing. And yet, these men show up from nowhere having everything they need. This is not fair. I am always starving, and I have to steal just to stay alive. They show up out of nowhere, and the townspeople give freely to fill their stomachs. I can't remember the last time I had a full stomach.* Just then, his stomach growled as though acknowledging his words.

The boy watched the whole scene carefully through the light of the night as more food kept coming in from everywhere. The town elder stood in the center of all the commotion, ordering entertainment for the evening while the tired and tattered men ate and were served precious wine.

The younger unmarried women came out in fancy clothes to dance for the men as the townsmen brought instruments and began to play music to entertain the soldiers. Suddenly, one of the soldiers, who looked much more distinguished than the others, got up and asked one of the men playing a harp if he could play it.

The boy drew in closer with all the excitement and was now watching from a short distance in the dark, kneeling behind a small wall in a pile of straw next to a stable within the city walls. Though unable to hear the conversation between the men, he was able to hear the incredible sounds coming from the harp when the handsome soldier passionately started to play. Everyone stopped to listen. The troops and townspeople alike listened intently to the soldier's beautiful music and incredible singing, telling a sensitive story.

When he finished his song, he declared, "Praise to the Lord of heaven's armies for the people of Shechem and their blessings of food, wine, and entertainment for the mighty warriors of Israel!"

All the soldiers instantly went to one knee, first bowing to the man who just sang and then standing to shout with pride, raising their cups of wine. "Praise the Lord of heaven's armies for the people of Shechem!"

The town's elder quickly stepped up to the soldier who had sung and gave thanks, dropping to both his knees in the dirt and bowing low to the ground.

The soldier looked down at the man kneeling, glanced to the other soldiers' faces reflected in the firelight, and silently gave them a message. The soldier said softly, "Stand up." But the man did not move. He repeated himself, commanding, "Stand up!"

The town elder slowly raised his head, saying with a jittery voice loudly enough for all to hear, "I did not know you were with your soldiers when you came into our city. Your men only identified themselves as the mighty warriors of Israel."

The boy continued to observe, still hidden in the dark, far enough away that he was not able to hear the conversation. So he decided to move closer to get a better look at these powerful men and what might be in their carts. When he moved, he kept his eyes keenly focused on the activity, not realizing someone had soundlessly stepped next to him where he was hiding. The orphaned boy suddenly bumped into a sturdy, hairy leg of one of the warriors who stealthily kept watch over his fellow soldiers.

Stunned, the boy looked up to see what stopped him, felt jolted off the ground with powerful arms, and found himself face-to-face with a man—a man who could kill him.

The elder, still kneeling in front of the melodious soldier, shuddered for a moment, not sure if he should say anything else after seeing the reaction of the other soldiers. Looking up into his eyes, he understood that this soldier wanted him to say what was on his mind. The town elder blinked a couple of times and gaped at his people who were unsure what was going on and said, bowing his head again, "Many years ago, I heard you when you were a boy, playing the harp for King Saul and singing him the same song."

Instantly, when the townspeople realized who their elder was talking about, everyone went to their knees as well.

As it went silent, all the soldiers relaxed, understanding that the townspeople did not set them up but were honestly scared to death of their presence. They proceed to sit back down and continue eating.

Still bowing, the kneeling man asked, "My king, why did you not send messengers ahead before your arrival? We would have set you up in the best accommodation we have and held a formal celebration of your presence in our city."

King David held out his hand to help lift up the older man and answered, "Because of exactly what you said you would do. We do not want any special attention taken away from the Lord of heaven's armies. He alone has given His army and mighty warriors a victory in battle against the Arameans from Damascus up north. Additionally, this group of men are special warriors who take very good care of their king, who must blend in for his own safety and protection." King David looked sternly into the older man's eyes, letting him know he, in fact, gave his identity away, which put him in harm's way. This could prove problematic as they made their way secretly back to Jerusalem while most of the Israelite army took a more direct route to Jerusalem on the other side of the Jordan River.

The man stood respectfully, lowering his head, saying, "My life is for you to take; do with it as you please."

King David reached out, lifted the shorter elder's head by his chin, and replied with a smile as the firelight flickered on their faces, "Your life is God's and not mine to take. I am a servant of His as you are to me. Go tell your people the soldiers of Israel thank them for their generosity of food, wine, and entertainment."

The elder smiled with several teeth missing, giving the king a grateful acknowledgment. "I will, and please let me know if there is anything else you need...soldier," he said, careful not to reveal King David's identify any more than he already had.

Just then, another soldier who was taller with more prominent muscles (although not as handsome as the king) came walking up to the two men holding a ragged, skinny boy by what little clothing was covering his shoulder. He said to King David with a smirk, "Look what I found outside of camp strategically coming in under the cover of darkness to ambush us."

Already scared, with wide eyes looking back and forth among the three men, the boy was suddenly horrified at what he was being accused of. He had been in trouble before but never with broad, strong men carrying weapons that still had dried blood on them.

The town elder looked at the young one, knowing exactly who he was. Embarrassed, he seized the frightened boy by the hair, pulling him out of the soldier's grasp, and interjected, "Sorry, this one will not bother you, men." He shoved the boy to the ground away from the soldiers and then kicked him in the rear as a signal to run away. "He is a city rat that sneaks around in the night, stealing food and whatever he can get from those who work hard for what they have."

On the ground with skinned knees, the boy looked at the men behind him, not sure what he should do, as fear gripped him. The soldier who had played the harp had a kind expression behind his magnificent black beard as his eyes met the boy's, confusing him. Then he kneeled on one knee to be at eye level, asking the town elder, "Does he not have parents and a home?"

"His mother abandoned him in our city years ago. People have taken him in, but he always runs away. So now he lives outside the city like a rat in a hole, robbing honest people." The old man kicked the ground, spraying dirt into the boy's face, roaring, "Get out here! You're embarrassing, Shechem!" He looked to King David, still kneeling, and added sarcastically,

"He probably came in to steal from you, most honorable soldiers. I apologize on behalf of our city." He then gave the king a slight bow as though asking for forgiveness.

As the boy wiped the kicked dirt from his eyes and tried to reverse his tongue-tie, the king asked him directly, "Boy, why would you run away when people took you into their homes to share what they have with you?"

Now trembling, the young one glanced up to the town elder. "No," the kneeling soldier corrected. "Look at me and answer from your heart." Not to scare the boy but to emphasize his request, he slowly reached out to touch his chest. The boy's wild eyes followed the warrior's finger until it gently pressed up against his bony frame. When his body was touched gently only with the tip of a finger, a surprising and swift feeling pierced him to his core, vanishing all fear he had.

Infant memories of his mother and father flashed through his young mind, rushing down to his heart as the gentle touch from the powerful man reminded him of when his mother and father would gently care for him.

He looked back up, surprised by the breathtaking moment, to see the kind and brazen soldier. Relaxing from the soldier's demeanor, the boy turned completely to him, sitting on the ground, and said, "I was made to work like a grown man and was never treated as family. They would"—his eyes quickly glanced at the town elder, knowing he was about to shame the city—"beat me all the time." He had subconsciously leaned toward the soldiers as though they would protect him.

It went eerily silent in the low light of the night. Then the town elder inhaled and clamored in defense as he lifted his lower leg to kick more dirt at the boy. The boy saw what was coming and swooped his head away, but no dirt flew his way. Instead, he heard a metal thump as the old man cried out in pain. Hesitating, he turned to see what was going on and found himself staring again at the large, muscular leg of the soldier he had bumped into when he was hiding.

The soldier had swiftly stepped over him, drawing his sword, and thrusting it into the ground to where the town leader was going to kick up more dirt. So instead of kicking the dirt, he had kicked the wide side of the metal blade, jamming the toe sticking out of the end of his sandal.

The painful cry caught everyone's attention. The townspeople who were serving and playing music came over to help their elder but instantly backed away when they saw the scene. The soldier was pulling the tip of his sword out of the ground as he ominously stared him down without remorse.

Several soldiers walked through the cowering townspeople to see what was going on. Stepping up and seeing their fellow warrior in such a posture, one spoke up in a loud, joking manner, "Uriah has finally found a child apprentice! He is now a father!"

A cheer rose from the soldiers with their deep voices, putting the townspeople in a panic because they did not understand what was happening.

Uriah, a soldier, put his sword back into its sheath across his back and stepped next to King David, who was still kneeling with the boy. The king looked up at Uriah with a joyful grin, agreeing with the statement.

Uriah knew before the statement was publicly made that he had found what he had been searching for ever since he was granted the honorable title of mighty warrior almost two years ago. He had killed over three hundred enemy warriors by himself in one battle to earn that title.

Still in a protective mindset, Uriah looked down, asking him with a raspy accent (Hebrew was not his first language), "How were you beaten?"

It was a very odd question at first but grasped everyone's attention as it went quiet once more. The boy now knew he was being protected as a strange feeling of comfort and power overcame him as a result of the kneeling soldier's kindness. He turned and lifted up what little clothing he had covering his torso.

The soldier who had spoken up in the jolly manner saw the boy's back glistening from the firelight. He turned to the now-mortified town elder and commented under his breath, "You better run for your life."

The old town elder did not move, not quite understanding why he would say such a thing since he didn't fully comprehend the conversation going on between the soldiers.

Uriah focused fully on the boy and turned around, lifting several layers of armor to expose his own back. The boy's mouth opened wide. He stared up, seeing the broad, muscular back of the soldier as light shone off his sweaty skin. The boy slowly stood with King David, following his lead.

Stepping up to the big soldier's bare back, he hesitated. Then he lifted his hand as his finger followed the long, scarred lines crisscrossing his back that matched his own. The boy realized this powerful man was showing him that he had experienced the same brutality at the hand of a whip. Instantly, he found himself feeling a true connection and brotherhood for the first time in his life. Nobody understood what they had been through, but now they shared this bond that no one had shared with them before.

The soldier lowered his body armor, straightening up his attire, and turned back around. When he fully faced the boy, the young one was no longer frightened. Instead, he was relaxed as if he was with actual family.

King David lifted his hand, placing it on Uriah's shoulder, saying, "I believe the God of our forefathers, the God of Israel, is blessing you with your legacy, Hittite."

The king turned to the town leader. When their eyes locked, the older man knew something bad was coming. The king said sternly, "Bring to me the fathers of the families this boy was with…right now!" The man cautiously bowed his head, acknowledging the king. Then King David added, "You will be accompanying them when they get here."

The town's leader started breathing heavily as sweat appeared on his forehead. David looked over to a couple of the mighty warriors listening and told them, "Send your sons with him to make sure they do not run away. And if they try, they have my blessing to kill all of them."

The rest of the mighty warriors who were still eating and drinking heard shouting, looking for two boys. Two obeyed right away who were ten and thirteen years old. After they were explained what to do, they politely replied to their mentoring warrior fathers, "Yes, sir!"

The older leader now appeared faint, understanding how bad

the situation was going to get because of the scraggly, young thief. He was pushed away from the group by the two intimidating and fearless boys who stepped up very close to him. They were wearing identical military attire and adjusted knives and swords to fit their smaller body size. Anyone seeing them might first think the boys were playing dress-up, but their attitude, movements, and body language were telling another story.

Years earlier, when David was not yet officially crowned king of Israel, he was in hiding from King Saul in the cave of Adullam. It was a cavern hidden deep within the mountains of Israel. People would have to crawl a long distance through a narrow tunnel a little wider than a man's shoulders. Many of these natural caves were scattered throughout the region. The mouth of the tunnels was easily camouflaged by rolling a sizeable rock in front of it.

David's family came to live there with him, safely away from any battle areas. As time went on, over four hundred men who were in trouble, had debts, or were simply discontented joined David, slowly building an army—a very special army.

In the cave, God did great things with David and those who joined him. It isolated them from the outside world in a healthy and productive way. It gave them a place for sanctuary to regroup and refresh themselves, transforming them into honorable men who walked with integrity and ultimately lived for a purpose other than themselves. They completely changed their identity and became men surrendering to the Lord of heaven's armies. They served him and the nation of Israel while simultaneously raising the bar for what it meant to be 'chosen men' promised to their great ancestor, Abraham.

David himself had an incredible reputation for killing Goliath when he was a young teenager. That bloodshed started his career as a warrior, and he continued to successfully fight every battle since then, having no equal in Israel or any other country. He was one of unfathomable, fearless qualities: strong yet agile as a leopard, kindhearted but deadly when necessary, consistent in glorifying the Lord of heaven's armies, and humble but unafraid to utilize the power of God flowing through him in everything he did.

God-like expectations kept growing in his heart to the point that everything he did was purely extraordinary. A master on the battlefield, David raised the bar, encouraging his men to be extraordinary as well. He came up with a goal for his small army of soldiers: If a soldier killed three hundred or more enemies in one battle, that soldier would be titled forever a Mighty Warrior, given the highest of honors that came with grand rewards.

Since the time of the Cave of Adullam many years ago, only thirty-seven men acquired the coveted title. Seeing that it was very difficult for most his men to accomplish such a victory, David reflected inward to see if he could identify the root of success. He himself had been a young shepherd boy who spent countless days and nights alone, fighting off lions and bears.

Other accomplished "mighty warriors," he concluded, had the same common thread: the power of God working through them as well as the necessity at young ages to scrape and fight to survive. Most did not have parents to support and guide them as children.

With this young and deep-rooted natural instinct to survive, he came up with a strategy (once he was fully crowned King of Israel) to increase the warriors' success rate, which would strengthen the Israelite army to be the greatest in the land. Once a regular soldier became a mighty warrior, that warrior had to take on a homeless, orphaned child living destitute, scraping and fighting to survive. This child would permanently shadow the mighty warrior's life on and off the battlefield. They would learn how to be a Hebrew man by experience, first loving and honoring the Lord of heaven's armies and then practicing everything firsthand what it takes to be a lethal killer.

As for the disheveled nine-year-old boy, abandoned and homeless this very night in Shechem, he had no idea he was about to begin a new and extraordinary journey. King David's heart had led him to help the poorest of his people to grow into the fiercest and most respected men in all the land.

"My king, please wait!" the town elder shouted as he was being prodded by the young warriors. "We meant no harm. I apologize for what has been said and done to the boy. It is hard on families to feed and clothe another, especially one that is not blood-related."

David could not believe what he was hearing. Stopping the young warriors from taking the elder away, he stepped up into his face, looked down on him, and yelled, "We are all blood family coming from the same ancient forefather: Abraham!" It went silent in the town of Shechem as all the warriors lifted their gaze to their king, who rarely raised his voice.

Quieting down, still staring at the town elder, he told the young warriors, "Bring these men and this one back to this boy here"—he gestured to the shabby, homeless boy—"so he may do what he pleases with them." Then David pulled out his battle knife from his hip, throwing it into the ground next to the boy's feet for him to take. No one said a word as everyone watched. The three walked away to gather the other men.

Uriah, the warrior who was to be the new stepfather and mighty warrior teacher to the orphan boy with torn-up clothes, knelt next to him, pulling the king's knife out of the ground. Handing it to him, he said with an accent different than everyone else there, "This is a great honor, boy. The king has presented his personal weapon for you to use on these men who beat you."

The boy's eyes were wide with questions, not sure what was really going on. He fearfully reached out, taking hold of the heavy knife with a gold handle decorated with gems of green and red all around it. Feeling the weight of the great weapon, the boy looked back to the large man, asking, "What are you wanting me to do?"

Uriah looked up to King David with a shrewd smile and then back to the boy, answering, "Moses wrote in the holy scrolls 'an eye for eye, tooth for tooth, hand for hand, foot for foot, burn for burn, wound for wound, and bruise for bruise.' You are to repay these men for what they did to you."

The boy stared at the man, hearing but not believing what he was being told. Thinking for a moment, he responded in his soft, child's voice, "But this is a knife. They used animal whips."

Uriah smiled, saying, "These are grown men, much bigger and stronger than you. But most of all, you were their responsibility, and they abused you. The blade on that knife makes it an equal trade-off." Then he winked at the child.

Now understanding what was expected when the men arrived, he took hold of the golden handle, testing its weight and moving it back and forth. Never having such a grand object in his hands, he began to smile, admiring it. His eyes flickered as the shiny blade reflected glimpses of light from the flames of the fires nearby.

Just then, a scream of pain came from a man in the direction the town elder and two young warriors went. Shortly thereafter, five people approached, with one new man limping. When they came up to the group of people waiting, the three men stood, lowering their heads and not making eye contact. Suddenly the three found themselves flopping to their knees in pain as the two young warriors swiftly swiped the sides of their swords to the back of the men's legs. "Kneel to your king!" they demanded.

As the men recovered, one of the warrior fathers standing nearby asked the young warriors why one of them was limping. The older boy replied, "He did not take us seriously even when the elder told him he needed to obey. He tried to slam the door of his house on us, but Azriel," pointing to the warrior boy next to him, "underhandedly threw his bolas between the narrow opening as the door was closing. He was hit in the knee, knocking him to the ground."

All the warriors around grunted, pleased at his clever reaction. One warrior spoke up, saying, "I would have put a sword through the door!"

The younger warrior bowed in respect but replied with, "Our king would have been upset. We needed him alive so the new student could be the one to kill him."

The group around the area, except for the three men kneeling, broke out in laughter at the boy's quick-wittedness as King David commented, "You are seeing clearly at your young age to never spoil the king's intent, unlike others...." He tilted his head toward the grown warrior who commented, raising an eyebrow as though this wasn't the first time a foolish thing had come out of his mouth.

Uriah interrupted the side conversation, ready for this new apprentice son of his to have a go. He said to him, holding the knife to his side, "These men have done you wrong..." Uriah suddenly realized he didn't know the boy's name and asked, "What are you called?"

He answered, "My mother called me Jonathan." Then the boy's eyes flashed to the three men kneeling and added, "But they called me Kelev."

Uriah's eyebrows narrowed as he growled at the kneeling men, "You called him a dog?!"

Interrupting Uriah's growing temper, King David was curious about the boy's name and asked him, "Do you know how you got your birth name, Jonathan?"

The boy glanced away, thinking. Then he said, "My mother told me my father named me after his distant relative that was the son of a king."

David's eyes went wide, reflecting years back to his close childhood friend Jonathan who saved his life when they became young men. Later, he was killed with the rest of his family, whose father was King Saul. Instantly he dropped to a knee, bowing low to the boy. All the warriors watching saw what their king was doing and quickly followed suit.

The homeless boy was now completely confused about what was going on. He stood taller than all the mighty men around him and asked, "What are you doing?"

CHAPTER 3

The scraggly boy who had been whipped over the past years by families who had taken him in as a slave was standing alone with King David's knife in his hands, staring around at the formidable soldiers bowing to him.

He had asked the king, who started this unexpected motion, why they were doing this. David raised his head and answered, "You are royalty. You are from the family line of King Saul."

"King who?" he asked innocently, cocking his head in question.

David stood, coming alongside the boy who said his birth name was Jonathan, and answered, "The first king of Israel. The king before me. Jonathan, his son, was my best friend. They are all dead now."

Awkwardly, boy Jonathan turned, looking up at the tall, handsome David, and asked, "If I am royalty, why were my parents poor, and we continually seemed to be hiding all the time?"

The king put his hand on top of Jonathan's head and answered, "That will be a question we will answer in time. Right now, you need to take action against these men that harmed you permanently." David turned Jonathan's head to look at the men kneeling in front of him.

The men quickly stared back down at the ground when Jonathan looked at them. All three had gaped at Jonathan upon hearing who this past slave boy was. "You may do anything you want to them, even put them to death! You tell us what you want us to do to them," the king stated.

The words sounded harsh but inviting at the same time. Jonathan looked down at the magnificent knife in his hand and then up at the three, moving his eyes back and forth. Finally coming to some conclusion, he said, "I cannot kill the men that took me into their homes. They have children. I don't want them to end up like me, poor and homeless."

The mighty warriors who listened glanced at one another with expressions that conveyed they saw wisdom in this young boy.

"If I kill the town elder, the God of Israel might get mad." Now a flow of murmuring was growing louder around the warriors' camp inside the city of Shechem among all the townspeople who had been feeding and entertaining them. They were shocked at the deep wisdom coming from one so young.

"It sounds like we have a king in training?" David commented. The boy appreciated the kind words and how he was being treated. Hearing the answer to his dilemma, he replied, "But I'm not a king; you are. What am I to do?"

A friendly laugh came from many of the robust men now standing around, hearing their king put on the spot by a child. David replied quickly, having been put in this position more times than he could count, "God speaks to us in our hearts to tell our minds what to do. This helps us not to react with our emotions or selfish desires but rather tells our minds what to do with compassion and wisdom. What is God telling your heart?" He pointed at Jonathan's chest.

He hesitated and answered, "I hear nothing."

Several sighs of relief could be heard from the men awaiting their demise.

The king, having an idea of what might happen, stepped to the side away from the men on the ground and said, "If we hear nothing, then we do nothing and wait patiently for God to speak. Sometimes it's not verbal, but a life circumstance or situation that dictates our reaction and gives us wise direction."

Jonathan stared up at the king, enjoying the calm, engaging conversation he had longed for from anyone who would be friendly to him.

"God has already spoken to me!" Uriah shouted, taking a step toward the men on the ground and kicking the middle man in the face so hard it sent him back several feet with blood splattering. Then each of his large fists slammed into the other two faces. Now all three men were lying on their backs, so Uriah drew his sword while no onlookers had any intention of stopping him.

King David thought this would be the reaction from the foreign Hittite who had been with them since he and his small army left the cave of Adullam years ago. He proved that he would serve Israel and its king faithfully until his death, accepting the God of Israel as the greatest God of all the lands. Now having just found out that he would be the warrior father to this young, innocent boy, he took his duty to protect and prepare even more seriously.

"Jonathan," Uriah said, turning to the boy who was somewhat frightened of the massive warrior. "Tell me what your mind is saying to you?"

It was silent as everyone, including King David, waited to

hear if more surprising wisdom was going to arise.

It took a moment for him to respond. Then he awkwardly stepped to the side of Uriah, reaching up and lowering Uriah's hand that held the large sword. He said, "I will not have you do what is my responsibility." He looked to the three men, sitting back up on their knees, adding, "They will no longer work to feed and clothe only their own families. Until their death, I want them to clothe and feed all people of the city who have no food or clothes."

He looked up to King David as though needing approval. David's body language spoke volumes as he straightened up his tired back and shoulders, raised his eyebrows, and smiled adoringly. Jonathan smiled back, understanding that the king approved. He lifted the knife up as though giving it back. David began to reach for the knife, but the boy suddenly turned to the three men at perfect height and sliced the sides of each of their faces.

The men screamed, reaching up to their cheeks that now bled with wide gashes. Still looking at the men, Jonathan screamed. Uriah and David jumped back; Jonathan sounded like a crazed animal, and they half wondered if they themselves might get a lashing from the knife.

Jonathan cleaned the knife off with his dirty clothes. Then he purposely reached up higher to the king so he would understand this time; he was truly giving the knife back and said, "Now, my king, we can identify these three the next time we come through this city. Now they and the people of Shechem see they are permanently marked to serve the poor and needy."

King David slid the knife into his sheath, stunned at what happened and the explanation why. Everyone looked at one another in awe at the shocking end of their long day.

Uriah yelled out in excitement, "He will be my son!" causing everyone to flinch as he bent down, grasped the child, and raised him in the air, showing him off as a prize. Jonathan gazed around, wide-eyed at being held high, with cheers erupting from around the camp.

The smaller group of mighty warriors had met up with the large force of soldiers that had gone a different route home a day earlier. Now together, they marched through the main gate of Jerusalem as crowds of the city had gathered to cheer their soldiers and king, who were returning with another great victory. Jonathan had bathed and was given clean, new clothes from the townspeople of Shechem, along with many other gifts in attempt to apologize for how they treated him.

Uriah rode close to the front, following proudly behind King David, showing off his soon-to-be apprentice warrior son on his shoulders. Jonathan, on the other hand, was consumed in amazement at the great wall surrounding the city. When inside, Shechem, the only place he knew, now appeared in comparison to be only a grain of sand amid a field of wheat.

Nearing the end of the parade, deep within the city, a large portion of the regular foot soldiers had already peeled off, going to their homes to be with their families.

Guards were waiting ahead at the base of a magnificent building with a wide flight of stairs at its foot, announcing the end of their journey, which had started over four months ago.

When Uriah and Jonathan got down off the horse, Uriah said, "We have explained to you: you are to be my apprentice, my trainee, to become a mighty warrior like us." He swung his hand around at the remaining eighty-seven (who always stayed together until their king dismissed the highest honored of all Israel's army at the palace).

Jonathan looked at all the warriors; half of them were shorter and close to his age or slightly older. He now understood that they were students as well to their adopted warrior fathers. They would continue to be apprentices up until they themselves were able to kill over three hundred enemy soldiers in one battle without assistance from another warrior.

Once they had accomplished that, they were honored for the great achievement by being anointed by the king as a mighty warrior and then allowed to live on their own, have a family, and eventually adopt a homeless, orphaned boy, repeating the warrior training process all over again.

A shout came out in front of them as the king turned his horse around to see all his warriors' faces. "Mighty warriors of Israel! My brothers in battle! You have again proven who you are in the victory in Damascus, killing more than 20,000 enemies of Israel!" Raising a hand over them, he said, "May the Lord of heaven's armies bless you greatly and keep you strong in the battles to come, and," he paused to capture their full attention, "in your homes and in your beds!" A roar of deep cheers issued from the yearning group of men as their king smiled wide. David finished by pulling back the reins of his horse so it would rear up on its hind legs and said loudly, "But first…we have a ceremony to perform that is a very long time coming for the Hittite, Uriah!"

King David got off his horse, handing the reins to a servant. The group followed him up the large stairs into the fancy building. Bending down to Jonathan as they entered, Uriah whispered, "This is the king's palace. We are going to a special room to anoint you to be my warrior son and to ask the blessing of the Lord of heaven's armies to come upon you to aid you in becoming a fierce, mighty warrior!"

Jonathan's little heart was beating quickly as more extraordinary changes were happening. He couldn't understand how he could possibly be fully clothed with a full stomach and how this man could be excited about him and treat him like his own son, having only met him days ago by accident. It was as though he and all the soldiers had been family all his life.

Inside the biggest building he had ever seen, Jonathan walked down a large hallway on a bright, white, smooth marble floor; he felt like he should be tiptoeing. But with soldiers and palace guards surrounding the king and servants following close behind, their footsteps echoed loudly, creating an orchestra of hundreds marching along.

They soon entered an open room with a large, highly decorated chair at the far end. The king led the way and gave instructions to four servants waiting at the entrance. One briskly went into a room on one side while another went in a different direction, almost running. The other two followed the king, continuing across the open room to the base of steps that led up to his throne.

King David stopped and turned around, spreading out his arms and legs before going up. Without hesitation, all the servants converged on him and began to remove all the body armor from head to toe. Then they removed the first layer of softer but dirty and sweaty clothes against his skin. Once completely undressed, the servant who had left the room on side returned with another servant holding body-washing items and a set of fresh, light, and comfortable attire. They nimbly washed his body and dried it before putting his new attire on him.

A guard holding his arms out, surrounded by other guards holding long, golden spears, came marching out of the same side room. Stopping in front of the king, the surrounding guards spread out, leaving the center guard holding a purple-colored pillow. Little Jonathan leaned sideways, craning his neck to see what was on the pillow behind the guard in the way.

His eyes went wide for the first time when he saw a king's crown. It was round and made of shining, polished gold with many colored stones embedded in it and spike-looking pillars all the way around it.

King David saw the child stretching his head around to see what was happening as an idea came to him, and he said, pointing out, "Jonathan, distant relative of King Saul." Heads quickly turned from servants and guards who were not in Shechem to stare at the boy the king had just mentioned. Then all at once, everyone except for David, Uriah, mighty warriors, and their sons went to their knees, bowing toward Jonathan.

A moment passed, and Uriah said in his accented, deep voice, almost annoyed, "Everyone, rise! Jonathan is to be my warrior son!" He looked to David, giving him a nod to finish what he interrupted.

Gratefully acknowledging how Uriah handled that, he nodded back and said, "Jonathan, come here."

The boy shyly looked around at everyone staring at him. He was suddenly the center of attention again, just like he was in Shechem and when his small group met up with the large army. That one had truly scared him—a rustling of thousands of soldiers had gone to their knees with armor and metal weapons clanking together as a dust cloud arose.

He walked around the guard holding out the crown, hopelessly looking up at the king. With perfect timing, an older man looking very distinguished and wise, wearing a fancy robe and head covering, walked in with the assistance of a staff. His hair was grayish white, matching his full beard. He was followed by the servant who had run off in the opposite direction of the servant who fetched the king's fresh clothes.

David raised his hand, waving him in, and said, "Thank you for coming so quickly, servant of the Lord. This is a unique moment and unexpected situation." As the old man got to the side of the king, he looked down at the child as David continued, "The boy here is a distant relative of Jonathan, after whom he is actually named." The priest raised his eyebrows, looking at the king with a questionable gaze. David nodded, answering the unspoken question, and responded, "Yes, Jonathan, the son of King Saul, my friend who has long gone to be with the Lord."

The priest looked down at the boy as David added, pointing to Uriah, "He will also be the warrior son of one of my mighty warriors here."

The old man looked up to the powerful soldier standing behind the guard who was holding the crown. "Ahh, the Hittite!" he said with a smile as he glanced down at the boy and added, "You are a very blessed boy to have an adopted father such as this mighty man." The priest looked back, deep into Uriah's eyes, and stepped up to him face-to-face. Out loud for all to hear, he stated, "Uriah, be patient with high expectations. Be gentle with a strong hand. Be firm with a soft voice. Lead without pulling him. Discipline without hurting his heart. Finally,"—the priest looked back to the boy—"love him by clearly demonstrating the great love the Lord of heaven's armies has for him."

The old man nodded to himself, still looking at the boy, giving him a confident smile. He looked back at Uriah, patted him on the shoulder, and added in a joyful tone, "You think being a warrior is hard work...." He didn't finish the sentence and walked back to the king, laughing under his breath.

Uriah had a blank look on his face as his eyes followed the priest, hearing others agreeing and trying not to laugh. The priest stepped up to the king who had seated himself. Then David asked, "What are we to do about this situation, wise one?"

The priest looked down at the boy standing next to the crown that was not yet on the king's head; he looked at the crown and back several times. Coming up with a solution for a potentially major problem of someone else's bloodline in the way, he privately whispered into David's ear, "Without question, God anointed you king of Israel by Samuel years ago. But minds can get confused or be misled, especially if they are in disagreement or confrontation with you, my king. The best way to kill a snake is to cut off its head. The boy must be renamed, and all knowledge of this must be severed now and forever!"

David leaned his head over to his other hand as his arm rested on the throne, thinking, stroking along his face and beard. With a deep sigh, he began shaking his head in agreement. He stood looking at the boy and then spoke harshly to make a point of hierarchy, "Boy of Shechem, step up here!" He motioned for the guard holding his crown and Uriah to step up as well.

Standing in front of Jonathan, the king suddenly went to a knee in a compromising position. Everyone gasped at what they were seeing, even Uriah. Uriah, not comprehending what was going on, took a step to the side. He drew his sword and looked around for something or someone that would make his king do such a thing, ready to defend not only his king but his mighty warrior brother as well.

"Uriah, put the sword away," David said softly. "All is well. A statement needs to be made to clarify who reigns."

Uriah, with a confused look on his face, slowly slid his sword back into its sheath. He still surveyed keenly, indicating he would not hesitate to kill them for his king.

The priest, fully understanding, said firmly to the boy, "Jonathan, put the crown on King David's head!"

Everyone, including Uriah, relaxed with a sigh of relief. With all eyes watching intently, the boy took the heavy, golden crown and gladly placed it on the head of the man who protected him a few days ago—a kind man who spoke to him as an equal and was very friendly when they first met, not judging him or sending him away but giving him a gift of a father. And he wasn't just any ordinary father; he was a mighty warrior.

When the crown was placed firmly on David's head, he rose with extreme confidence as the guard holding the empty purple pillow stepped away. He opened his arms out for the boy to come stand next to him. Once there, he turned the child to face everyone, placed his hands on the boy's shoulders, and said, "This boy from Shechem is to be anointed as the warrior son of Uriah!" A shout of excitement burst forth.

"Also…" The king raised his hand to quiet everyone and added, "He will be renamed!" There was a pause; everyone wondered what this was about. "He will be granted a new life and a new future, and his past will be completely forgotten!" King David now glared at everyone, sending a message that would not be misunderstood as he moved his hands gently around the boy's neck like he was going to choke him to death.

It went silent as everyone clearly understood the message. He relaxed his hands, giving the boy a pat on his shoulders, and said, "I, King of Israel, am renaming this boy"—he looked to Uriah—"Shuriah!"

Taking a moment to let this unexpected event soak in, Uriah put on a grand smile, bowing to the king for honoring him. Applause erupted within the great room, acknowledging the wisdom of their king. Once it quieted down, David said directly to Uriah, "His past is now forgotten. Any thought, talk, or action about his blood or past will only end in…" He slowly and softly put his hands back around Jonathan's neck.

Uriah clearly got the message, nodding his head in understanding as David added, "I hold you fully responsible, Hittite, to sever any head…." Pausing to make a statement, he flexed his arm and hand muscles while gritting his teeth; he added, "That of a warrior brother, Israelite, foreigner, or…." Without saying his name to frighten the boy, who did not know the strong hands around his neck were positioned to immediately end his life, the king tilted his head down, looking directly at the top of the boy's head. Then he lifted his eyes only back to Uriah.

They looked at each other for a moment. Then, Uriah went to a knee, stating for all to hear, "Yes, my king!"

Seeing Uriah in that position, all the other mighty warriors and palace guards demonstrated they would follow the orders as well by going to their knees and repeating the same words, "Yes, my king!" Seeing that he got his point across, David let go of the boy and sat back down on the throne.

Glancing at the priest, David said, "Please continue with the anointing of Shuriah to become a warrior son, training to become a great mighty warrior with his new warrior father, *Uriah*!" He ended with an uplifting tone of joy.

A cheer went up in approval with all the warriors. The servants and palace guards all backed away as the group of mighty warriors moved forward to the base of the stairs. The priest moved Shuriah and Uriah in front of the throne so the king could observe the anointing and the crowd on the main floor at the same time. He never liked having his side or back to anyone, unable to see everyone at once, even if he was being protected by his own people. It was a learned behavior going way back to his own childhood when he watched his father's sheep by himself in the wilderness.

The priest stood between the two, withdrawing a lengthy, tethered, and braided rope made of human hair from a pouch hanging from his hip sash. He slowly threaded the rope through his hands, admiring it as he asked Shuriah, who was curiously looking at what he was holding, "Do you know what this is?"

Shuriah quickly answered in a childlike manner, "Old rope!" The warriors in the room let out a muffled chuckle so as not to interrupt the ceremony as the old man replied, "Not just any old rope but rope from the strongest man to have ever lived."

The boy, looking at the priest, obviously not knowing who he was talking about, eyed the powerful, mighty warrior and asked excitedly, "My warrior father, Uriah?"

King David was the first one to give a boisterous laugh as all the warriors joined in, reveling in the boy's naïveté. The priest lifted his hand to Uriah's broad shoulder, answering, "Uriah is a very strong man, but he is not the strongest man to have ever lived." Giving Uriah a friendly gesture, he looked back at the boy. "Let me explain; I am from the tribe of Dan. There was a man, a judge. I knew when I was your age who was as strong as ten Uriahs put together. He killed a thousand men in one battle!" He pointed one finger in the air with excitement. "But not with a sword, knife, or bow and arrow like these warriors," he said, gesturing his arm to the group watching attentively. "But with the jawbone of a donkey." Shuriah pulled his head back, giving him a look of unbelief as the old priest replied, "It's true. He was the first of all the mighty warriors of Israel. God of heaven blessed this special man named Samson with great strength… through his hair!"

Naïve of his people's history, the boy looked up to the king sitting on his throne. Here was the first man to treat him kindly, resulting in blossoming trust for the first time since his mother left him, but Shuriah gave him a puzzled expression as if to ask if this was really true.

King David returned a smile the boy had seen days earlier,

nodding his head 'yes' with confidence.

Not sure what to do with this information, Shuriah went along with the priest, imitating the king's smile and nodding his head as the priest continued, "Samson's strength did not come from having special or magical, long hair alone but from obeying God to never cut it off.

"For as long as he never cut his hair, instructed by his mother before he was born, God would always be with him. Obedience to God and following His instructions were extremely important for Samson—and for us. For God had plans for him to be His servant as a judge for the nation of Israel.

"God proved his faithfulness, giving him great strength up until it was cut off."

The priest hesitated, thinking what to say next, but the boy had a question. "Why did he cut his hair?"

The old man appreciated the question and answered, "He didn't; someone else did."

"How could they? He was the strongest man; who could overpower him to do such a thing to him?"

Many of the men around the room gave out a distasteful grunt as the priest replied, "A woman!"

"A woman?" the boy responded with a quirky frown.

"Yes, a woman. You see, Shuriah, a woman can do things even to the strongest man in the world, tempting him to become as vulnerable and weak as a child."

Shuriah wrinkled his brow and cocked his head to the side, expressing a feeling of confusion. So the old priest redirected the conversation, "I will let Uriah explain that subject with you some other day. The point I am making is as long as you are obedient to God's laws, the ones He gave to Israel through Moses, to the king of Israel, and to your warrior father, then power beyond your imagination will be with and in you and always!"

The priest quietly looked down in his hands at the rope of hair, feeling the texture and imagining (as he has many times) where it came from and the extraordinary feats that happened when God was with Samson.

Suddenly, he called a servant waiting in the room from which he came to bring the anointing, sacrificial lamb. Then he told Uriah to kneel (so his head was the height of the boy's) and criss-cross their hands, grasping each other's wrists, fumbling for a second because of the drastic size difference. Finally, they were securely interlocked.

Working the rope of hair, the old man wrapped it in one direction around their wrists. Then he worked it in the other direction until all the rope was intertwined, locking them together. Then he withdrew a decorative knife from a hip sheath and told the two to lean forward, touching each other's heads and looking down at their tied hands.

When the servant stopped at the side of the priest holding a small lamb in his arms, the priest raised his hand with the knife and openly prayed, "Lord of heaven's armies, David, the king of your chosen people, cries out to you! We are asking for your favor on this boy and man bound together to be father and son. He humbly asks you to bless this bond to be as strong as the strength you gave Samson. Encourage them to never let go or sever what is being anointed with blood in your presence. Their heads are bowed, staring at the rope made from Samson's hair wrapped around their arms. May their minds' eyes remind them that when one becomes weak, the other is there to hold them together, for they are bonded for life. But most of all, remind them that when they become weak, it is by the strength of the Lord of heaven's armies working through them that makes them strong—not their minds filled with their own wisdom or bodies mounting with muscle as you reminded Samson when his hair was cut off, and your presence left him...."

The old man lowered the knife, gesturing for the servant to hold out the lamb over the heads of the two tied together. He looked up to the king as David nodded approval and then swiftly slit the neck of the lamb as blood spouted out, covering both heads.

Instantly, shouts echoed within the great room from all who witnessed the bonding ceremony of the new father and son. They cried out, "Praise to the Lord of heaven's armies! Praise to the king of Israel!"

Still touching, Uriah shifted so they were eye to eye. Then with an almost crazed look in his eyes, he said loud enough for Shuriah to hear over the shouting, "My son, Shuriah! It is now time for you to learn how to kill!" Fittingly, bright, warm blood dripped down their faces as the ceremony came to a close.

CHAPTER 4

The new warrior son and mighty warrior father walked away from the palace with their bonding ceremony complete. Uriah directed them a little way to the Spring of Gihon to wash from being drenched in lamb's blood. The sun was getting low in the sky as they walked quietly while Shuriah tried to understand in his young mind everything that was going on. It was happening so fast, a blur, like it was only a dream.

In just days, he went from sleeping on the ground in little, cold, small caves by himself, with no one to call family or friend, and stealing food and clothes to survive to a full stomach all the time, nice, warm clothes, and crowning a king who gave him a father. Not only that, but his new father appeared sincerely proud to have him and cared for him as a real father—unlike the other "adopted fathers" in Shechem who treated him like a slave and a burden to the family, embarrassed to have him in their home.

One thing stuck in his mind that he didn't understand about this man who was now his father. Out of nowhere, he asked, "Why do they call you 'the Hittite?' What is a Hittite?"

Uriah looked down at his new son, understanding he was very naïve of the world outside of Shechem, and calmly answered, "I am from a place far away called Hatti, the land of the Hittites. My people are from a different bloodline than you "Israelites." Many generations back, more than we can count, my people occupied this land. Your ancient forefather, Abraham, settled in this area amongst my people, and he was a very good man. Everyone liked him. As generations passed, the Hittites were pushed out of this land and now live far north from here where I came from."

"If you are from far away, why are you here and not with your people?"

Uriah paused; he was about to open a wound he never wanted to go back to. But he knew this special boy of his must know the truth. "I left my people some years back for doing horrible things their gods demanded from them. As you know, I was treated the way you were, whipped on your back. But it wasn't because I was abused as an orphan. They whipped me as a young man because I wouldn't do the terrible things they were doing to please their gods. I left my own people, seeking refuge somewhere else, hoping to find a people that would have me, even if it meant being a slave."

"You're a slave?"

He looked down at the innocent boy and answered with a smile, "No, I am not a slave."

Shuriah asked, "What terrible things did they want you to do?"

Uriah inhaled deeply, fighting the desire to withhold an answer, and explained, "I was married, and we had a baby boy. The Hatti gods, of whom I never speak their names, demanded sacrifices of babies born on nights when the moon shines full. Our baby was born on such a night. The priest came to our home to take our baby, and I wouldn't let them. So they had their guards take me to a prison and whip me. My son was sacrificed anyways and…" Uriah hesitated, scrunching his face to fight back tears, and added, "They sacrificed my wife as well because we were disobedient."

The young boy understood this was a very difficult and sad thing that happened to his new father, so he stayed silent. They got to the spring, and Uriah began taking off his dirty armor and his undergarments as he continued the conversation. "I left Hatti and traveled for over a year, looking all over for a place I could fit in or where people would accept me for who I was. Then unexpectedly, I found myself in the middle of a small battle outside a town near Damascus where we just were…which is where my life and story begin with King David."

Uriah walked into the cool water and sat down with only his head sticking out, and began washing himself. Shuriah hesitated following him, but Uriah raised his hand to wave him in, saying, "Get in here, son. You need to clean off all that blood." Out of character, he smiled and splashed up water in a playful manner, changing the atmosphere.

Shuriah seized the lighthearted gesture and quickly took off his clothes, jumping in next to Uriah and splashing him back. Shuriah stood facing his new father with a smile and suddenly saw the large man stand up with a serious scowl. He shriveled down into the water, peering up helplessly. Not able to hold the intimidating posture any longer, the big man crinkled his face and began to laugh.

The boy, not quite thinking it was funny and that he was going to be punished, suddenly found himself lifted high out of the water and tossed away, crashing back in. Popping back up and gasping for air, he wiped his face and understood this man, called his warrior father, had a gentle and fun side he had seen many times in other families who cared for one another. Now he had the same thing he had yearned for all his young life.

They washed themselves, dunking their heads in and out of the water, scrubbing off the dried blood. Stepping out of the spring and putting their clothes back on, Shuriah asked, "So what happened when you met King David?" Before Uriah answered, Shuriah added, "I like him; he's a nice man!"

Uriah grinned at his comment, agreeing, and answered, "I had been walking through the wilderness alone, following a road from a safe distance, which led to a city about which I overheard people talking weeks earlier. One evening, still a half a day's walk from this city, I saw a small band of people sitting around a fire, having a meal surrounded by several tents. I watched them, trying to decide if I was going to meet them or go around them. That is when I spotted movement surrounding the group, like someone sneaking in, crawling low to the ground, ready to rob or even kill them. It wasn't just several people but about a hundred men."

Shuriah was looking up to his side, intently listening to the story as they walked back near the palace, getting close to several smaller buildings off to the side. "As I stood there, I couldn't let these innocent people be ambushed, so I started to run to warn them. But before I took one more step, the bush next to me reached out, pulling my legs out from under me as the rock on the other side grasped my mouth, holding me tight and low to the ground."

Uriah stopped, turning directly to him. The boy's eyes were wide, completely engulfed in the words of his father. "Taking me off guard, I first thought I was going to be killed, but one of the hands from "the bush" let go, and a finger lifted. It pointed up to be quiet as a face finally came into focus. The eyes of the face looked toward the small camp, and my eyes followed what the finger was pointing to.

"I stopped struggling as I watched those sitting next to the fire. When the men surrounding the camp got close, suddenly, the innocent-looking men sitting down stood loudly, throwing off robes and blankets. To my surprise, they were fully clothed for battle, raising swords and shouting a frightening battle cry.

"The camouflaged rock and bush holding me down let go and suddenly stood as well. Men ready for battle appeared all around me. They had been in hiding, waiting for the large group of bandits to take advantage of the helpless ones. The soldier who looked like a bush patted me on the shoulder and said in an uplifting tone, 'Now you can join us and kill those who were sneaking up on the small camp.' Then he ran off, screaming and brandishing his sword back and forth to fight.

I watched the battle begin and decided to join the fight. All I had with me as a weapon was a long spear I had also used as a walking stick. I caught up with the man running ahead, who was easily going through the enemy; bodies dropped to my side without me doing anything.

"It was unbelievable how he was fighting, like nothing I have ever witnessed in my life. I stopped and looked around, realizing all the soldiers who had been in hiding were fighting the enemy the same way—with a fearless fury and swift agility, moving in acrobatic ways I never knew were possible, all while using multiple weapons at once.

"As the battle was ending, several friendly warriors were left, finishing off the final adversaries as other warriors searched around for more to do. When the last soldier finished killing his opponent, he looked around to find that all his warrior buddies had watched him finish the kill. Suddenly, boastful cheers rose, and clanking of metal weapons echoed.

"As I absorbed this incredible show of military action, little by little, eyes were now turning my way. I turned around, realizing I was in the center of all these warriors looking inward at me.

"With all eyes on me, no one saw one of the enemies creep up who had been lying down, assumed to be dead. He raised a knife in his hand. I knew this person needed to be stopped, so I lifted my spear, and swiftly, it arched high over all the soldiers' heads.

"Knowing the spear wasn't meant for them, they watched it fly over, impaling the enemy in the middle of the chest even as he still held his knife back, ready to throw. Without a sound, he fell back dead with my spear sticking straight up in the air.

"It went silent, and then a roar of cheers exploded again as two people walked over to me. One was the man who still had remnants of the bush covering his body, and the other was a handsome and very confident man who appeared to be in charge."

"King David!" Shuriah interjected in his childlike voice, knowing the description of the man.

"That's right, but I didn't know he was the king. He asked me, 'Who are you?'

"During the short battle, I quickly realized who the enemy was by the language they spoke and their clothing, which completely gave their identity away.

"Afraid of what the reaction would be, I went to my knees as they stared me down—curious. I raised my hands out and said the best I could in broken Hebrew, 'My name is Uriah, I am…a Hittite. But I am not like these men here.'

"All the men stiffened up, ready for another battle, whispering among themselves. Then the king raised his hand, and they instantly went silent. He asked me, 'Why are *you* here, Uriah… the Hittite? You are a long way from your home.'

"I thought for a moment, and then I lifted off my upper body covering, exposing my back and bowing my face to the ground."

"Your back is like mine!" Shuriah exclaimed, almost excitedly, as they had this in common.

"Yes, like yours…." Uriah paused to confirm their unfortunate connection. "I sat up and told King David, 'I was whipped by the guards of the priests for not obeying the rituals the gods demanded from our people: human sacrifices. I escaped prison and had been traveling through other nations, looking to find a new people and a new place to live. Even if I am to be a slave.'

"It was silent for a long time as each of these powerful warriors softened his spirit toward me. Then one by one, all the warriors came up to me, putting their hand on top of my head, saying, 'Brother.' Then they each walked away, gathered together, and waited for everyone to finish."

"Why did they do that, Father?" Shuriah purposely said *Father*, unsure if it was going to be appropriate.

Uriah gave a slight smile and a nod that it was okay to be addressed as *Father* and answered, "All the soldiers were giving their approval to accept me as one of their own. For you see, son," Uriah winked, "most all of the mighty warriors serving the Lord of heaven's armies under the command of King David had lives somewhat similar to mine: discontented, in trouble, or in debt, looking for a family, a home, and a purpose."

Uriah patted the top of Shuriah's head, saying, "Just like you. We're giving you a family, a home, and a purpose."

Shuriah thought through the story and asked, "Who were the men they killed?"

"They were Hittites!"

"Like you! That's why you were scared to answer the king," Shuriah replied.

Uriah thought to himself, *He's a curious and smart boy*. Nodding his head "yes," he added, "The king explained they had been hunting these men for a while because they had been raiding farms and small towns, killing and stealing from the people of Israel. So they set up this helpless pretend camp near the road three days earlier, knowing the raiders were somewhere in the area. The rest of the warriors stayed hidden, blending in a ways outside the camp for days, not moving."

Shuriah looked up surprised, saying, "For three days and nights, they never moved, waiting for these bad men to show up?" Uriah proudly said, "Yes, yes, they did! The mighty warriors are very patient, prepared, determined, and most of all, disciplined!" He bent down to one knee, looking straight into Shuriah's eyes, adding, "Being patient, prepared, determined, and disciplined are the first lessons you will learn, Shuriah, in becoming a warrior." He looked away in hesitation and then back, saying, "These four things will be your worst enemies from now on until your mind and body are trained and tamed and your spirit is ignited with wisdom and faith. Your lack of understanding of these four mountains will encourage you to quit and give up. Even at times when you are tired or in pain, you may hate what you are doing and who you are doing it for. They will whisper to you, *there is a better and easier way to be a mighty warrior than being patient, prepared, determined, and disciplined*. But you will learn these valuable lessons, I pray, sooner rather than later." Uriah changed his tone harshly to make a point. "But there is *no* easy way! It will take everything you have to accomplish these, my son, and become a mighty warrior!

"For now, you must know in here"—he tapped the boy's chest and then his own—"that I care for you as my own son. We are bound together for life, as the priest said when he anointed us with blood and tied our hands together with Samson's hair. I will always be for you, not against you, just like the God of Israel, whom I have come to learn is *for* His chosen people. Do you understand?"

Shuriah simply nodded 'yes,' though he did not fully understand the depth of what Uriah was saying.

Uriah grinned, accepting the naïve boy's answer, knowing he really had no idea how hard his life would be from now on, and it started tomorrow.

For the first time that he could remember in his young life, Shuriah woke up warm with a thick wool blanket covering his body as he lay on a low, comfortable bed of soft blankets and rugs inside a small home.

The sun had been up off the horizon for a while as he studied the small house, focusing on the details of the inside. (He couldn't see any of it last night in the candlelight.) Distracted by his new surroundings, it took him a moment to realize his warrior father was not there. As he sat up in bed, a knock came from the front door. "Shuriah, are you awake?" a young voice asked, using his new name.

Answering, *Yes, just a moment!* he quickly put on his new clothes and tied the sandals strings up his legs. Opening the door, he squinted his eyes, shielding the sun that was shining straight in. Through the bright light, it appeared only one person was standing in front of him. He was taken aback, realizing more than twenty-five other kids behind him, varying in age, staring at him.

The boy in front was older and had no expression on his face. He said sharply, "We must go now! You are making us late, new warrior boy. Our morning duty must get done before we eat and do today's training."

Shuriah recognized him as one of the older boys back at Shechem, who brought the two abusive stepfathers to the king.

The boy turned and started jogging away as the other boys followed closely behind. Shuriah stood there, watching until the last boy in the group, closer to his age, said, "Hurry, you must come with us!"

Shuriah left the home, next to the last boy heading to the other side of the city. After a little while, they got to an area cluttered with small homes, looking obviously poorer than other areas they passed along the way. The lead boy stopped, and the crew following halted in orderly lines. He turned around, saying, "You know what this job is! Fill as many empty clay pots on the doorsteps of these homes full of water from the wells as you can. The person who fills the most pots and returns them to the doors of the houses will become the lead warrior of the day tomorrow!"

Shuriah wasn't sure what was going on and leaned over to ask the younger boy next to him, "I don't understand what we are—"

Before he finished his questions, all the other boys instantly went running off as the lead boy said, "Go!"

He watched the boys swarm in every direction, and he found himself standing alone. They were running from door to door of every house that had empty water pots waiting for them. They grabbed the pots and ran off to where he assumed the wells were. Soon, some boys returned, carrying a heavy pot or two, trying their best not to spill a drop.

"You better hurry and grab a pot, new warrior, or you don't eat today!" he heard from another boy racing by.

Shuriah raised his eyebrows, looking around for a door with an empty water pot and not seeing any. His heart began to race as anxiety built at the thought that he wasn't going to eat today. He darted here and there, going around several buildings but did not see one empty pot. He realized he was alone down a side street, looking in all directions. He skirted around a corner and suddenly bumped into a much older boy, maybe sixteen years old, carrying two large clay pots. The taller boy stumbled for a moment to keep his balance with the extra weight and said, "Watch where you're going, young one!"

Shyly, lowering his head, he replied, "Sorry, I didn't mean to bump you."

They made eye contact for a second, and then the taller boy asked, "How many pots have you filled and taken back?"

"None. I didn't understand what we were doing at first. They are all full."

The older warrior boy looked around and said, "Here, carry this one for me." He leaned over, handing a full pot to Shuriah. Surprised at the kind gesture, he grabbed the heavy pot and followed the boy, taking the pots to their homes before going back to where all the boys were assembling. They got back in line as Shuriah proudly stood next to the older boy. Once all the boys were together, the daily leader of the group called out, asking who had filled the most pots. In order, going down the line, each one declared a number. When it got to the older boy who handed a pot to Shuriah, he proudly announced, "Six!"

A murmur erupted with all the boys impressed with the highest number so far, with the average being two or three. The lead boy looked to the new warrior boy and asked, "How many did you fill?" Before Shuriah answered, the older boy next to him said aloud, "He carried one of mine back to a house. He did not fill one bucket!" Laughter broke out as Shuriah realized he didn't do what was directed, as it appeared the older boy only took advantage of him.

Humiliation swallowed Shuriah from head to toe, as his facial expression instantly telegraphed how he was feeling. A different boy in line said, "Oh, look, he's going to cry!" Laughter broke out again, this time with all of them pointing at him.

Shuriah looked up to the older boy that gave him the pot with a questionable look of "why did you do this to me?" The boy tilted his head down close to his ear, privately saying, "You have lessons to learn! I am helping you."

Shuriah could not control himself. He had been raising himself for the past years, learning he couldn't trust anyone. And again, it showed its ugly face as anger exploded within him and leaped up at the older boy in wild frustration.

Before he got a full step forward, halfway swinging his fists, the older boy swiftly planted his foot in the middle of Shuriah's chest, knocking him to his back, gasping for air. It went silent as all the boys surrounded him, looking down with determination. Once he was able to fill his lungs, he sat up with all the boys peering at him with fists, ready to attack as an organized army. The only thing coming to Shuriah's mind to protect himself was the big man that had taken him in as his own son. He exclaimed, "My father will beat you all for this!"

The boys looking down suddenly relaxed, standing straight up, glancing at each other, and then began snickering at the one on the ground as a different older boy leaned down, saying sarcastically, "Your warrior father, the Hittite?" Laughter spouted Shuriah's direction as he became more and more confused about what was going on. He thought these new people were to be family, looking out, caring for one another, not hurting and making fun of each other.

The lead boy stepped through the crowd that had gathered around tightly. He crossed his arms, snubbing his nose at Shuriah, and said, "Your father, the Hittite, will do nothing! He is a mighty warrior of our king and knows the ways of the Israelites.

You are the one who doesn't know anything and must learn everything. Don't you ever threaten one of us again!" The lead boy glanced up at a couple of boys standing next to Shuriah, nudging his head toward him.

In unison, the two boys hit Shuriah with loud *smacks*, knocking him to his back. He felt instant pain on both sides of his face, and his nose began to bleed; Shuriah started to cry. The lead boy turned, giving another order to leave and follow him, so all the other boys got in an orderly line and began jogging away.

Shuriah lay there with tears and blood running down his wounded face, thinking he should run as well, but the other way. This place wasn't any different from Shechem. Suddenly, he felt himself being lifted off the ground with two hands under his arms from behind. He looked back only to see the older boy who had him carry the pot of water. Surprised at the gesture, he was unsure why the boy had helped him up. The older boy met his gaze and said kindly, "I told you: you have lessons to learn. You can run away and hide, which you are probably considering; I thought that when I was your age. But if you do, you will remain weak and homeless your whole life with no purpose for living. Or you can run forward, joining them and beginning to grow strong and wise with a purpose for your life. Your choice, son of Uriah!"

He thought for a second, wiping the watery, red blood from his face with his forearms. Then the older boy gave him a kind grin and pushed Shuriah to encourage him to move forward and catch up with the others.

They caught up with the other boys jogging across the city to a large, enclosed area behind the palace. That area, a training arena, was a courtyard walled in that was about a hundred feet by a hundred feet. There was a moderately-sized building inside against one wall, and the back wall was the high outer city wall.

The other walls were half that height and wrapped around, secluding everything inside. At the front, four large, wooden doors wide enough for two men to run through dropped to the ground from the top like a drawbridge every twenty-five feet. In the middle of the front wall between doors was a round tunnel at ground level. The width and height were a little bigger than a large armored man's shoulder width.

The group of boys formed a straight line just before they got to the hole in the wall. The daily leader of the warriors' boys stopped and turned around, standing to the side of the hole and watching over the group. To Shuriah's surprise, all the other boys dropped to their knees when they were next in line at the hole and then proceeded to crawl through instead of going through the closed doors. When it got to be his turn, he hesitated, not sure of what was on the other side. The leader glared at him and nodded for him to go through.

He knelt and surveyed where he was going. He only saw legs, so he slowly started to crawl through but was kicked in the backside, jolting him forward. He knew the leader was the one to hurry him through, so he scurried to the other side.

Standing, Shuriah looked around, beginning to understand what this place was.

The leader came in from behind and ordered him to get in line as he was shoved in the back to get out of the way. He watched the boy walk around to the front of the line, boasting out orders, ending with "Everyone, to the dining hall!"

The group took off, anxious to have their morning meal. "Shuriah!" the leader shouted out. "Come with me."

They walked in the same direction as the others, but when they got to the dining area of the side building in the courtyard, the two went into another room where a fire had been going. Several women, clearly servants, had been preparing the meal. As they approached the hot, intoxicating aroma of baked bread and roasted lamb, the leader said, "You will serve all the warriors' sons today—all day! Then you will clean up after them." Stepping up close and looking down at the new Israelite boy, he said sternly, "You will eat *nothing* today because you did not fulfill my orders to fill a pot full of water. You only carried one back to help another who will be the leader tomorrow because he filled the most!" He then shot an angry frown toward Shuriah. But Shuriah thought the facial expression was meant for the older warrior child he had helped, not him.

The daily leader turned away, going into the dining hall as an older woman approached him with a large basket of bread. She handed the basket to him, asking with a big smile, "What is your name, new one?" She reached out and stroked his long, scraggly hair away from his face to see him clearly. Before he responded, she called back to another woman to bring a wet cloth. The much younger woman stepped up to them with a wet cloth and took note of the mess on the boy's face. She bent down and gently cleaned the drying blood and said under her breath in a disgusted tone, "They are only children!"

"Now, now, Bathsheba. Watch what you say. You know this is the best way to create mighty warriors such as your father to protect our people and to conquer other nations with power and speed."

"I know, but it's hard for me to see them hurting themselves or each other at this age. They are so young."

The older woman, humored by her comment, responded with, "You're not much older than today's lead warrior boy, Bathsheba." The older girl stood up, finished cleaning the boy's face, and answered with her hands on her hips, "I might be younger and unmarried, but I'm definitely more mature!"

Shuriah had not stopped staring at the older girl who had cleaned his face. Even in his young years, he knew what a beautiful woman looked like. And the most beautiful one he had ever seen was just now touching his face and standing tall, fully developed, less than a half step from him. He was watching her face as she talked with the older lady. The older lady nudged the basket in his hands, saying, "You need to get the bread into the dining area and stop staring…." She hesitated, remembering she hadn't gotten his name, and asked, "What was your name, boy?"

"My new name is Shuriah. I am the warrior son of Uriah, the Hittite."

CHAPTER 5

It was a very difficult and painful day for Shuriah. He didn't know what he was supposed to do or what was going on most of the time. The other boys either ignored him, made fun of him, or made his day worse. The daily leader never let up, pushing him to do things or correcting and disciplining him in front of the others—purposely humiliating him.

They never left the training facility or saw another adult except for the women who prepared the meals. He was the only one who served the others, cleaned up each time, and never ate.

They spent the whole day only conditioning their bodies, never touching a weapon. Continually, the group ran around the arena. They raced one another, ran as a group in orderly lines, and even practiced running as close to one another as possible without tripping over each other. They also did so many different exercises that they could hardly lift their arms or legs.

Shuriah was always last at everything and, most of the time, couldn't finish what the group was doing. His body felt like it was going to collapse from fatigue. Every time he attempted to drink a lot of water to recover and fill his empty belly, he would throw it up. Halfway through the day, he thought he was going to die. The older boy he had helped earlier in the morning was the only one to give him encouragement.

Finally, before the sun set on the other side of the city wall, it was time for the last meal, which ended the daily training. Because he was barely able to walk or carry the food items, the women had to help him. The cruel words from the boys making fun of him for having women do his job didn't bother him. He was so lethargic he couldn't concentrate on anyone or anything. Finally, after all the boys were fed, he took a seat on the floor next to that older boy, dropping his head and falling asleep.

The boy nudged Shuriah not to fall asleep and slowly moved his hand so no one could see him place a sizable piece of meat under Shuriah's leg. It took a moment for Shuriah to understand what he was doing. As he reached down and felt the chunk of meat, his eyes popped open. He looked over, surprised. The older boy gave a slight wink and turned away, adjusting his body to hide the new, young warrior from sight. Shuriah looked around, making sure no one was looking, and then leaned farther behind the boy, popping the much-needed gift into his mouth.

After the boys were dismissed for the evening and Shuriah was done cleaning up the dining area with the women, he painstakingly walked home, exhausted, discouraged, and feeling completely defeated. For a young boy who had been living alone, freezing at night and hot during the day with very little food in his stomach and no one to call family, he was beginning to think this new life was worse.

When he finally found his home, he walked in to find Uriah kneeling next to the fire, cooking his dinner. Uriah looked up and saw the unfortunate (but expected) condition his new son was in. Every first day for all young ones starting training as a warrior son is a confusing and painful day. They do not know what is going on or why they are doing it. And they are pushed further physically than they had ever been in their lives.

"How was your day, Shuriah?" Uriah asked calmly, looking back at his cooking pot.

It took him a moment to answer as he sluggishly dropped onto his new bed, putting his head down into his arms. "It was terrible, Father."

There was silence for a few minutes as Uriah filled a bowl of food for himself and went to sit next to his new son. First taking a couple of bites, he chewed methodically and asked (though he knew the answers), "Tell me about the whole day."

Shuriah had been crying softly in his arms. He sniffled and managed to slur out, "They took me to the other side of the city. I didn't understand what they were doing, running around filling water pots from different houses. By the time I figured out what to do, I was tricked by an older boy to carry a pot for him; then, I didn't get the credit. Since I didn't fill a pot, I wasn't allowed to eat all day."

"Why did the boy trick you?" Uriah said gently. "He told me he was helping me learn lessons."

"Did you learn a lesson?"

Shuriah raised his head, saying sarcastically, "Yes, don't trust anyone here! It's no different from Shechem."

Uriah turned away, smiling, knowing these were normal things that happened during training. But most of the time, this led to purposeful growth, in the end, building strong relationships and, ultimately, mighty warriors.

Turning back to his son, he asked, "So you didn't eat anything all day?"

Shuriah dropped his head back down, saying, "No." Then, he popped it back up, adding with slight enthusiasm, "Except at the last meal a short while ago. After serving everyone with the women, I sat down next to the older boy, who was now being nice to me after he tricked me. He secretly gave me a piece of meat to eat."

"Did you eat it?"

"Yes. I was careful the lead warrior boy and the others didn't see me put it in my mouth."

Only slightly surprised, he asked, "So...you weren't supposed to eat anything, but you did?"

In the moment of the stressful and dramatic day, his mind had been clouded until now. From the way his father stated the question, it hit him he had done something very wrong. He looked into his father's eyes, believing he was going to be punished, expecting to be backhanded and whipped based on past experiences with other men who said they were his father.

But instead, Uriah handed his full bowl of food to him. "Eat. You will need all you can get into your body. For tomorrow will be just as bad or worse, depending on which boy is going to be lead warrior. Do you know which boy it will be?"

Shuriah paused, putting a handful of food in his mouth, saying, "The older boy who gave me the piece of meat."

Uriah raised his eyebrows, understanding his naïve son didn't realize he was tricked again and waited for him to put the puzzle together.

Shuriah gulped down a couple more bites and realized Uriah had been waiting for him to respond but didn't know why so he asked, "What is it, Father? I know now I did wrong eating the meat, but he was being nice helping me because I was hungry and hadn't eaten all day."

The big man stood up and went to his cooking pot, dishing himself out some more dinner. He held off responding until he was next to his son, who was rapidly finishing his bowl of food.

Uriah spoke softly, "Have there been times when you haven't had anything to eat all day?"

He raised his drooping head, widening his heavy eyes, and said, "Yes, many days, especially when living outside Shechem by myself. Many times, I wouldn't have any food for a day or two! One time I hadn't eaten for four days because some of the townspeople had their dogs chase me far away!" He spouted out with a small boast of energy, "But I ended up killing one of them and ate it!"

Uriah let his son think about what he had just told him before replying, "So what was different about today than any of those other days you didn't eat that you were used to?"

"We ran all day long in all sorts of ways." He frowned, not understanding why they did the things they were doing, and added, "Then we worked our arms and legs over and over until we couldn't lift them. I was exhausted, and my body was shaking from not having any food. I even vomited several times."

Uriah was not surprised at what the boys did; it was routine physical conditioning the first week of a new boy joining the warriors. But he did ask, "Is that reason to disobey the lead warrior boy's instructions for not accomplishing the morning duty?"

He sat there, thinking, and then answered, "I guess I didn't realize it was a big deal as long as I got away with it and no one knew."

"Oh four actually know, Shuriah!"

He looked up to his father, proudly blurting out, "No, no one knows. I made sure no one saw." Then he gave a confident smile, believing his father would be proud as well.

Raising an eyebrow and tilting his head down, he answered, "How about the one boy who gave you the food?"

There was silence as the young boy was trying hard to stay awake and put together the conversation and everything that happened throughout the day.

Uriah raised a second finger as though counting and added, "You know, Shuriah."

Shuriah crinkled his face, thinking to himself, *Of course I know!* Uriah held up three fingers now and pointed to himself, saying, "I know. But most of all…the Lord of heaven's armies knows," Uriah said, coming full circle in the conversation, lifting a fourth finger.

The more his father talked, the smaller Shuriah felt himself getting. "When we disobey an order, no matter how small it might seem or how big it is, there is always a consequence—a consequence we must live with for the rest of our lives."

"But I only ate one piece of meat?" Shuriah said, looking up innocently.

"It has nothing to do with the food, Shuriah. You chose to let the weaknesses of your body, hunger, and exhaustion, control your mind and moral values, which could take your heart down a wrong path in life, making you a weak man. You might have been very tired and hungry, but you just told me you have been there before many times, and obviously, you're still alive."

Shuriah tried hard to understand; his head was swirling in a fog from being so tired. He could hardly keep his eyes open, and his satisfied stomach put him over the edge. His father took his bowl, telling him to go ahead and fall asleep, for tomorrow will be another big day.

Just before drifting off, Shuriah asked with concern, "So what is the older boy going to do to me for disobeying the other leader?"

"He is not the one to worry about. Yes, he trains your body

and mind to learn to always obey the leaders God puts in your path. And your leaders must know they can trust you, no matter how bad things get, especially during a battle. But your main concern needs to be with the Lord of heaven's armies. For God sees a man's heart"—Uriah gently tapped the boy's chest—"and knows what it is filled with. And that's what always controls our lives. What is in your heart, son?" he asked. Pausing, he finished with, "When your heart is clean and filled with truth, the power of God is very strong in you!"

The large number of ships on the Mediterranean Sea started to rock up and down more vigorously the closer it got for the sun to rise off the horizon. A knock came at the cabin door of General Shuriah. "General, your assistance is needed at the stern. A storm is coming our way."

Shuriah raised himself out of bed away from the warm blankets and his wife, Tara, and replied groggily, "I'll be there shortly!"

He rose, stretching his old, muscular body. With age came the pains of life in his joints and the many battle wounds marked by scars on his arms, legs, and torso. He looked back down at his beautiful wife of many years. She was still sleeping as he gently covered her back up, thinking how blessed he had been with Tara in his life. She bore him many children over the years who were all adults now—two sons and several daughters who were joining them on this epic journey.

Always dressed battle-ready, he wore thick animal hide foot coverings that thinned out as they extended up tied tightly just below his knees. Protecting his shins over the hide on the front side of his legs, iron leg guards plated in gold with artistic designs were firmly strapped on.

His peplos waist wrap that covered his groin tunic was belted, skirting loosely to his knees and patterned with many Israelite designs and configurations. Attached to the side of the belt was a sheath with his battle knife in it, along with two smaller throwing knives that were hidden and secured on his lower back upside down. They crisscrossed each other at an angle for easy access; he simply had to reach low behind him to draw and kill.

Strapped to his back at another angle was his wide-bladed sword—handle sticking up next to his head to be drawn out over his shoulder.

On his core frame against his body, he wore a soft lamb's skin sleeveless shirt, on top of which was multilayered body armor fitted over his head, draping down the front and back. This first inner layer of armor against the lamb's skin was three thick layers of tough animal hide, and the second outer layer on the back and front comprised iron that was gold plated and secured to the animal hide.

Again, artistic designs swirled around in the gold, matching the leg protectors, which matched his final armor attire of iron forearm shields plated in gold. They were secured firmly over animal hide against his skin as well.

He also had a thick, animal-hide helmet with gold-plated iron plates surrounding the outside. But he didn't put that on unless he was in an actual battle.

Dressing for the anticipated weather on its way, he put on a heavy, long-sleeved robe with a hood that had an oily, waterproof coating on the outside. It was striped with two wide bands dyed red that spanned from the bottom of the back over his shoulders to the bottom in the front. Golden thread was widely woven the width of a man's hand around all the edges of the robe, top to bottom.

After putting everything on, he looked into the reflective mirror made from pure silver attached to a wall in the dressing area. Adjusting his stance to keep his balance with the ship rocking up and down, he combed out his long, black, and grayish-white hair, tying it together in the back. Then he combed out his large beard over which he prided and which matched the color of the hair on his head. As he finished getting ready, the general stared at himself for a moment, asking humorously, "What have you gotten yourself into this time? He called it an epic journey?"

Lifting his hand, he looked at the new addition to his body—the large signature ring of King Solomon. Clearing his thoughts, he realized he had been dreaming throughout the night about his childhood when his father, Uriah, and he first met and when he began his adventure to become a mighty warrior.

Stepping up onto the upper deck, a gust of wind hit him. He didn't let one drop of the salty sea affect his demeanor, for he was the one with ultimate authority. He walked powerfully to the stern, where a young ship captain and one of his regular soldiers were doing their best to keep the ship in formation.

Peering around to the open sea, he saw his fleet attempting to navigate the high-rolling waves as the morning sun dimmed by way of dark clouds marching across the sky. Shuriah asked calmly, "Have instructions been given from the forward lead ship to maneuver into defensive positions against the weather?"

"No, General."

"Call out, and make it happen!"

"Yes, General," the captain replied weakly.

Shuriah looked into the younger captain's eyes, seeing he needed to build confidence in him since this was his first time as a full-fledged captain—the captain of the General's ship, no less. He added, "Fear is not an option! Do your job as if you are doing it for the Lord of heaven's armies, not me or our king!" Shuriah raised his hand with the large ring on it, making a point, clenching a fist toward the captain's face. "The might of God is revealing that He is with us! Not the worthless powers of darkness that are against us!"

Releasing his fist and putting his hand on the young captain's shoulder, he ended by saying, "Embrace God's might, for He loves going into battle with His people!" Shuriah bared a determined grin of anticipation, excited for what they were about to go through.

The captain's body language suddenly changed, standing more erect, inhaling deeply, puffing out his chest, and yelling to the men while grasping tightly to the sides of the ship, waiting for instruction.

"Call out to the fleet, and order everyone into weather battle formation!"

Hearing the confident tone of the captain, all the men hurriedly began their specific duties. Some dropped any remaining sails that were up, while others double-checked that everything was tied down and securely anchored.

At each end of the ship, loud rams' horns could be heard, blasting out instructions to the other ships near them that could hear over the windy sea. Instantly, the surrounding ships sounded off with the same message, repeating the process until all the ships were informed.

Large, brightly-colored identification flags were set in place, each with Solomon's mark in the middle. A red one stuck out high at the bow, a green one at the stern, and a yellow one was placed at the top of the mast. The different colors helped other ships locate and understand what direction the opposing ships were heading in order to avoid crashing into each other under low visibility.

Shuriah's ship was in the center of the forty-five, sailing north. After the rams' horns stopped blowing and the flags were raised, ships began to gradually disembark from eagle formation. The purpose of the message sent for battle against the weather was to spread out from each other until the nearest ship was at a good distance on the horizon. The original shape of an eagle transformed into that of target rings billowing out from Shuriah's ship in the very center. In this arrangement, most of the ships could keep an eye on one another and stay in a group without veering away.

Once the outer ring (which was all Israeli warships protecting King Hiram's cargo ships) was formed, they blew the rams' horns again but in a completely different melody—one that informed the inner ring's ships that they were in place and prepared for battle against the storm that was now directly above them.

The storm lasted throughout the day and all the next night, showering rain with waves arching over the side walls as wind continually fought to control the direction the ships were going. When the invisible daily sun set, bringing complete darkness to the world at night, every ship lit its large signal torch that was centered in the middle of the boat. This was positioned in a manner so that from any angle and distance, other closer ships could see the flames and would have a better perspective of where the center of the ship was on a stormy night. This gave better awareness to stay an equal distance away all around the torch.

Lightning bolts whipped across the sky, screaming the power of God throughout the sea as thundering explosions vibrated the wooden vessels, penetrating every heart that was submitting to the Creator's supremacy.

Throughout the rough day, Shuriah walked placidly around

his water-soaked ship that was being tossed around, encouraging the crew to be strong and courageous. He did not show one sign of fear or worry as they continuously bailed water. It didn't surprise the soldiers to see their general this way—in control with peaceful emotions, which was the complete opposite of when they were in battle in hand-to-hand combat.

That's when he switched into a completely different human being, inside and out—one with the appearance of a fighting tiger and a heart empty of compassion or remorse. He relished war, and the more fighting he was involved in, the happier he was.

No one ever wanted to get on General Shuriah's bad side during times of battle (or peace). And when someone was out of line, needed discipline, or was complaining, his mighty warriors knew to attempt to take control of the situation before it got to him because if it did, usually someone died by his hands. It wasn't that he had an uncontrollable temper; it was that he had such high expectations of himself to succeed and conquer that he battled unobtainable expectations from everyone else.

He was never lazy or weak and never made excuses for himself. He always lived with Godlike expectations, which are limitless—unlike feeble, human expectations. That was why he was always successful in war and brought prosperity to Israel, making him a great general.

Fortunately, the tranquil side of him was seen more often because the people who knew him knew his expectations and worked hard to achieve them. He also had a very sensitive heart for those who truly could not take care of themselves and needed help, young or old.

Finally, the storm subsided, and the sea began to rest once again. It was early the next morning, as a sliver of light was scarcely seen on the horizon as the sun pushed hard to start a fresh, new day. One by one, torches began to appear at farther distances over the serene water now absent of waves. Excitement built within every ship when another torch was seen, confirming more of their fleet was still alive.

In one direction on the outer ring of the ship's target formation, a few men yelled out, "General, signal arrows have been shot in the air!" As soon as they said that, rams' horns bellowed as loud as they could, only faintly heard from the large distance.

When a ship wasn't in formation or seen by the surrounding ships, it was assumed to be lost after a storm. The protocol was for the adjacent ships to shoot arrows into the air as high as they could with a large flame lit at the tip. Then the ship would blow deep blasts from rams' horns to attempt to locate the lost ship and notify the rest of the fleet that a ship was missing in their section.

Shuriah and the rest of the soldiers on deck looked in the direction the men pointed. Still looking outward, the general asked sharply, "What are we to do, Captain?"

The young captain knew he was being tested and replied assuredly, "Maintain our heading as we reconfigure into eagle battle formation, General! The lost ship knows to continue in the direction of our destination. It could take one or two days and nights for them to catch up or find us. By the third day, if they have not shown up, we move forward at full sail, leaving our prayers behind for them to find their way safely!"

The general turned around without changing his facial expression, replying, "Well done! Forward to success, Captain!" He walked down to his private cabin where his wife and his youngest (unmarried) daughter were—safely staying out of the weather.

Once in the cabin, Tara helped him take off the heavy-hood-ed robe, all the metal armor, and the rest of the clothing, leaving just his groin tunic. After a brief conversation and a meal with his family, he lay down on the bed as the sun rose outside. He was tired from no sleep, having helped his soldiers battle the storm since it started more than a day ago.

Ready to get out of the cramped cabin, Tara and their daughter went up to the upper deck to help care for the other soldiers who were tired, wet, cold, and hungry.

As the general drifted off to sleep, his older body exhausted, his mind kept moving, catching up to where he left off in his dream as a child.

It had been over a month since the new warrior boy Shuriah arrived in Jerusalem. He caught on quickly to the daily routine of extreme physical exercise, as well as the different morning jobs they had to do around the city before the training and morning meal.

He did have to forgo more meals for not accomplishing other new duties that he didn't understand. But once he understood the job, the young warrior excelled at completing it.

By the fourth time he missed the daily meals, Uriah helped him to understand not to focus on hunger or food and let it control him but to redirect his thoughts and energy from his stomach to his mind. They strategized to do the jobs faster and better to beat all the other boys, making it his goal to be the daily leader, even though he was one of the younger boys who never seemed to achieve the honor.

Uriah would always end their evening discussions by giving him strong encouragement with this statement: *Always work hard, be wise, and be honest as you do everything wholeheartedo-*

ly as though you are doing them for the Lord of heaven's armies. He pounded his chest in emphasis and added, *For God can and will defeat any giant in our lives for those who are faithful!*

Every time his father made that statement, it was said with passion and complete trust, as though he had lived it and experienced the defeat of many impossible giants in his life.

For the past month since he arrived, the group of boys had been training very hard by running and exercising to build strength and greater stamina. Shuriah was always kept in the dark about why this was the only thing they did day in and day out, never seeing a soldier or a mighty warrior in the training area. He also wondered why they were not training with weapons or doing other fighting events he expected to do in becoming a warrior.

They were keeping it from him, purposely helping their weakest warrior to catch up in body strength, endurance, and speed with the others who were already amply conditioned for their young ages. It was all so he could become 'an equal' in the group as quickly as possible. Then once they started all the other training and exercises with hand-to-hand combat, weapons, horses, and battle strategies, the new warrior-to-be would not hold them back. Despite their strict discipline, they did not want him to fail… even though they could all be called to war at any time.

Meeting up with all the warrior children on the outside of the training wall, they lined up next to the tunnel leading into the arena before taking off to do the morning duty somewhere in the city as the sun rose to warm the day with its bright glow. The new day felt different when Shuriah arrived, though; he could tell something was unusual in the atmosphere from the other boys' demeanor and facial expressions. They reflected uneasiness and a touch of fear he had not seen before.

Once all the boys were lined up, the lead young warrior of the day (who happened to be the same older boy who helped him his first day) walked over and stepped up very close. He paused and said, "Shuriah, warrior son of mighty warrior, Uriah, today you must prove you are worthy of being a warrior son. Up until now, you have only been chosen because of your life situation as an orphan living homeless like all of us did at one time." The older boy looked around, eyeing and pointing to all his fellow warrior brothers.

"We have worked hard so you would quickly become as physically strong and fast as we are. Only half of the new warrior sons ever get to this day. They usually give up and run away by now, only to be cowards begging for handouts the rest of their lives."

Pausing again and narrowing his eyes, he tried to maintain his composure, having become fond of the new young warrior child. "Even fewer warrior boys live past this day!"

Shuriah frowned, looking up, unsure if the older boy was perhaps playing a joke on him with such dramatic words.

"Today will prove to King David…and your mighty warrior father, Uriah"—the young leader turned to look up at a private balcony where the two aforementioned men stood as the older boy bowed and the other boys imitated—"if you are worthy of continuing on as a fully trained mighty warrior son."

To this point, no mighty warrior, regular soldier, or guard had observed or instructed the warrior children on anything (except for the women cooking inside the training facility). It was only the daily leaders who guided everyone.

Every day Shuriah was disappointed not to see an adult soldier or mighty warrior inside the compound. He wanted to do something other than the boring, painful, and exhausting workouts. Constantly he asked his father 'why' when he got back home every evening, to which Uriah would repeatedly reply, "Focus on working harder every day, getting *stronger* and *faster* as you build endless *endurance*. Understand *you* have the *strength of the God*"—Uriah always emphasized the words by pounding his chest with his big fist—*"of Israel in you!* For a day is coming soon that you must prove yourself worthy!"

Shuriah never pressed him for a better answer because he knew from his demeanor he couldn't say anything more. Also, his statement closely matched the words of the songs they would chant during the workouts to keep their minds off of what their bodies were going through to help pass the time.

The lead boy continued, "Shuriah, you alone must now go into the arena. You will find twelve mighty warriors spread out evenly against the walls, representing the twelve tribes of Israel. Each adult warrior will have a different weapon in his hands. You must choose wisely a weapon with which to defend yourself.

"Once you have chosen a weapon, you must go to the center of the arena, where you will have to defend yourself against what is waiting for you in the cage."

Shuriah blurted out, "Defend myself? Against who? With a weapon? But we haven't trained—"

The older boy cut him off. "We have all gone through this, asking the same questions." He pointed to the other boys, still watching intently, and said, "You do have one chance right now to give up and not continue your training to be a mighty warrior. But once you crawl through the tunnel entrance, there will be no turning back." The taller, mature boy crossed his arms, shifting his tone and posture. "If you want to be one of us like our warrior fathers, the fiercest fighters of all the nations, then you must go through the entrance and kill what is presented to you in the center of the training facility—covered up and in a cage."

Still crossing his arms, his tone became sarcastic. "*Or* you can walk away now only to become a poor commoner at best, maybe becoming someone's servant or slave."

"How am I to make a decision on what weapon to choose when I don't know what I have to kill?" Thinking this through, he added, frightened, "You first said to defend myself. Is this person or animal going to try to kill me?"

The older boy, remembering many past children losing their lives violently, tried not to put on a regrettable expression, answering plainly, "Yes…yes it will."

Then he shrugged his shoulders, giving him an encouraging smile, completely believing what he was going to say next from personal experience. "But what does it matter if *you*"—he now pointed to Shuriah's chest—"believe in your heart you have the strength and power of God within you?"

When the older boy poked him and delivered those words, Shuriah suddenly knew this whole time that the daily conditioning, singing, and encouraging words from his father collectively had purpose. But still, it was unclear what that purpose was. Then the leader added, "The Lord of heaven's armies rules all beasts and men with a simple weapon. What weapon do you think our God would use?"

Thinking about the question, Shuriah looked up to the balcony, seeing his warrior father and the king, who were staring down at him. Trying not to become more scared than he already was, he looked back down at the leader of the young group and attempted to decipher what weapon he was talking about. Then he turned and crawled through the small tunnel into the arena.

Once inside, he saw the mighty warriors standing proudly yet patiently in their battle gear along the walls all the way around, each holding a different weapon to use against whatever was in the covered cage in the center of the training facility. The cage was quiet, as though there was nothing inside it, which gave him hope that it was empty. Maybe this was only a test to see if he was bold enough to move forward with the horrifying thought of being attacked or killed.

The fierce warriors waited motionless for him to decide on a weapon. Slowly, he walked around the arena, stopping in front of each warrior, admiring the powerful and spectacular weapons they were holding. First, there was a large, shiny sword, then a long spear with a sharp bronze head on it, then a swirling slingshot with smooth stones, then a battle knife, and then a bow and its arrows. Shuriah was stumped at the next thing he was staring at because it appeared to be out of place. Looking at a full-sized sheep herder's staff with a large, curved hook at the top, the warrior son was perplexed at why a mighty warrior would be holding a lowly sheep herder's staff as a weapon.

After taking a moment, he continued around, viewing the rest of the exciting weapons of war he had never seen before during his life on the outskirts of Shechem. When he came full circle back to the sword, he narrowed his choices down to two: the sword and the long spear. His young mind thought they were the easiest for him to use that would also do the most damage to kill anything. Looking up at the burly warrior with the sword, he asked in his higher-pitched voice, "Can I hold this first before I decide?"

Without saying anything, the warrior handed the sword to him. The weight of the shiny metal sword surprised him, and he almost dropped it. He struggled to bring it up and tried to swing it around in a defensive manner.

But it was awkward and clumsy for him, and suddenly, he felt foolish having it in his hands. He struggled to lift it back up to the mighty warrior. Then he stepped to the man next to him with the spear. This warrior did the same thing, handing the long-shafted spear with the solid, bronze, sharp head at the tip.

Shuriah did not grab it up higher for better balance; instead, he grabbed it low (at his own height) when the tall warrior let go. The heavy spearhead plummeted sideways, rotating the long weapon until the bronze head hit the ground. He flushed red as he slid his hands up the shaft, struggling to lift the weapon into a position that was comfortable to use it properly.

Handing the spear back, he turned around, looking at all the different weapons the warriors were holding, realizing the only one he could actually use effectively was the long, light-weighted shepherd's staff.

CHAPTER 6

Shuriah walked across the training arena to the warrior holding the shepherd's staff. When he got to the proud man, they locked eyes for a moment. Then without emotion, the mighty warrior slowly handed the staff to the boy as though it was very valuable.

Grasping the staff with both hands, it instantly felt right. It was solid and well-balanced but not too heavy. His eyes followed the length of the long stick, noticing it was well used, as evidenced by scratches and a darker stain in the middle from being handled more often than other areas.

Looking up, Shuriah candidly asked, "Why is this old, used, and made out of wood when all the other weapons are new, shiny, and made out of metal?"

Taken back, the warrior replied in a deep voice, "Does it matter what a weapon looks like or how old it is if one knows how to use it?"

The boy looked down at the aged stick and asked another question, "But this isn't really a weapon like the other things. Isn't it made to help and save sheep?"

The warrior began to admire the boy for thinking things through as he replied, "A weapon is anything that helps and saves people. What do you think a weapon is made for in the first place?"

Disconcerted at the profound thought, Shuriah clarified, "Even though a sword or spear is only used to kill, it is saving the lives of who they are protecting."

The man kept his stern demeanor and only nodded that Shuriah was right. The warrior son looked back down at the staff in his hands. He twisted it upright and stabbed it into the ground. Looking up at the mighty warrior, he asked, "I choose this as my weapon. Now what?"

Sticking to his stiff posture, the large man answered, "Now you will go to the covered cage in the center and face your first adversary."

"My what?" he asked with a frown.

"Your first enemy. And you must kill *it* before it kills *you*," the warrior cautioned sternly as his eyes drifted to the cage.

Shuriah followed the man's eyes to the cage, hearing words echo in his head from today's daily leader: *While even fewer warrior boys live past this day!*

Fear began to quicken Shuriah's heart. He was not sure what to expect, and at the same time, he asked himself why any of these mighty warriors would put him in any danger when he was working hard to be one of them.

Looking back up again, the tall warrior only nudged his head for him to go to the cage. Immediately responding, Shuriah tried his best not to show that he was afraid in front of all these warriors, piercing him with their eyes. Once at the cage, he heard something large move and sniff the air hidden under the cover, letting Shuriah know it knew he was there. Widening his eyes for the unexpected, his mind was swirling with nightmarish visions. Then he thought, *I'm only a kid. Why would these so-called warrior fathers want to put a warrior son in harm's way? Especially when they protected me from the people of Shechem, and they want me to be one of them?*

Holding the shepherd's staff out in front of him, he waited for something to happen, glancing up over the wall hiding the training arena where King David and Uriah were still standing on the balcony watching him. Shuriah caught Uriah's eye, and Uriah just barely moved his hand as though sending him a private message from a distance—like he was pounding his chest.

Shuriah straightened his back, knowing exactly what he was telling him—the same thing he saw every evening. Suddenly he felt himself stand up taller and straighter, seeing in his mind his father's serious face, believing that made him a mighty warrior. As inner confidence was growing to face whatever was in the cage, Shuriah repeated his father's words in his mind. *Always work hard, be wise, and be honest, as you do everything wholeheartedly as though you are doing them for the Lord of heaven's armies. For God can defeat any giant in our lives for those who are faithful!*

Without warning (his head was still turned to the palace), the cover of the cage was swiftly pulled off with a snap by one of the mighty warriors. He had pulled on a rope from across the arena that was attached to it along the ground. Instantly, the cage door facing him was assaulted by a full-grown leopard, springing full force to attack him.

Shuriah tumbled backward onto his backside, dropping the shepherd's staff. Horrified at what was only an arm's length away, all logical and wise thoughts disappeared as complete fear exploded throughout his body. As the cage held firm, a mighty warrior stepped up between the cage and Shuriah. He looked down at the boy, smiling, and held his hand out, saying, "Shuriah, warrior son of Uriah, you have successfully passed your first test to be a mighty warrior. Bent over, Shuriah stared wide-eyed at the man and tried to understand what was going on. He looked around the man at the leopard, pacing back and forth, snarling and hissing, showing its teeth, and thought to himself, *How did I pass the test? It scared me to death.*

He then looked around at all the other warriors around the training arena, who were now in a casual stance, smiling and raising their hands in victory for him. Glancing to the palace, he saw King David clapping, and his father was nodding his head that he had done well.

Looking back to the warrior who was still bent over with his hand held out, Shuriah started to ask how he passed the test when out of the corner of his eye, he caught something else behind the man. When he had bent down to help Shuriah up, the sword on his hip (which stuck out past his backside and lifted behind him) gently lifted the cage latch that was holding the door closed.

The door had begun to swing open slowly and quietly as the leopard crouched, waiting for his moment to leap onto the man. Unable to utter a word of warning, he grasped a handful of dirt. Simultaneously, he spied a knife handle sticking out of a sheath strapped to the side of the man's lower leg; he rolled forward, snatched the knife with his free hand, and threw the handful of dirt directly into the large cat's face right as it began to leap.

Being fast himself, Shuriah leaped onto the man's thigh that was halfway bent, leaned forward, and pushed off into the air, spearing the knife and meeting the leopard in midair. The dirt thrown hit its mark just in time for the cat to lose enough focus that it didn't see the long knife coming. It was impaled down its throat as it had opened its mouth in anticipation of biting the prey in front of it.

Shuriah screamed in pain because the cat had swiped his arms with its dangerous claws. He fell to the ground, and the leopard ripped at his hand with its exposed teeth. The mighty warrior, not realizing what happened, swung around to see the cat out of the cage and the boy's body wrapped up in its legs. Without thinking, he dove straight for the small boy and grasped the paws as he planted his foot forcefully down on the neck of the cat, yelling, "Get out of here, boy!"

Shuriah rolled around on the ground, screaming in agony from the deep scratches down his arms and the puncture wounds on his hand. Instantly all the mighty warriors ran to give aid as Uriah yelled in horror—heard across the back of the palace and the training arena.

The daily leader and all the warrior sons heard the screaming came out of the arena. They all went to their knees in prayer, knowing what had happened. They had seen this many times when new warrior boys made the wrong decision about which weapon of war to choose. Then the animals inside the cage were let loose, making the boys defend themselves as punishment for not using wisdom in selecting their weapon…they had to prove they could physically protect themselves with their chosen weapon.

All the warriors inside the arena were at Shuriah's side, making sure his wounds were not life-threatening. Then they attended to their warrior brother, who had several minor injuries.

The group of men calmed Shuriah down, letting him know he was safe and was going to be fine even though he was in pain and still bleeding. They helped him stand. Trembling from the pain and fright, they still directed him to step to the cat lying dead with the handle of the knife sticking out of its mouth and blood seeping onto the ground so that he could observe his first kill.

Carefully, the mighty warrior that Shuriah saved picked him

up and put him on his shoulders. All at once, a roar of shouts came from the arena as all the warriors chanted their victory song in unison like they do after a battle and stabbed the sky with their swords and spears.

King David and Uriah stood at the edge of the railing, gaping in shock at what they had just seen. Then David turned to Uriah and placed his hands on top of both shoulders, saying, "Today we saw a giant be killed by an innocent boy. It reminds me of another boy who killed a giant, and God made him great!"

Uriah knew exactly who he was talking about. He smiled back and said, "Praise to the Lord of heaven's armies. For we need great people as you lead the nation of Israel."

"Leading *our* nation of Israel, Hittite. You are one of us!"

Days passed while Shuriah stayed at home, recovering from his wounds. During this time, there was an unexpected victory celebration in the palace—partially for the wise decision in choosing the correct weapon but mostly for putting himself in harm's way to protect a fellow warrior by killing a ferocious animal.

Within the group of young, mighty warriors-to-be, there was a new and great respect for the warrior son of Uriah the Hittite. They would come by every evening after their daily training to see how he was doing and to tell him they couldn't wait for him to be able to join them when he was healed.

Uriah was a very proud father. It took everything in him not to boast of his wise and courageous son, especially since he was the newest, and one of the youngest, of all the warriors' sons in training.

King David had given him a special gift at the ceremony in the palace: the shepherd's staff Shuriah chose as a weapon. It was his personal one from when he was a young boy watching over his father's sheep. The king told exciting stories the night he gave it to him about when he was a boy alone in the wilderness and when animals would try to take his father's sheep. He would have to save the sheep by chasing the wild animals away or fighting them to the death. It got really exciting when he told them he had killed lions and bears, sometimes with his bare hands.

These images created excitement, courage, and great expectations for Shuriah as he began to understand the purpose of the training he had been going through and the meaning of the latest test. He also suspected other tests that were hinted to come by some of the other warrior sons.

As soon as his wounds were healed, he was thrown back into the daily training of running and working out. His muscles were treated as though his exciting victory and brave moment never happened. The only difference he did feel was an underlining respect and confidence the boys now had in him. They no longer talked to him as though he was young and naïve but as an equal warrior son, training together as a unified army.

Once Shuriah caught up with the other boys and had reached the expectations of the mighty warriors in physical conditioning (leaving no one as a weak link), the mighty warrior fathers systematically changed the training to hand-to-hand combat—the second stage of training. Then after weeks of this grueling training of how to defend and kill with bare hands, weapons were slowly integrated—knives, then swords and shields, spears, bows and arrows, and so on. The weapons, along with body armor, were made specifically for the size of each boy's body.

This system of all the boys going back and retraining when a new warrior son was adopted was the natural process to bring a new boy into the fold of warriorhood to grow them together as a group.

This wise process for the young boys was crucial to make

sure their abilities were as equal as they could be. So when engaged side by side in battle with their warrior fathers, everyone was confident during the frenzy of warfare with what to expect out of every boy just in case something went wrong.

This also strengthened the sons as a unified army, keeping them in healthy relationships to help each other get better as a group and not solely on an individual basis. All the while, they still acknowledged and greatly appreciated that each boy had their own individual talents. One is better with hand-to-hand combat, one is better with a sword, and yet another is better with a bow and arrow.

Knowing these individual strengths, the unit's confidence in strategies using their strengths while knowing their weaknesses helped the warriors to make quick and precise decisions for victory, whether they were boys or full-grown men.

Since Shuriah showed up about a year ago, it had been quiet—no major battles among the surrounding nations of Israel. Shuriah began to grow in strength and wisdom in his young years, completely changing the direction of his future from his trajectory in Shechem.

He was the last warrior son to have been adopted, and probably would be for a while since all thirty-seven mighty warriors now had an adopted son to be trained in becoming a mighty warrior. Uriah had been the only one left not to acquire a son until Shuriah came into his life.

This time of year in early spring, King David would always lead four hundred traditional soldiers chosen out of his tens of thousands who had not yet achieved "mighty warrior" status to a very special place of his called the Cave of Adullam. Included with these soldiers were the thirty-seven warrior sons. With their fathers left behind in Jerusalem, this was the only time they were apart from each other. All the boys except for Shuriah had already been to the Cave of Adullam.

This trip was extremely important to David since he had spent much of his young adult years (before he was protected) hiding from King Saul in a sanctuary of refuge while he and his small, growing army of four hundred grew closer and stronger to each other and most of all, to God. After several days of traveling there, they would spend six days in the cave that was in the mountain wilderness—about a day and a half east-southeast of Bethlehem.

In the moderate-sized hole inside the mountain, the presence of God was overwhelming to all who entered it through the long, narrow tunnel. Everyone had to crawl awkwardly on their hands and knees to get through. God spoke through David, the one man who boldly, courageously, and passionately served the Lord of heaven's armies. David's heart, powerful for the Lord, was very persuasive and determined for all to follow the instructions and laws of God. But most of all, he had a passion for loving his Heavenly Father and wanted everyone else to experience the same relationship he had with God.

When they were in Adullam every spring, they would go into deep meditation with the Lord. The cave was cramped when they were all in it. It smelled musty, and every sound echoed. It was an uncomfortable and irritating place, making some very claustrophobic.

Yet with nothing else to distract them from the outside world, the irritants and clutter would gradually disappear as they were able to forget what was outside and focus on what was going on inside the solemn sanctuary of refuge: the love of God transforming minds as their hearts were being opened and guided to new heights. With renewed vision and purpose inspired by David, who lived close and faithful to the Lord, God would clearly present Himself by building excitement in a new relationship these men had never experienced before. This began to grow fearless courage and establish high expectations of what they could accomplish in this world if they were serving the Lord of heaven's armies, just like boy David with Goliath.

Shuriah marched within the group of warrior boys, following most of the soldiers on foot while a handful rode horses with King David and his bodyguard. They were all in full battle gear, and the soldiers' horses were loaded with extra supplies. Shuriah was continually filled with excitement even though they marched through clouded, dirty air from the horses and soldiers in front of them.

The world had seemed to become small after being in the city surrounded by high walls, but now he was able to see far into the distance (even with dirt-filled eyes). The scenery of the wilderness suggested new adventures as he proudly walked in his battle uniform with a miniature sword strapped tightly to his back. He also had a battle knife strapped upside down on his chest, a shield, and a bow and quiver draped on his back over his sword to leave his hands free.

In the late evening on the second day, the boys talked about all the different battles they had shadowed their warrior fathers as they sat around small fires, eating the last meal of the day. Shuriah was quickly drawn deep into these stories that sounded like fictious dreams. But as the details of battles were revealed, his mind ran rampant, imagining the cries of pain when an adversary was stabbed or their arm was cut off, followed by a shout of victory as the warrior advanced forward to slay another enemy of Israel.

Shuriah was enthralled with the many different stories to the point that he couldn't get enough. He continuously asked questions, wanting more details of the fighting: Who were these enemies of Israel? What did a battle of thousands sound like? What did it look like, and how did it feel to shadow their fathers as they fought in front of them? But what he wanted to know most of all, he asked with enthusiasm, "What does it feel like to kill a grown man?"

Right as he said that in the confidence of the circle of boys sitting around their fire, a soldier who was walking to his tent for the night instantly stopped when he heard the question. He turned to the young boy, irritated at the notion that they now had the responsibility of babysitting even though they were trained soldiers themselves. Then, having drunk too much wine, he answered loudly, "What? Are you street rats planning on killing one of us real soldiers?"

All the warrior sons sitting around nearby fires heard him. At first, it was silent. Then the older boys began to stand one by one, facing the soldier as the younger ones followed suit. Shuriah, looking around, was the last to stand. The man staring him down suddenly found himself the center of attention as the many eyes of the small army of kids, no taller than his shoulders, turned toward him.

The silent commotion caught the attention of soldiers, and the king himself, who were purposely in a wide, protective circle around the children. (King David was once again dressed the same as his soldiers in order to blend in and confuse any adversaries since he didn't have his full army with him.)

One of the older boys, who was at Shuriah's fire, replied confidently, "Sir, we were having a simple conversation about great battles that the army of Israel has had and our victories."

"*Our* victories, you say?" he questioned as his hand went up to the handle of his sword, strumming it with his fingers.

"Yes, sir. We are you, and you are us. There is no difference except for our age. We are *Israel*!" the boy yelled, raising a fist in the air.

The soldier whispered under his breath. His mind was clouded from too much to drink, and he had an obvious chip on his shoulder. "You are *not* me."

King David silently smiled at the boy's answer as the light from the flames flickered off his face. He was very proud of him, but most of all, it confirmed that the training they were going through was producing exactly what he planned and prayed for—a wise and strong army for Israel that was also faithful to God in the *unity* of the chosen people.

All the warrior boys, even Shuriah, chanted with fists raised, "We are Israel: servants of the Lord of heaven's armies!"

It went silent again momentarily as all the soldiers in the large, protective circle were gazing at the boys, holding their ground against a fellow soldier. Then as the boys lowered their arms, they were shocked when the wall of soldiers around them bellowed the exact same chant in grand, deep voices.

As the echo of voices quieted down in the cooling night air, everyone was standing except for the proud king, admiring his army. As his eyes wandered through the crowd, they stopped dead at the man facing the newest warrior boy. The soldier was now looking down at him in anger, thinking it was this child's fault for making him the center of attention. Under the influence of wine, the angered soldier bent down and whispered to the boy, "I should kill you...." His hand was still grasping the handle of his sword, and he started to slide it out.

Shuriah and the boys next to him stared in disbelief. Then an embedded instinct was triggered from their intense training over the past year. Shuriah suddenly leaped in the air as high as he could, reaching back with one of his legs and, with the speed of light, whipped it forward and planted the top of his knee at the base of the man's chin. The soldier was not expecting such a quick response, and his head snapped back with such force that his body collapsed backward.

Shuriah landed straight back down on both feet in a low crouch, having drawn his knife from his chest when he was in the air, ready to defend himself again. It was like slow motion as all the soldiers watched the small boy leap into the air like a lion, attacking with his strongest muscle against a giant, by comparison, who flailed backward to the ground, bouncing until he stopped as though dead.

All eyes were staring, stunned, at the soldier lying there knocked out. The older boy who first spoke to the soldier cracked the silence by shouting orders. In perfect unison, all the warrior boys drew their miniature swords and surrounded Shuriah, waiting for another attack from another soldier. The remaining 399 soldiers could not believe the incredible devotion the boys had for one another, not to mention their fearless courage, willingly to engage grown men in battle.

The soldiers were not sure what to do except to burst out in laughter at one of their own, drunk and stupid. There were cheers for the warrior boy for what he did and great sarcasm for the soldier lying completely helpless at his feet.

David rose, nodding to his bodyguard next to him as the guard commanded, "Our king!"

Instantly everyone went quiet and to their knees, even the boys. The king's identity wasn't ever exposed unless he gave the command, which he had just done. David strolled over to the warrior boys, stopping and looking down at one of his soldiers who had been assaulted.

Breathing deeply, he tried his best to contain his pride in the boy and not favor him in front of the regular soldiers. The anticipation was building for the king's response. Finally, he ordered, "Shuriah, look up at me." Skittishly, Shuriah obeyed, not sure what to expect. "You hurt one of my men. What am I to do?" The king stood there as they locked eyes. There was silence. Then the king added, "You may speak."

Shuriah contemplated and responded, "We have been training to be unified—helping the weaker ones to be as strong as the strongest."

David only nodded his head in agreement, waiting for more, still trying to contain his emotions.

Shuriah looked at the soldier, still unconscious. "This soldier was the weakest of all who are here." He pointed around to include the warrior sons. "Up until moments ago, I thought I was the weakest one until I had to kill him to protect myself as he was drawing his sword!"

There was a murmur and snickering from the surrounding soldiers at his comment.

"But Shuriah, warrior son of Uriah the Hittite, you only knocked him out with your knee; you didn't kill him." Shuriah asked if he could stand. David nodded that it was okay.

After Shuriah stood there for a moment, he raised his knife for the king to take. David took the knife but didn't understand until his eyes caught a glimpse of what was on the tip of the knife. Taking him by complete surprise, David stepped to the fire to shed light on the end of the knife to clearly see what he thought was there.

Nobody understood what he was doing until they noticed the blood streaming down the small blade. David whirled his head back to Shuriah in disbelief. Gasps of breath were heard all around him.

Digesting this drastic turn of events, David told one of the boys to grab a stick of fire and come with him. He stepped to the lifeless body, took the stick from the boy, and scanned the body, looking for the puncture wound. He found where the blood pooled but had stopped oozing because the man's heart wasn't beating anymore; it had been stabbed.

The king stood as Shuriah, unsure what would happen next, kneeled in submission. Unexpectedly, David's tone was very calm, almost cheery, as he asked, "When did you stab him? I didn't see you do it. I only saw your knee hit his chin."

Shuriah cautiously rose, keeping his head down as though he was in trouble, and answered, "I drew my knife going into the air because I knew I was too small and weak to overpower him. I kept my hand at my hip when his head snapped back so that when his chest lurched forward, it helped the knife to go in smoother, faster, and almost by itself."

King David turned to everyone and asked, "Did anyone see the knife in his hand as it went into the soldier's chest?"

Everyone, including the boys, looked at each other, shaking their heads "no."

David went to his knee to be face-to-face with the boy. Everyone else did the same (as it was custom that your head was never to be higher than the king's). Then he asked, "When we get back to the training arena, you will teach me this move."

Shuriah didn't know how to reply, still not quite sure if he was in trouble. Then David gave him the same smile he got almost a year ago when he rescued him from being a homeless orphan in Shechem. He proceeded to add, "You did the right thing today, Shuriah, by protecting yourself. But please, try not to kill any more of my soldiers. Just knock them out." Then he patted his shoulder and shouted orders for someone to take care of the dead body as he handed the knife back to Shuriah.

CHAPTER 7

Days had passed since the first storm of the voyage. The young captain walked up to the general seated at the back of the ship on the top deck. "General Shuriah, the forward ships are signaling that there are oncoming ships headed directly at us."

"How many?" the general asked, showing no concern.

"They see three."

"Go into forward swarm with the first line of both wings."

"Yes, sir." The captain left for the front of the ship, instructing the flagmen to signal the message to the closest ship, who then continued the message until the front outer ships received it as well.

Soon the eagle-shaped fleet appeared to be flapping its wings with only one layer of feathers from each wing as the head of the bird looked like it was retreating like a turtle's head. Soon the three ships were surrounded on both sides, as the whole fleet came to a halt. The lead ship at the head of the bird approached the center of the three ships that were tightly squished together, so they wouldn't be able to maneuver without the surrounding ships allowing them.

A blast from a ram's horn came from behind the front ships, signaling a message that three other ships now were approaching on both sides of the fleet's eagle-shaped formation, and they were to secure the first three until further notice.

Back at the general's ship, he gave more attention to the ram's horn and the flag messages coming in from both sides that more ships were approaching. Again, his instructions were to swarm them on both sides with layers two and three of the wings, completely dissolving the "wings" of eagle formation.

"Tell the lead ship to find out who these people are and why they have approached King Solomon."

The captain shouted out the orders to the ship's flagmen. Thinking strategy, General Shuriah decided to change the tail formation of the eagle, instructing the ships to straighten out backward, extending itself to look like legs with talons. He thought it was best if they were being flanked, keeping the possible enemy at a distance from the body and the heartbeat of the fleet.

Finally, information came in from the front ships explaining who these people were and what their intent was. It took a while to interpret the signals as they were passed from ship to ship. The captain took the information and approached the general. "General Shuriah, these are Phoenician trading ships headed to Egypt."

"Ask them why have they surrounded our ships in such a manner."

After some time, the news came back. "General, their large fleet started to travel in groups of three, spread out to the far horizons to not appear aggressive and frighten smaller incoming ships that wanted to trade. Then if a very large fleet such as ours is confronted, they are to come together for protection."

The general thought for a moment, understanding this strategy of deception in warfare, knowing many more ships could be out there working their way in and following the ships on the horizon. General Shuriah thought the situation through; he didn't want any more interruption in their journey, but he also wanted to make sure his fleet was safe by always having the upper hand. Just then, a soldier from the side of his ship urgently came up with information from a close-by cargo ship of King Hiram. He said in a skittish tone, "General, one of the captains from Tyre said these ships of Phoenicia have been encountered several times over the past two years, and there could be three times the amount of ships we have out there slowly coming in on us!"

General Shuriah studied the soldier, sensing fright in his voice, and gave him a questionable look. He then asked loudly enough so all (friend or foe) could hear. "Are you so easily persuaded to fill yourself with fear, which only makes one weak?"

The young soldier was instantly swallowed up with guilt and embarrassment. Before he could respond, the general stated, "Fear only demonstrates that you do *not* believe the Lord of heaven's armies is all-knowing and all-powerful. Or that *I*, the general of Israel's army appointed by King Solomon, have the wisdom, strength, courage, or experience to lead to victory!"

The soldier was frozen, knowing again what the general said was true, and fell to his knees, bowing in submission.

Seeing the soldier in such a state, the general wisely empowered the humiliated young man by saying, "Stand. Go back to your station and send this message to the Tyre captain, 'Message received by the general. The Lord of Israel *fears* no one!'"

The soldier stood there for a second as confidence flooded back, and he was instantly ready to go to battle. "Yes, General!"

One could hear *Yes, General* murmured all around under men's breaths; the seven simple words, "The Lord of Israel fears no one," held so much power. All the men suddenly appeared as if they wanted to go to battle right now.

Turning to the captain, who had been relaying messages from the front ship, the general told him, "Tell the Phoenicians we apologize for delaying their trip to Egypt and ask if there are any supplies they need for their long voyage. Supply them with what they need. Then give them a gift of 500 pieces of gold and 1,000 pieces of silver. Then tell them to give this message to the Pharaoh from General Shuriah, his friend. Your daughter Ahura, wife of King Solomon, is with child, and he will be a grandfather midsummer."

The young captain stood there, puzzled and wondering why he would be giving gifts, let alone personal information about their king, to these strangers.

Shuriah exhaled loudly, seeing hesitation and questions in the captain's eyes. The captain questioned no more and responded, "Yes, sir!" Then he quickly turned and went to the front of the ship to the signaling flagmen.

Shuriah eyed the captain all the way to the front, knowing he was going to have to do something about this fear and doubt that seemed to be poking their heads up here and there. They hadn't even been close to any threatening situation that would call for it.

Later that evening, Shuriah invited the young captain to have the evening meal with his family. Midway through the meal and small talk in the general's quarters, Shuriah bluntly asked, "Why do you not trust me, Captain?"

Stopping mid-chew, the young captain swallowed hard and answered defensively with wide eyes, "I do, General!"

Shuriah countered, "A person who trusts another's wisdom, intent, and experience never hesitates to think or evaluate what and why. They only believe and obey without question. And in our case, it is the orders I give to you and your crew."

Taking another bite of meat and chewing hard, the general looked up, asking open-heartedly again, "Why do you not trust me? I do not hide anything from anyone. Have I not proved myself to be a fair and worthy leader, equally working alongside everyone? Not deceitful but honest, not stealing but giving, putting the Lord of heaven's armies, the God of Israel, first before all else?"

Eager to defend himself, the captain anxiously said, "But I do trust you, General!"

Shuriah's wife, Talia, glanced up at the captain just as his daughter did and then back down at their meals. This was not the first time a conversation like this was brought into their home around dinner with a weak leader in the Israelite army. The leader of their family was a master at encouraging and building relationships with the ones of whom he was in command.

Calmly and in charge, the general said, "You say you do… but your body language says otherwise."

"I…I do trust you, General. It is the…*unknown* that I do not." Shuriah's wife raised an eye to her husband at the young captain's wise and honest response.

"And what makes you afraid of the unknown?" As Shuriah asked the question, diverting the captain's attention, he pulled his battle knife out of its sheath attached to his chest and gently laid it on the table between them.

His daughter understood what her father was doing and knew what was going through the other man's mind; she was trying her best to not snicker out loud in laughter.

"Well, I…I am not sure. Maybe because I cannot see or hear what dangers are heading our way, and I do not have time to prepare."

"Jazelle, please sharpen my knife."

The young man watched wide-eyed as the general's daughter took the knife that had killed hundreds, if not thousands, of men in battle and went to the other side of the room to begin stroking the impressive weapon with a sharpening stone. The sound of each stroke of rock and metal grinding together gave off a heart-searing and ear-piercing trill of death.

The captain took a bite of his meal, and his hands began to shake. His body squirmed in his chair, and he did not understand why this was going on during this meal. Suddenly fear washed through him, and he wanted to run for his life out of the cabin.

The three quietly ate until Jazelle stopped sharpening the knife. Then she walked to her father, handing it to him and saying, "I am done, Father."

Shuriah took the knife and stroked it with his thumb from the side to feel how sharp it was without cutting his skin. He stood and slowly walked around to the backside of the young captain, who was stiffening up, suddenly terrified of what was going to happen.

Speaking in a firm tone, Shuriah probed further. "*Trust*...my young captain, is *earned* but can be scarred or easily taken away. Trust demonstrates that one believes not only in a man's abilities but in his character as well. And when one's character, that is to say, *my* character, is honestly reflecting that of God, why would you not trust me?" He paused for a moment and added, "Which leads me to ask the question: how strong is your *faith* in God?"

Again, there was silence as the young man was trembling, thinking he was going to pay the price for not trusting his general. Shuriah stood behind him, admiring the long, shiny blade of his knife and stroking it with his fingers.

"Captain, *faith* has nothing to do with man. It is completely the power and strength of God working in and through us. By faith, we *do not need* to know, see, or hear what dangers are coming our way. We only need to *trust* through faith in the Lord of heaven's armies that His power will conquer anything or anyone that comes our way. Being afraid, as you are now, is *only* an illusion that will always be your demise if you choose fear over faith."

The general stopped talking as he reached his powerful arms around the neck of the captain with the sharp knife glistening from the reflection of the candle on the table. The eyes of the captain went wide as his worst nightmare was coming true. He watched the deadly weapon cross his face and then clinched his eyes shut, waiting for the worst.

Shuriah gently grasped the ends of the captain's young, scraggly beard hanging down to the top of his chest. With ease, he slowly worked the sharp knife, painlessly cutting the ragged ends and pruning them.

As the general made his way back to his chair, he put his knife securely back up into the sheath on his chest and sat down. He took a big bite of food, folded his hands in front of him with his elbows on the table, and glared at the captain, who was trying to regain his composure.

The captain glanced at the two women staring at him and then looked away, embarrassed. Talia stood, leaning over to take his plate of food that now had trimmings of his beard in it, and said, "I will get a clean plate of food for you, Captain."

When she came back with a new plate for him, she looked at her husband and said, "Next time, not over a meal."

Shuriah gave her a smile and looked back to the young man saying, "Captain, you must choose right now: are you going to live by fear or faith? For the illusion of fear will get you and others killed. Faith prospers your life.

"You thought I was going to kill you because you were afraid. But what I did was help with your sloppy appearance. My job is to help my men be the best they can, even if it is trimming their beards."

The captain took a deep breath, sighing with relief as the general explained, "The reason I gave the Phoenicians supplies is that they have traveled far and have a distance to go to get to Egypt, which demonstrates we have concern for their welfare. The reason I had you give them gold and silver was to pay them for wasting their time when we appeared to be hostile toward them.

"Finally, I gave them a message that our king's wife, the pharaoh's daughter, is with child. It was to send a clear message that the Egyptians are our friends, and if their intent is to harm them in any way, they will have to deal with King Solomon and the nation of...*Israel!*" he finished loudly as he slammed his hand on the table. The sudden gesture made the young captain and his family jump back in their seats.

Composing himself, Shuriah said, "Starting tomorrow, I will not see one"—he lifted a finger in the air forcefully toward the young man's face—"of your crew hesitating or questioning my orders. If I do, you and he will be giving the mighty warriors on board some battle practice. And I guarantee you, there will be two sliced-up bodies littering the ship's floor for the rest of the crew to feed the sea."

King David, his bodyguard, the remaining 399 soldiers, and all the warrior sons were halfway back to Jerusalem, slowly marching through a valley. Their six-day refuge of meditation and prayer with God in the Cave of Adullam was an extraordinary experience for them all. David shared exciting stories from his life that gave them encouraging wisdom. They could see the Lord of heaven's armies larger and mightier than they ever imagined Him being.

In the distance, a horse was running with all its might toward them across the broad wilderness valley, leaving a long cloud of dirt hovering low but filling the air behind it. Several of the soldiers riding horses in front of the king raced forward, going directly for the rider on the horse to intercept them before they reached the king.

The horsemen soon recognized the rider, the Israelite symbols on the horse, and the rider's clothing. The rider was waving and yelling out, "Let me pass! I need to see the king!"

Seeing the urgency in the eyes of the rider, who had come a long way to deliver a message, they all turned and went to King David.

As the four approached him on his horse, the messenger jumped off and silently knelt low, waiting for permission to speak.

David idly got off his horse, walking up to the noticeably tired soldier. "Rise." Then he turned, signaling for his bodyguard to stay behind, and said to the rider, "Walk with me." They went a short distance away to talk privately.

Stopping, David turned to the soldier, "What news do you have for me?"

Still trying to catch his breath, he said quietly, "My king, our spies from Gath arrived yesterday with news. The Philistines from the west have been preparing for war again and will begin to head to Bethlehem today. Then they will move on to Jerusalem, approaching from the south."

The king's heart sank, but he did not let on. Bethlehem was where he was born, and he still had many friends and distant relatives there. He took a deep breath and asked, "How many soldiers are they coming with?"

"They said approximately 15,000."

David slanted his head back, thinking, and asked, "Do you know why they are coming with so few soldiers?"

The messenger's eyes indicated he knew something, and he continued, "Our spies from Kir-hareseth returned with news two days ago, saying the Moabites on the other side of the Dead Sea are coming for war on Jerusalem, approaching from the north. But they are delaying the attack until the Philistines have gone through Bethlehem. Then they will meet up with them, surrounding our city and combining forces to attack at the same time."

David knew these nations and their intentions very well (to take over Jerusalem). He carefully thought through the timeline from leaving their posts in foreign lands to getting back: *From Gath would be a 3- to 4-day march for 15,000 Philistine soldiers. Then fifteen to seventeen days for an equal-sized army of Moabites from Kir-hareseth.*

Looking past the rider into the wilderness, David smiled to himself, thinking about God's perfect timing of things. He realized his small group of soldiers left the Cave of Adullam yesterday; they were less than a quick, half-day march north over a short mountain range, and they would be able to intersect the Philistines before they got halfway to Bethlehem.

Looking back to the rider, he asked, "Were you given information from General Joab for me?"

"Yes, Master. As soon as he received the news about the Moabites, he sent 20,000 soldiers and twelve mighty warriors led by Jashobeam and Shammah to ambush them when they cross the Jordan River before it flows into the Dead Sea."

David briskly asked, "Why is Eleazar, the third mightiest of the warriors, not going with them?"

The rider hesitated, not knowing what the king's response was going to be, and then answered, "He told the other two he wanted to fight back to back with you again against the Philistines as you two did several years ago. He said it was his most exciting time as a warrior."

The king let out an unexpected outburst of laughter as he remembered the battle. He replied joyfully, "That was a great battle! We killed so many Philistines, I cannot believe they are coming back for more punishment!"

Regaining his composure, he asked, "So what's Joab's plans for coming to Bethlehem?"

"Yesterday, he immediately sent a group of fifty riders, ten who are mighty warriors, to prepare and form a front line with the soldiers in Bethlehem and the surrounding countryside. Then he is marching 15,000 soldiers with two mighty warriors all day and night to get to the city by tomorrow night."

"He left thirteen mighty warriors and the remaining soldiers back in Jerusalem?"

The rider bowed with an affirming "Yes!"

"Good, good. Who did he leave in charge?"

"Benaiah, the captain of your bodyguards."

Again, David laughed. "Oh…I bet that made Benaiah mad." The rider, knowing all the personalities of the leaders and how much they enjoyed going to war, understood the king's merriment at the situation. Benaiah was one of the most honored warriors who had accomplished a great deal of feats during battle for being so fierce.

"Thank you for your loyalty to me and Israel, soldier. Trade for a fresh horse and get back to Jerusalem right away to inform Benaiah that we will be intercepting the Philistines before they get to Bethlehem. Also, tell him that I am sending a messenger directly to Joab, informing him of our status and devising a plan to wipe out the Philistines before they get to Bethlehem."

"Yes, my king!" He bowed low and turned to trade horses.

David turned his attention back to his soldiers, patiently waiting, and got a glimpse of the warrior boys behind them. Suddenly a thought came to him. "Do you know where the Hittite mighty warrior, Uriah, was appointed?" he asked the rider.

As he was getting on his new horse, the rider replied, "Joab made sure he was going to Bethlehem to be with his son, who has never yet gone into battle."

David nodded with a smile, acknowledging the wisdom of Joab, and waved the rider on, saying, "Go with the Lord of heaven's armies!"

As the rider left promptly in the direction he had come, David stepped up to higher ground, motioned for his bodyguard, and said to him, "Gather the warrior boys up here—up front and close to me with the soldiers surrounding them. I have great news!"

David turned his back to his men and knelt with his eyes to the sky as the guard gave out the instructions. He began to pray, seeking the will of God and His favor. Once done, he rose with his eyes closed, inhaling deeply. He blew out forcefully to rid himself of any fear that tried to encroach on him, knowing God loved him and was with his people.

Turning, he contemplated the questioning eyes of the boys and the grown men as he smiled wide, drawing his sword from over his shoulder. "Soldiers of Israel, yesterday we came out of the Cave of Adullam, a special place where God has done mighty work in soldiers before you and in you as well if your heart was open. You know the ritual of and purpose for this journey; every spring, four hundred soldiers are given the same opportunity as other men before you to become great men for God, working to become mighty warriors for Israel!"

A cheer of confirmation arose from the soldiers as many raised fists in the air, wanting the chance to become a mighty warrior.

"You heard my stories as God whispered loudly to your hearts. You know what it will take to become a mighty warrior of Israel." He stabbed his sword in the air, answering, "You must fight through battles fearlessly with courageous swiftness and strength, following the Lord of heaven's armies and killing three hundred or more enemy soldiers. We are His chosen people, and we will not allow a nation with pagan gods to defy the God of Israel!"

Again, another cheer went up but louder and with more emotion. The warrior boys heard talk like this often during their training, and they nearly put the grown men to shame with their staggering excitement. There was no fear in their eyes or body language. All of them except Shuriah had been in a battle. But after Shuriah's encounter in the mystical Cave of Adullam and the drunk soldier, he had blossomed with new self-confidence.

King David continued, "Unexpectedly, God is giving you an opportunity right now"—David stabbed his sword into the ground to make a point as he yelled out—"to set yourself apart to become a mighty warrior, to engage this new relationship you have with the Lord of heaven's armies, and to be a man that you never knew you could be!

"The Philistines are marching right now to Jerusalem, as are the Moabites from the other side of the Dead Sea!"

Soldiers turned to one another with questions as all the boys' eyes stayed glued to the king's every word.

"The Philistines are going to go through Bethlehem first, which is their second mistake! The Lord has positioned us here perfectly to intercept them! We will do a short, straight march north over the hills." David pointed in the direction they would be going. "We have a half-day advantage right now, so we must move swiftly. Part of our army will meet up with us at Bethlehem, but before they arrive, we are the first line of defense to slow them down."

He paused for a second, filling his chest with pride and giving all the men a look that he believed in them. One of the boys closest to the king knelt, signaling he wanted to speak.

"Rise, warrior son. What do you have to say?"

Innocently, he asked, "You said 'their second mistake.' You never mentioned their first?"

The great king motioned for the boys to gather closer. Then he knelt down to them. They all automatically knelt to stay lower than him as he replied in a boisterous tone, "Their first mistake"—he peered around, building the excitement, and added—"is deciding to go to war against the Lord of heaven's armies!"

An eruption of energy from all the soldiers and boys burst forth, knowing they were going to war with the power of God led by King David. This was the same God, David had explained in the Cave of Adullam, who killed Goliath when he was the age of many of the boys kneeling in front of him.

David dismissed the small army of 399 men to ready themselves for the march through the wilderness. They needed to be ready to fight at any moment, but he had the boys remain behind to have a talk with them. Once the men left, David sat down on higher ground and told the boys to sit below him.

In a relaxed manner, he began to talk not as a king but as a father saying, "My young warriors, you are not with your warrior fathers as we go into battle. It is my responsibility to protect you, for you are the *future* warriors of our nation."

He could see the faces and body language begin to shift to disappointment. They could tell where he was going with this talk, and they did not like it.

"I am not allowing you to engage in this battle." He paused, eyeing each boy, making sure they all heard the order. He continued as he pointed to his bodyguard, "My bodyguard will lead you safely back to Jerusalem the way we came through this valley."

An older boy squeezed himself forward and bowed to the ground, wanting to speak.

"What is it, child?"

"Master, you just said we have the power of God in us. We can fight just as you fought the Philistines and killed their giant!"

David smiled and said gently, "I know you can fight, and I know you can kill. I have seen many of you do it and do it very well! But...we need to be wise. Without you being in the shadows of your mighty warrior fathers, you will be in danger because these soldiers"—he pointed over the children's heads to where the men were—"have not proven themselves as mighty warriors yet. They will be looking out for themselves and not for you as they have not trained to battle with you as their shadows."

"We understand, our king, but—"

David quickly held his open hand toward the boy's face, stopping his next words, and stood, retrieving the sword he had stabbed into the ground.

He looked deep into the boys' eyes and walked around the group, holding all their attention firmly as if he was talking to adults. "You have learned the importance of authority and knowing your place, have you *not*?"

They all nodded reluctantly, seeing the king's attitude change. "If you ever disrespect a king, you better be ready to receive one of two things." He had walked back around to the boy who had been talking and quietly raised his sword to his neck, saying, "You could have your tongue cut out or your head removed."

There was dead silence among the young ones as they all bowed low in respect and submission. David looked in the direction of his bodyguard, who was listening close by, and winked, giving a slight smile that he was teaching them a lesson. The guard nodded in agreement, returning a smirk.

He lowered his sword and sat back down in front of the group, knowing it was his responsibility to lift the boys' spirits back up, and said, "I said you are the future warriors of our nation; that is the truth. From boys like you, men will arise! And not ordinary men, but *extraordinary* men!" David pulled his shoulders back, making himself appear bigger. "Men of greatness who will protect our people and the future kings to come. Men who will bring down the enemies of the chosen people of Israel, continuing to give future boys as yourself the opportunity to be mighty warriors!" He stood, raising his fist in the air as he said the last words.

The boys responded, knowing it was an appropriate time to stand and cheer at their king's wise and encouraging words.

As the thirty-seven boys quieted down, David secured his sword and told them, "On your journey home, you must keep a close watch for our enemies. We are not the only ones with spies. They could be watching us right now, especially since two of our adversaries have decided to go to war with us.

"I have watched you constantly during training, and you are a deadly army to deal with, to say the least." Instantly, many of the boys stood up straighter with pride. "Stay in a battle formation, keeping your shields up to the side, ready for any silent arrows headed your way. Listen carefully to my bodyguard and obey him at all costs. If he does go down in battle, the oldest of you will be next in charge. Who is that?" David asked, already knowing the answer.

The oldest boy of sixteen years raised his hand. David said, pointing, "And if he goes down, the next oldest is in charge and so on. Do you understand?"

All the boys nodded "yes."

"Good, now prepare for battle. When ready, line up with my bodyguard, and you will be on your way!"

The oldest boy yelled out, piercing the sky with his sword. "For the Lord of heaven's armies!"

The rest of the boys followed suit, echoing the statement several times, and did as their king commanded.

CHAPTER 8

David's bodyguard was a great, accomplished soldier who came from a long line of warriors that excelled in hand-to-hand combat. He was not a mighty warrior mainly because he was busy watching out for the king (who was a magnificent warrior himself) and not focused on engaging in battle to slaughter the enemy. He and the warrior sons took off toward Jerusalem, leaving their king and the 399 soldiers to intercept the Philistines on their way to Bethlehem.

At first, they started in a quick, organized jog, staying two body lengths from each other in two separate lines, side by side. As the day progressed in the hot sun in the dry wilderness, they had stopped again, taking their second break to catch their breath, drink some water from a cool spring, and eat some dates to keep their energy strong.

The bodyguard was on constant watch, peering up at the mountains and down the valley, looking for anyone or anything out of place. As the boys were getting rested and replenished, the guard caught a glimpse of something dodging from boulder to boulder on the southern hillside, after which it disappeared.

He thought at first it might be a wild animal since he didn't get a good look at it from two full arrow flights' away. Just then, from the last place he had seen it, there was movement, but this time, there were two things moving. He clearly saw they were walking on two legs, hunched over as though sneaking around.

"Warriors, we have company," he whispered in a manner so as not to attract attention. "Eyes on me. Do not look around!"

"We are being followed, and I don't know who they are or how long they have been tracking us. We are going to spread out five body lengths and trot in snake formation back and forth to be hard targets for arrows. Stay in two lines side by side, keeping your shields up to the outer side of the formation as you have been doing to protect your head and body.

"We have been following the same route to Jerusalem as we came, so if we are attacked, and something happens to me, you know the way home." He paused, looking into the young eyes and seeing anxiety, which was not much different from what he saw in normal soldiers. He knew it was his duty to mentally place these kids in the proper mindset just as their warrior fathers would do (who, at this point before a battle, were like rabid dogs fighting to control themselves, excited to go kill their enemies).

He brightened the appearance of his face, saying, "Each and every one of you has been specifically hand-picked to be a warrior son. You have been chosen by God to represent and protect Israel. You were fighters before you were trained to fight. When the Lord of heaven's armies chooses someone for a job, He knows you have the extraordinary abilities to do the job. He is a wise God.

"As our great king teaches, *fear* is only an illusion! You must choose now if you want to live or die! Follow the lead of the Lord of heaven's armies, trusting that He will give you protection, speed, and strength that always lead to…." The guard narrowed his eyes, gritted his teeth with a savage expression, and drove his long, deadly spear into the ground, finishing, "Victory!"

Under their breath, all the boys started to chant *victory* as the mood erupted. The viciousness the guard had needed to see in the boys' faces finally showed up.

"In service to the Lord of heaven's armies for Israel…we are warriors!" the guard affirmed, though quietly. Then he turned and started the quickened formation, smoothly weaving side to side like a snake in the sand.

The group had been traveling for a short time when the guard in the lead saw in front of him six men blocking their path. Wanting to keep distance from danger, the guard suddenly turned to the left, heading north up the mountain—opposite the hillside he saw movement earlier.

Just before they made it to the top of the ridge, a horse crested the other side with a Philistine soldier sitting proudly, surprising the small band of soldiers. With precision, the small group of warriors immediately stopped and angled their shields forward simultaneously. The rider looked down at the guard, smiling big as though he was victorious, and said, "Where do you think you are going with those children? You must be their nurse maid!" Then he laughed out loud.

Everyone paused, waiting for the others to make their move, and then the Philistine added, "Do you think you're the only ones with spies?" He gazed around, finishing, "Where is your king hiding?"

Before another word was said, a small arrow silently flew out of the group of boys, hitting the rider at the only vital spot exposed: his throat. Both of his hands reached up, unable to do anything about the profuse bleeding and blockage of air as he slumped off the horse, hit the ground in the fetal position, and jerked around until he was dead.

The guard hastily turned to see where the arrow came from, only to see the same child who had killed one of their own soldiers a few days ago standing proudly as he lowered his bow. Nodding his head in approval to Shuriah at his timely action, he instructed the boys to get into a tight turtle-shell formation, holding their shields for a domed, protective barrier and to move together to the top of the ridge. He then grasped the Philistine's horse and sprung himself up onto it. Spinning the horse around to get an eagle's-eye view of the enemy around them, he witnessed a picture he didn't want to see.

On the other side of the ridge was a small group of soldiers getting close, working their way up, while the six men on the other side (who had blocked their way in the valley) had suddenly turned into about twenty.

As the boys crested the ridge in their tight formation shoulder to shoulder, the guard told them, "Remain here! Do not let the enemy get too close, but when they are in range for a clean kill, use your arrows as the new warrior did.

"If they get too close, go into porcupine formation, walling yourselves in with all your swords pointed out. Do not engage one on one; they are too big for you. If 'porcupine' fails, run the 'leopard,' vanishing into the wilderness to never be found!"

He glared at the young warriors, boldly giving them courage through his eyes. Then he turned the horse and headed down the backside of the mountain where the closest enemies were.

The group of boys huddled tightly as the oldest boy took charge, saying, "Warriors, you have been in battle before!"

Before he said anything else, they heard a powerful scream, then another, and another from the direction the guard had gone. The tension in the group grew in the darkened inner shell. All the boys peeked out between the cracks where their shields came together, clanking into one another. They searched in all directions for the enemy. The boys facing the hillside from which they came saw the opposition working their way toward them with swords drawn.

The lead boy yelled, "Five arrows at the ready!" Five of the older boys had younger ones hold their shields to keep them in a protective position and nocked their arrows. "On my order…" He reached around, touching the shoulders of several boys facing in the direction of the oncoming soldiers. "Lower your shields. Then the five archers quickly rise, find your target, and kill the enemy!"

Looking toward the front of the approaching men, he stated, "For the Lord of Israel…now!"

Instantly three shields lowered, and five bows rose up, giving a breath of a moment before letting the arrows fly to zero in on their targets. Hearing the wisp of the arrows flying away, the shields instantly went back up.

Two groans of pain were heard as they watched two soldiers flinch with arrows sticking out of their midsections. One other fell dead on his back with an arrow sticking up out of his eye socket.

"Again repeat, five at the ready!" Pausing, he ordered, "Now!"

They were functioning exactly as they were trained. From an untrained eye watching from afar, one would think it was a group of grown soldiers with years of experience.

Again, three out of the five arrows hit their mark, with two dead and one injured. As the lead boy was about to order another arrow rally, another boy spoke up who was facing the side parallel to the ridge. "Enemy running in!"

The boy next to him saw the same man who had snuck in

close, raising his sword to come down on the turtle shell of miniature shields. Seeing it, the lead boy yelled, "Snake-bite!"

Without thinking, only reacting to the command, the two boys moved their shields to the side, exposing their miniature swords, and pointed straight forward at the oncoming soldier. Together they sprang forward, extending their bodies full force with lighting speed, each spearing the man—one in his stomach and one deep through his thigh.

The soldier toppled forward and came down on the back of one of the boys. His sword hit the boy hard, forcing the young one to the ground. The soldier groaned, attempting to swing his weapon at the other boy who stabbed him, but he was met swiftly with a sword, piercing upward through his throat and into his skull; another boy on the other side had sprung forward powerfully, spearing him to his death.

As the boy's body hit the ground, the two boys on either side of him slid his body back into the protection of the turtle shell.

To their surprise, the boy eased his way up, catching his breath; the air was only knocked out of him when he was hit. The sword blade had twisted sideways, hitting him with the flat side of the metal sword.

Seeing that everyone was all right, there was a brief cheer of victory inside the dome from many boys, "Praise be the Lord of Israel!"

The lead boy remained focused and signaled out, "Archers, ready…." Swiftly the group reset into battle mode and reacted at once to the next order: "Now!"

The five raised their bows, releasing the deadly, small arrows at the men rapidly approaching uphill. This time, four men were hit in their chests, two of which were fatal.

With the enemy so close, the lead boy yelled out, "Porcupine formation!"

All the boys speared out their swords as far as they could reach to the sides of their shields. The lead boy looked around for more enemies and only saw the remaining of the original twenty charging in. "Wall this side standing!" he commanded.

The reactions of the small group of boys took the men running in by surprise. They saw more than thirty shiny daggers suddenly facing them at stomach height.

All the men halted, almost bumping into each other, squinting in the boys' direction. Some turned to run away, but others got in a crouched position, ready to face whatever was coming.

Their reaction bewildered the boys until one said loudly, "They are scared to attack us, the mighty warriors of Israel!"

Most of the boys started to chime in, but something else caught their attention: they glimpsed a spear flying over their heads before it hit the closest soldier in the center of his chest, knocking him backward to the ground, dead. As they turned to see where the spear came from, they saw their guard had returned, racing his tired horse past them in an attempt to pursue the band of soldiers.

He stopped at the dead man. Leaning over, he pulled his spear out of him and raced after the Philistine soldiers who were running back down the hill. Given the turn of events, the boys were instructed by the lead boy to go back into turtle shell formation.

Scanning all over the place, the boys looked for more soldiers coming from different directions. One of the boys said, "Did you see the guard?"

Another answered, "Yes, he's a great soldier!"

"He is, but did you see all that blood running down his leg?"

There was silence in the huddle. Then one boy said, "Maybe

it was from the men he killed on the other side of the hill."

"Maybe, but it looked like it was from him when he rode passed."

Soon, the guard galloped back on his exhausted horse, who was breathing heavily and trying to get air into its body. All the young eyes looked up at the guard, whose face was now colorless. He gingerly dismounted, and when his feet touched the ground, his legs could not support his weight, so he promptly collapsed.

Initially, the boys hesitated. Then one of the younger boys busted open his section of the protective mound and said, "Stop the bleeding!"

The guard raised his hand, pointing for the boys to come to him. They surrounded the dying man as he pushed out, "They are all dead. You are safe for now." Pausing to catch his breath, he added, "But I saw," pointing with his finger, "farther down the valley in the direction we are going, there are more Philistine soldiers waiting for you just in case we got by these soldiers.

"We have to change plans for you to live...." He tried to keep his eyes open as his head drooped to the ground. He moved his finger in the other direction and continued, "Go back toward the king...stop when you can see them from a distance...watch and wait. You...you will know what to do...mighty warriors..." His body went limp.

The lead boy knelt down to the guard to cover his open eyes with his hand and shut them. The boy stood, trying to gain as much confidence as he could. "We need to do what he said." Most of them verbally agreed as they adjusted themselves and checked their weapons and supplies. As the older boy looked around, he told the five boys who had shot the arrows to go to the bodies downhill to retrieve as many arrows as they could find.

Shuriah walked up to the body of the Philistine horseman he shot in the neck and stared at him for a second. Then he drew his sword. Several of the boys watching asked, "What are you doing with the sword? He's already dead." Shuriah glanced from them back to the corpse. He raised his razor-sharp, miniature sword high, and then with both hands on the handle, he came down as hard as he could to severe the dead man's head. It went deep into the neck before he pulled back, releasing it. He knelt down to cut away at the muscle and windpipe until his arrow was free.

One of the older boys walked up, telling him, "All you have to do is push the arrow through, then pull it out the other side."

"I know," Shuriah said calmly, staring at the dead man.

"Then why did you do that?"

He answered in a matter-of-fact tone, "I wanted to know if I could cut a man's head off." As he walked away, cleaning the arrow and putting it back into his quiver, he added, "I need more practice and a much bigger sword."

Many of the boys who saw and heard him were now staring at the newest warrior son in admiration. Yet in the back of their young minds, something gnawed at them as they thought to themselves, *Should we be concerned? Less than a year ago, the warrior son of Uriah killed a leopard in the arena without training. Then during our training in hand-to-hand combat or using weapons, he hurt many of the other boys by being too aggressive and intense—almost not caring if he was disciplined for doing so.*

Now he's killed an Israelite soldier, was the first to make a deadly move without being instructed (killing the Philistine on his horse), and has mutilated that same man with no remorse just to see if he could cut off his head.

Young Shuriah checked his armor and weapons, looked

around at the other boys watching him, and asked nonchalantly, "Are we ready to go?"

The lead boy refocused and said aloud, "Let's get into normal formation and head back to where we left our king and the soldiers as the guard instructed."

They all started to line up, but Shuriah stood there looking around the valley they had just come from and asked, "Are you planning on marching the same way we came here?"

"Yes, now line up," the lead boy stated.

"That would not be wise," Shuriah responded, holding his ground as the older boy stepped up to him.

"You will follow orders; get in line!"

"No disrespect, but that is not a wise move."

"And why not?" the lead boy asked sarcastically, tilting his head and putting his hands on his hips.

"We will be seen, and if we are seen, we could be killed. We need to hide all the way back to be safe."

"Mighty warriors, do not hide!" the older boy responded. The others agreed with him, crossing their arms and laughing.

"We are not mighty warriors *yet*; we are sons of mighty warriors." Shuriah glared boldly into the older boy's eyes and added, "We jog in snake formation to confuse the enemy trying to shoot us with arrows. We strike at the enemy low like snakes because we are smaller than grown men." He pointed to the dead Philistine, who was able to sneak up on them from the side but was stopped. "We need to survive like snakes, hiding among the rocks on the sides of the hills to stay out of sight if *we*, mere boys, are to stay alive. If we are in the open, they will see us and cut off our heads"—he pointed to the decapitated body—"like we do to snakes that are in our paths in the open, which is where you want to put us."

There was silence as the newest and one of the youngest boys shocked them with his wisdom. *Perhaps there may not be anything concerning about him after all.*

The older boys looked at one another and agreed with him, nodding as the lead boy patted Shuriah on the shoulder, saying, "That is very smart, Shuriah. I am glad you are on our side." Giving him a quick smile, he turned to all the others and said, "We will stay higher up on the hillside, moving from boulder to boulder or bush to bush.

"I will take the lead, watching and waiting to spot any enemy that is hiding in our path or that may have seen us and is coming our way. I want six of our best archers to follow closely behind me with arrows nocked."

He looked down at the dead but courageous guard and then up to the horse that had time to catch its breath as an idea came to him. "Take the guard's upper body armor vest off," he ordered.

The other boys looked at each other, wondering what he was doing. Shuriah was the only one to immediately follow his order, kneeling and trying to untie the thick, leather outer cover. He was having trouble because he didn't have quite enough strength in his fingers; he looked up at one of the older boys staring down at him and implored, "Help me; you're stronger."

Suddenly, most of the boys jumped in, taking the heavy armored vest off by rolling the body back and forth. One of them stood with it, about to ask what he was to do, but the lead boy took it from him at once with the reins of the horse in his other hand. Then he flung it over the saddle, opening it so it was draped on both sides.

He bent down to the dead guard respectfully, sliding his battle knife out. Turning to the horse, he engraved a six-word message into the leather, and then he stabbed it deep into the center of the thick saddle to hold the vest in place. Turning to Shuriah, he said, "Warrior son of Uriah, nock an arrow."

Automatically following the order, he crunched his face in concentration as most of the other boys wondered what he was doing. As he nocked the arrow, positioning the bow in ready position, the lead boy walked the horse up to the center of the ridge of the hill facing directly where they came from and tied back the reins, letting go of the horse.

A big smile came to Shuriah's face as he piped up enthusiastically, "Great idea! The Philistine horse will reach them quickly, and my short arrow will tell them the warrior sons are alive, but the guard has died in battle because of his armor!"

The lead boy nodded, smiling back as he winked to give the go-ahead to shoot the arrow. Shuriah stood farther back up to the ridge, aimed the arrow at the thickest part of the horse's rump, and then let the arrow fly. The arrow hit its mark as the horse shrieked in pain, rising up on its hind legs, and took off running as straight as an arrow along the ridge. It disappeared, leaving a trail of dust that slowly simmered back down to the ground.

All the boys watched as the plan unfolded perfectly. Walking down away from the exposed ridgeline, the lead boy broke the silence to begin their 'sneak and peek' journey. "Let's go, warriors."

It was the end of the day, and King David and most of the soldiers had made it through the hillside wilderness and were getting close to having a visual of the area where the Philistines should be marching through to Bethlehem. David knew the area very well and where all the great hiding spots were for ambushing an army. He had done it many times when he continually hid from King Saul, who was out to kill him in his younger years.

David and his small army were resting, looking down into a valley, waiting for news from sentinels he had sent out ahead in the direction the Philistines were coming from. He had also left behind soldiers periodically from where he had sent the warriors' sons away. This would allow them to make sure no one was tracking them and sneaking in on their backside.

The king heard murmuring behind him as a soldier he had left behind was making his way through the hundreds of men spread out on the hillside, hiding behind rocks and vegetation. As the soldier approached David, the king narrowed his eyes at what he was holding in his arms. His body language wasn't natural, and he had a weary expression on his face. The king stood as the soldier dropped hard to his knees, laying the items at his king's feet.

David looked down, knowing exactly what the items were, but he didn't want to come to any conclusions, especially with all eyes on him as they were about to go to battle.

"What is the story?" he asked in a demanding tone.

The soldier looked up, answering as respectfully as possible, "My king, a Philistine's horse was running directly to us, exhausted and injured."

"From what direction did it come?" David already knew the answer, but he wanted to make sure he saw a clear picture in his head.

"From where the warriors' sons went."

Whispering broke out among soldiers close by, listening in. David raised his hand to silence them and asked the kneeling soldier to continue.

"We stopped the horse, and your bodyguard's vest was draped over the saddle. His battle knife"—the soldier pointed to it lying on the ground—"was stabbed in the middle of it, holding the vest in place."

David asked firmly, "What about the small arrow covered in blood?"

"It had been shot in the rump of the horse, probably to get it to run for its life in our direction."

Without changing his expression, David silently agreed with why the arrow was in the horse.

"There is more, Master."

The king moved his eyes back to the soldier, asking without words, *What is it?*

"Inscribed on the saddle with the knife, there were six words: 'thirty-seven are coming your way.'"

Instantly, David twisted his head in the direction from which the Philistine army was coming. When he didn't see anything, he looked in the direction the warrior boys were heading to him. Wasting no time, he called out for the highest-ranking soldier.

Kneeling at his king, the soldier rose, waiting for instructions as David lowered his voice. "The warriors' sons are coming back. They have either been in battle with Philistines that have flanked us already or are possibly with spies that have been watching us this whole time. My bodyguard has been killed, but more than likely, he killed many Philistines that attacked them before he died.

"I must go to them. I will take two soldiers with me, and I want you to reorganize everyone and work your way quickly to Bethlehem. Meet up with the fifty horsemen and the local army they have gathered; General Joab should be there by tomorrow with 20,000 soldiers. If the general arrives before we do, tell him what has happened and that I will return with the young warriors in Bethlehem through the eye of the moon."

The high-ranking soldier cocked his head and wrinkled his eyebrows, giving it away that he had no idea what 'the eye of the moon' was. David gave him a sly smile, saying, "Don't let it concern you. The general knows what I am talking about."

David patted the ranking soldier on the shoulder. Then he pointed to the soldier who had brought him the message and singled out another specific soldier who was an accomplished archer and said, "You two, come with me."

Looking at the archer who had been with him for many years, he said, "Anasa, triple our supply of arrows and get me and this soldier bows as well."

"Yes, my king." He retrieved the weapons and handed them to the king and the other soldier as they quickly made their way back up the hillside to intersect the warrior boys coming to them.

The sun had set with little visibility when the warrior sons had finally slithered their way safely along the mountainside. They could be found just below the ridge and high above the valley floor where they parted from King David.

The lead boy squinted through the dim light, cautiously scanning the area in attempt to see any evidence of their king or soldiers. Then his eyes spotted a mound that looked like a pile of rocks on the ridge above them. As he stared at it, the silhouette began to take on a different, almost unnatural, appearance.

He looked back into the shadows of rocks and brush, saying in a soft voice, "Ready your bows. I am going to see if that's the horse we sent with the message lying up on the ridge. If you see anything else, move beside me. Let your arrows fly."

He heard quiet voices respond that they understood and would do as he said. Carefully the lead boy made his way, staying hunched close to the ground and trying not to cast a large shadow now that the light of the moon was overtaking the sun that had disappeared for another day.

When he was only a couple of body length's away from what he confirmed was the dead horse, he stopped and dropped flat to the ground out of sight, thinking he heard faint movement come from the other side of the dead animal. Waiting to glean more information, he watched closely with his chin nestled in the dirt and his hand in front of his head, clenching the sword he had drawn while sneaking in.

He heard whispers from a short distance on the other side of the ridge past the dead horse, but it was so quiet he couldn't interpret the words. Suddenly, he heard the rustling of multiple feet. He hastily moved closer to the horse, nestling in near its stomach between its outstretched legs.

He slowly tucked his legs underneath him with his feet ready to spring upward into "snake-bite formation" if his archers missed their targets. His breathing quickened, and he gripped the handle of his weapon tighter, holding it with both hands straight in front of him, staying as low as he could.

He could now clearly hear the words spoken and distinctly recognized one of the voices. Suddenly he had a deadly situation on his hands, realizing these two bodies would be visible to his archers if they took one more step; they would be silhouetted on the ridge. Without thinking and keeping his head down, he shouted, "King David! Drop to the ground!"

Bodies and clanking weapons came crashing to the ground as the swishing sound of arrows only an arm's length above his head flew past. Before he took another breath, a deep groan faded as a body thumped onto the horse, rolling off in the dirt.

It took a moment for the lead boy to clear his head. Then he asked loudly so all the warrior boys below could hear him, "My king! Are you still alive?"

There was a moment of silence. Unsure if he was being set up, the king and the remaining soldier wriggled their way back down to the other side of the hill. Then he replied wearily, "Warrior son, are you and the others alone?"

Relieved they didn't kill the king of Israel by mistake, he answered back, "Yes, we are!"

"Prove it!" a different, older voice replied.

The boy understood they were not out of danger; the king and his soldiers were taking precautions and could potentially shower them with hundreds of arrows, killing them all in one rally if they didn't trust them.

Without warning, the lead boy heard a young voice behind him before diving to the ground next to him. "You prove you are alone!" Then crunching into "snake-bite position," Shuriah looked at the surprised lead boy, nodding his head that he wasn't going to leave him here by himself. Boldly, Shuriah continued, "If you are not…the Lord of heaven's armies and his warriors will come to your rescue!"

CHAPTER 9

There was a moment of silence, and the soldier on the other side of the dead horse asked, "There were thirty-eight of you. How many are there now?"

The question was out of nowhere, and it took a moment to understand what they were doing. Then the lead boy, turning away from Shuriah, answered, "There were four hundred of you. How many are there now?"

Neither party wanted to divulge their numbers, so it remained silent. The two boys looked at each other, wondering what was taking so long to respond, when suddenly they felt a ghostlike whisper breathing on their faces. It shocked their heads upward, looking nose-to-nose at a man with a large beard and a bright smile. "Warriors, are you alone?"

In awe that their king had clambered his way around the dead horse so quickly and quietly, the boys paused before answering. Then Shuriah answered softly, "My king, we are alone, but your bodyguard is not with us any longer."

Still smiling, proud of the boys for their wise actions, David said, "Call off your invisible archers. There are now only two of us since you killed the third."

Shuriah inched closer to the king's ear and asked a question he was afraid to know the answer to. "Is the rest of the army dead?" The lead boy called back to the other warrior boys that it was safe to come out.

David quickly shook his head, saying, "No, they are heading directly to Bethlehem. The three of us came back for you, boys. We got your message on the horse—great job!" He looked proudly at both boys and then heard small footsteps gathering around them. He asked with some humor, "Is it safe to raise my head now?"

The boys looked up as the others gathered around them, and the lead boy answered, "Yes, King. Sorry, we killed another soldier. It is my fault. I gave the order for the archers to shoot anything that moved that was not me."

David shook his head as he stood, saying, "You were protecting yourselves. You had to do what you had to do. And thank you for your timely warning, which the dead soldier did not follow. You saved my life."

He looked around at the short bodies and knelt to talk. All the boys knelt as well to stay lower than his head height. "I'm very proud of you warriors—" David began.

Suddenly, they all turned. Hearing and seeing movement, some drew their bows back as others drew their swords. "Stand down, warriors!" the king said as his soldier walked around the dead horse. "We're going to need as many of our soldiers as we can have when we go to war with the Philistines. So far, you boys have killed two of ours in a week."

The soldier, Anasa, stood next to the king, handing him his bow and other weapons he had left behind to crawl to the boys. Reaching for his weapons, Shuriah asked bluntly, "Master, how were you able to sneak in so close when you're so big?"

The older soldier (who had been with David for quite a while) gave a faint laugh. David knew what he was thinking and said, "Tell them one of the stories, Anasa."

Anasa thought about it. He stepped back and sat down on the body of the dead horse. He understood the king was regrouping the boys after the tense moment and wanted to make sure they were rested. Soon they were going to be rushing dangerously through the night to join the rest of the army by morning.

The boys gathered close, just like all children who love to hear stories, and their eyes widened with anticipation.

"Do you have any food and water to replenish your bodies, sons of mighty warriors?" the soldier asked. "It is always vital to do so when you have a chance."

The bodies in the dark all grasped at something to eat and drink before getting back into position to hear another exciting story about their great king.

David nodded for him to start as he motioned that he was going to survey the area for Philistines. Inconspicuously, the older soldier nodded back and began telling a story as though he was their grandfather. "King Saul and his army had been chasing young David throughout the wilderness." He stretched his arms out in the dark to motion everywhere around them.

"One day, David and a few of his soldiers were hiding out in a sizeable cave that you did not have to crawl into like we did at the Cave of Adullam. It so happened that King Saul was on the heels of David, looking for him, when the king needed to relieve himself."

Many of the boys looked at one another, not sure what he was talking about. So he made it clear by motioning with his hand at his backside and added, "King Saul had to go…."

Many of the boys giggled but then quickly quieted to hear

the story.

"Well, David and his few soldiers were like mice, hiding and very quiet—so quiet and well-hidden that when King Saul looked around for a spot to go, he had no idea there was a group of men, let alone soldiers, in there with him.

"As he was in the middle of doing his thing…" Several boys smirked, and the soldier raised an eyebrow as if to say, *control yourselves*. He continued, "David made his way so close to the king that he cut off the corner of his robe without him knowing."

Shuriah, kneeling in the back of the surrounding group, had a good picture in his head and looked around for King David. When he didn't see him, he slowly and quietly left the group, trying to see where he was. In the dim light the moon was casting, he thought he saw him meandering around, looking for something. It struck him odd for the king to be by himself when there were enemy soldiers out there.

Unconsciously, he checked his weapons as he took the last bite of food and looked back to the group of boys, making sure no one saw him. Then he carefully made his way to the king. When he was getting close, David suddenly disappeared right before his eyes. Shuriah's stomach dropped, wondering if something happened to him as he twisted around back and forth, looking for him. All of a sudden, he found himself gruffly lifted in the air from behind, unable to reach for any weapon.

He was going to yell for help, but a familiar voice spoke into his ear, "Shuriah, you must not sneak up on a king unless you intend to kill him."

Relieved it was King David, Shuriah was quick-witted and said, "But you only cut a piece of King Saul's robe off. You could have sliced his throat. Why didn't you?"

Taken aback at the child's innocent response, he eased him

back down, thinking of how to respond. Kneeling to the boy's height, he answered, "Remember back in the cave and after a couple of days of prayer and fasting, the Spirit of God could be felt and heard deep inside here?" David had gently put his hand on Shuriah's chest, and Shuriah nodded in agreement.

"Good. I feel God and hear Him here, and here"—David pointed first to his heart and then to his head—"all the time. We have had a very close relationship ever since my father, Jesse, taught me about Him when I was a boy.

"Plus, God had told Samuel to anoint Saul to be the first King of Israel! Who was I?" David raised his shoulders and opened his hands. "Only a child of God and a servant to the king…even if he was out to kill me. It was not my place to take his life—only God's if He wanted it."

He pulled Shuriah close, making sure they were both seeing deeply into each other's eyes. "Do not believe you have any right to be God over anyone. For God always shows up to take care of His people. He is the one to teach them a lesson, allowing them to do things that do not make sense but will have purposeful implications later in life when He shows a new and better path to take…even in situations when He clearly gives the order for whether or not to slice someone's throat, which He definitely did *not* give me with King Saul."

Shuriah didn't quite understand what was being said, and David watched the young boy's face contort slightly. Patting his shoulders and letting go with a smile, David stood, parting his mustache and full beard. "Young Shuriah, who I am convinced will be a mighty warrior one of these days, live your life as though you must always follow in the shadow of someone." The king pointed straight up to the heavens making sure the boy did not mistake who he was talking about. "Then you will never deceive yourself that you can make Godlike decisions, always knowing who you are and what your place is in this world as a servant. Even if you are a king!" He now was pointing at himself, tipping his head to the side as he looked down in the boyish eyes.

Still curious, Shuriah asked, "So why did you cut off a piece of King Saul's robe?"

David laughed at the sudden change of the boy's thoughts and answered, "To let him know that I could have sliced his throat if God told me to without him knowing it."

"So you did it to scare him!" Shuriah replied with excitement.

"No...not all." David's face went blank for a moment and then turned stone cold. "To put the fear of God into him!" he corrected. The look, combined with his words, took the boy back; Shuriah widened his eyes, wondering if this big man was going to do something to him. The king promptly smiled and rubbed the top of Shuriah's head, saying, "We all need the fear of God put back into us, especially when we forget to be in His shadow! Let's get back to the group. We need to go; it's going to be a long night."

The young captain stepped up to the general in his normal sitting area at the back of the ship, which was higher and made it easier to observe his own ship as well as the others sailing around them.

"General Shuriah, may I have a word with you?"

The general glanced up and nodded while working on something.

"The men are getting tired. There has been no wind in our

sails for several days now. Should we give the fleet a break from rowing for a day so their hands and arms can rest?" he asked, believing it was responsible to look out for the welfare of the men.

The general raised his head at the question, changing his thoughts as he had been making more arrows for himself. It was a normal job for the weaponry masters to make and care for the weapons, but it was one thing he enjoyed doing because it always kept him calm and gave him time to think. He responded, "I'm not sure I understand the *intent* of the question, Captain?"

"Well, General, the men are getting tired after rowing all day every day, and it has been several days now, and the winds could fail us for many more days."

"Do we not give them breaks throughout the day, rotating fresh hands and arms often?"

"Yes, General, but it is beginning to affect their heads as well."

"Their…heads?"

He narrowed his eyebrows questionably and dropped his hands onto his lap with a tool and an arrow almost complete.

The captain was beginning to get uneasy, having learned in a short time that this general was no ordinary high-ranking soldier but a far superior master. His experience and knowledge continually kept him in suspense; his personality intimidated him down to his bones, to say the least. His voice quivered as he replied, "Yes…yes, sir. They are getting frustrated and doing a lot of talking."

"Talking…?" His expression remained subdued; he did not let the captain know if this information was surprising or not.

"Yes, they are saying things like, 'How much longer are we going to have to do this? And what are we doing this for? We don't even know where we are going.'"

The general peered at the captain with an awkward look and asked, "And this is concerning you?"

Flustered that the general was not showing concern, the captain answered, "Yes, I believe it is important to keep morale high and smiles on everyone's faces so they will put everything they have into doing a good job."

One of the two mighty warriors on the ship (besides the general himself) walked up just as the captain finished his statement. He came to ask General Shuriah a question but was asked one by the general first as he pointed up at him, "Hezro, while you're doing your job…you know, fighting and killing enemies' soldiers—do you put a smile on your face?"

He answered, "No!" then put on a stern look, adding, "I only smile when I'm done killing them all and adding up the body count!" He opened his mouth wide with a smile that was missing half his teeth and gave a boisterous laugh. He slapped the young captain on his back, knowing where the absurd question originated from.

As he calmed back down, the general asked him, "What did you want, Hezro?"

With a serious glare, Hezro looked at the general for a moment and answered, laughing again, "I can't remember! Must not have been as important as putting a smile on my face when I'm doing my job!" He turned and walked to the other side of the ship, chuckling along the way.

The general looked up, still seated with the arrow and tool in his hands, waiting for a response from the captain. Meanwhile, the captain was bewildered, trying to put together the pieces of the conversation. Shuriah said, "Work is work no matter what you do, Captain. Some people talk through it, some are quiet, some complain, and some encourage through it."

He stood, handing the arrow and the tool to the captain. He grasped his stout bow leaning against the wall and the quiver full of arrows hanging on a hook next to it and said, "What men think or say during work is *not* what is important." He looked over and eyed the captain, making sure he had his complete attention before he pulled back powerfully on the empty string of the bow.

"What *is* important is that the men *grow* mentally and physically during the work they are doing. If they *do not* grow, they will remain weak and ineffective, not reaching their potential. Only if they work hard through it all and finish their job will they achieve that. Without growth, eventually, they will fail their job when it gets harder, never realizing they could have been extraordinary at their job if only they would not have settled for less. Now break that arrow in half that I was working on."

"What?"

The general retracted the string to its straight resting position and said, "Just do it. You're not in trouble. You are learning a valuable lesson in leadership."

The captain hesitated. Grasping the arrow at its ends, he dropped the shaft of the arrow down on his raised knee, snapping it in two.

"Good," the general said as he took the half of the broken arrow with the arrowhead attached and pointed it out, saying, "Now I want you to pick out a target on that ship over there."

The young captain looked out across the water. Vibrations rippled from the ships cruising by with oars rowing uniformly that stuck out the side walls through little windows on each side of the ships.

With the distance between the ships, he saw it could be a hard target to hit, so he pointed with the back half of the broken arrow. "How about the plank in the middle of the ship just behind the last oar opening?"

The general shrugged his shoulders in agreement. He skillfully worked the broken part of the stick with his tool, forming a faint groove for the string. Putting the tool down, he took the bow and nocked the stunted arrow. Facing the ship, he just barely pulled back, stopping when the arrowhead touched the grip on the bow. Taking aim for a moment, he let go, but the arrow fell way short of its target, plopping into the Mediterranean Sea halfway between the ships.

"What just happened?" the general asked. "You fell short of reaching the target."

General Shuriah lowered the bow as he slid a full-sized arrow out of the quiver. "You need to look closer at the picture and come up with a different answer, for there is a great difference." Attempting to help the captain, who was wrinkling his forehead, the general hinted by nocking the longer arrow and drew it back several times towards the target across the water. Then he lowered the bow.

Then it hit the young man. "The *arrow* fell short of its target!"

"Correct, Captain—not me. There is a great difference." He lifted the bow up, pulling back on the string with the full arrow nocked, pointed at the target, and released the arrow. The arrow's flight was smooth and accurate, hitting its target dead on as the general asked, "And why did the arrow fall short of its target?"

Believing he understood the lesson, he quickly answered, "Because the arrow was too short and could not be drawn back far enough to have the power to hit the target you were aiming for."

"You are beginning to see the picture. The short arrow represents the men, the soldiers working the ship. The bow, on the other hand, is who?"

The captain thought for a moment and answered, "Me."

"Correct, and who is holding the bow up and aiming it?" Shuriah asked.

"That would be you, General." The young man was starting to concede that he truly saw the picture drawn for him.

"All right, now let's go back to why you approached me in the first place. What was it?"

"The men's morale getting low," he answered.

"No, no, that's not what you said. You said the men are getting tired, and their hands and arms are needing to rest. Then you suggested giving them a day off. Is that not what you came to me with?"

Hesitating, he suddenly felt the tables being turned on him, so he straightened his posture to save any dignity he had left and answered, "Yes, it is, General."

Shuriah inhaled deeply, letting his large barrel chest expand, standing to his full extent. He looked down at the captain and raised his finger, "We will not have *one* short arrow among my men that will fall short of doing their job and hitting their target when I aim them to go to battle, or they will die and put others in danger.

"The men are doing their tough job of rowing the ships right now because the Lord of heaven's armies has called off the winds, so they have time to get stronger in their minds and bodies, working together and not sitting around getting lazy and weak while God does all the work. How does that help His people grow and mature? For we haven't even begun the march to the battles we will be facing on this journey of all journeys.

"And on this journey, my young captain"—he took a step

closer, only a breath away—"you and the men are the arrows, I am the bow, and the God of Israel is the one holding us up, aiming to a target, which for us *alone*, without *him*...is impossible to reach."

The captain finally understood the whole picture. He nodded his head, not only intimidated by the general physically but also by the amazing wisdom He possessed.

"So, Captain, I am not concerned about what the men are saying or if they are smiling while they work because this is not work"—he pointed toward all the men rowing—"but a training arena on the sea for what's ahead of us!"

King David, Anasa, and the thirty-seven warrior sons were stealthily making their way through the wilderness in the dark of the night. David knew this mountain like the back of his hand, taking every step confidently, zig-zagging the group around the terrain. They were constantly going up and down, making their way as everyone following his black shadow was getting dizzy, trying to draw a mental picture of where they were going.

Once they got to a specific destination, he stopped, gathering them together to give instructions. "We are in a spot very few people know about, how to get through, or even try to go through." He turned, pointing in the dark. "This canyon gets very, very narrow soon to the point we will be walking single file and sideways. It will feel like the high rock walls are closing in on you and that you won't be able to breathe."

He paused to make sure he had their attention so he could give them confidence that they would be able to do this, especially in the dark, with just a sliver of the moon lighting the way.

"The things that will go through your head and what you will feel are *only* illusions, young warriors. Do not believe anything that says you cannot do it or make it. For I tell you the truth." He paused again to pierce their minds and hearts with what he was going to say next. "The Lord of heaven's armies does not know what 'cannot' means!"

He let the statement settle and added, "For there was a boy that was the same age as some of you that killed a Philistine's champion soldier that was nine feet tall. Then he cut his head off with his own giant sword, scaring away a whole army of thousands by himself!"

There was a silent cheer among the children as well as Anasa, who knew the story very well because he had been there to see it for himself when he was a young soldier under King Saul.

Confirming what he found out earlier in the day, young Shuriah thought to himself, *So, it does take a large sword to cut off a man's head...*

David continued, "And these were the same men that for days had been laughing at and taunting the Israelite army and defying God, telling the boy he could not defeat their champion: a giant soldier named Goliath. If you believe you *cannot*...you are a dead person in here"—he was pointing to his head—"and in here," he said, pointing to his heart.

He looked around in the dark and asked, "Is there anyone here that is dead?"

The lead warrior boy went to his knee, and all the others followed, including Anasa. He answered, "Our king, we are very much alive just as young David was, who is now King of Israel!"

David nodded with confidence, looking at every shadow in the dark, attempting to make eye contact. He said, "Good, we will now follow the Lord of heaven's armies silently through the eye of the moon. Do not talk at a normal volume while we are in there. If you do, it will echo so loudly it will drive everyone crazy." All the children nodded that they understood. As they were all standing back up, he turned to Anasa, saying, "Be the last one through."

"Yes, my king," Anasa replied, giving him a slight bow, which wasn't seen in the dark. He was curious about this place and where they were going, for he did not know where they were.

Gingerly, they worked their way through, and just as David told them, the canyon walls came together very tightly. From high above, they appeared to be at the bottom of a faint crack in the earth in the dark.

Because they were only able to take half a step sideways at a time, it was much easier on the younger and smaller ones. The two grown men were having the hardest time, and the king had slowed down the caravan of bodies significantly. He was still inching his way forward, but the last boy in line had lost sight and sound of Anasa.

There were a few moments when several of the older boys appeared to get stuck and began to move their arms around in a panic, pushing against the unmovable rock walls and trying to shuffle along. They would blow out the air of their lungs and stand on their toes, pressing up because the walls were slightly V-shaped—wider apart the higher the walls went.

More than halfway through the deep crevasse, it suddenly got wider for a short while, and David stopped to gather the children somewhat close to him. He pointed straight up passed the high, dark walls into the thin line of heavenly sparkles of stars densely scattered in the night's sky.

Motioning the boys to gather closer, he whispered so as not to start an echo while focusing his eyes upward. "If you look closely at the sky, you can see we are in a curve of the canyon.

This area we're standing in has faintly widened out. Then it gets narrow again shortly after we leave this spot."

The boy closest to him whispered with excitement, "I see it! The eye of the moon." A perfect sliver shaped exactly like a crescent moon was allowing the brilliant stars to glisten down at them. As all eyes were staring up, it gave the cramped Israelites at the bottom of the fissure a reminder of hope—that if they kept moving, the open world was still out there; they just had to keep going.

David looked around at the boys, who were energized that they had made it this far. He motioned for them to continue. That's when he realized Anasa was not with them. "Who was the last one next to the soldier?"

"Me," a soft, young voice replied.

"When did you see him last?"

"I don't know. It was a ways back when I realized I did not hear him grunt or see him anymore."

David looked up, thinking through the situation, and decided for the safety of the warrior boys, it would be better to continue and let Anasa fend for himself. There was nothing he could do if Anasa was stuck except to get stuck himself, leaving the boys alone again.

"He will make it. We need to keep going." Then he turned to continue. David felt one of the boys grab his uniform. Turning back, he asked with his eyes, *what do you want?*

It was Shuriah. He stretched up to discreetly whisper to the king, "I will go back for him. I am small. I will not get stuck helping him."

"No, young warrior. You are brave, but we must be wise in this dangerous situation and stay together."

Shuriah thought for a moment and asked, "You told us in the Cave of Adullam that you were a shepherd when you were a boy our age. And you would often leave the large, safe flock to look for a lost sheep. Help me be like you by experiencing danger so I can grow strong and go after the one sheep that could die."

David was stumped at his reasoning for one so young; it elicited pride in him. There was nothing else he could say for the boy trapped him in his own teachings to grow strong to protect the chosen people of God. With a serious look, he bent down saying, "Find him, and if you cannot help him, leave him. You must live, Shuriah!"

Excited to be granted to go back, he replied directly into the king's ear so no one could hear him, "I don't know what *cannot* means, my king." Again, Shuriah left David in awe.

Shuriah turned and began to shuffle his way back to where they came. After a while, he finally got to Anasa. He was exhausted and slumped down with his body smashed between the impenetrable walls. He was drenched with sweat, and his eyes were closed. At first, Shuriah thought he might be dead so he touched his arm.

Anasa jerked, looking in his direction in the dark. He let out a frightful bellow, "Aahh!"

It echoed loudly as his eyes adjusted to see what had touched him. He could finally see a dark figure the height of a boy. Trying his best to get air into his lungs, Anasa rasped, "What are you doing? Get out of here!"

"No, I'm here to help. The king's orders," Shuriah added, knowing that would hold power.

Anasa couldn't move; he tried to wiggle but was stuck as though he was in a tomb. He pushed the boy with his free arm and said in a shallow, wheezing breath, "Leave me, warrior son.

I am a dead soldier now. It is your time to live and fight for the Lord of heaven's armies."

Shuriah looked Anasa up and down, trying to figure out how he could pull or lift him free. Then an idea came to him and he said, "We can get you out, but I will need your help."

"No, no leave me. Our nation will need you when you get older."

"Our nation needs *you* now!" the boy whispered, persistent. "We are going to war with the Philistines."

Shuriah took off his miniature weapons, laying them all on the ground except for his knife. He reached up to all the ties and straps that were holding Anasa's thick, leather battle vest on him, untying the ones he could and cutting the others he couldn't. He had to climb on and over Anasa to get to all of them as the soldier groaned in pain.

Next, he worked at all the weapons strapped to Anasa—his sword, battle knife, bow, and quiver of arrows. He had taken his shield off a while back, leaving it behind. Getting the weapons out of the way so neither of them would get hurt, he began to pull at the front side of the leather battle vest wedged between the wall and his chest. He tugged, pulled, and even placed a foot on the side of Anasa's body. Pushing off, he was finally able to work it loose. He did the same thing with the back half of the vest.

Once done, Anasa felt a slight release of pressure from his chest but still couldn't get out of the tight wedge. Shuriah looked up and down the walls, knowing the higher they went, the farther apart they were. He looked down at the man's feet, seeing they could still move around and thought for a moment. "Can you raise your feet off the ground?"

"If I do, I'll get stuck even tighter."

"You're stuck anyways and will die right there if we don't

try something else. We need to get something under your feet so you can stand on it and push yourself upward where the walls widen."

Still gasping to get air in his lungs, Anasa whispered, "There's nothing here big enough to make a difference."

Shuriah looked at the weapons lying on the ground and the halves of the leather battle vest. The only thing that caught his attention was the dirt and some small, scattered rocks on the floor of the crevasse.

On the other side of the soldier where they came in from, Shuriah edged his own body sideways to touch the ground. Feeling the dirt was workable, he laid sideways all the way to the ground. He was cramped but was still able to squirm around with his head at Anasa's feet.

He began to dig under Anasa's feet using his knife. He pushed the dirt and rocks to the other side in the direction of King David and the warrior sons. After a while, he had a sizeable impression under the feet, but Anasa was beginning to panic as his body slumped down more, crushing his torso.

"Lift your feet up as high as you can," Shuriah whispered. Anasa struggled in the terror of the moment, knowing he would be suffocating soon if he couldn't expand his chest to breathe.

Anasa got his feet a little higher off the ground, and Shuriah quickly wiggled his body sideways underneath him. Once his shoulders were under Anasa's feet, he murmured, "Push your feet down on me and lift yourself up."

He felt the leather footwear touch and press hard on his upper arm. Suddenly he felt immense pressure on his whole body, unable to inhale. With the last bit of air left in his lungs, he groaned, "Push harder, or we are both going to die!"

The pressure was so intense he thought his chest was going to collapse, breaking all his ribs. And then the pressure left abruptly, as did the feet of the soldier. It was as if his body was now as light as a feather. He took in several deep breaths, sensing nothing was broken in his young body.

He worked his way up to see Anasa staring at him in disbelief, still standing on his toes on the mound of dirt Shuriah dug from underneath him to stay elevated. With the battle vest off and the weapons no longer weighing him down, Asana was able to maneuver more freely.

Extremely grateful, Anasa freely whispered, "Thank you, young warrior. This would have been a shameful way to die." He looked in the other direction down the narrow crack in the mountain. When he didn't see anyone else, he asked, "Are you alone?"

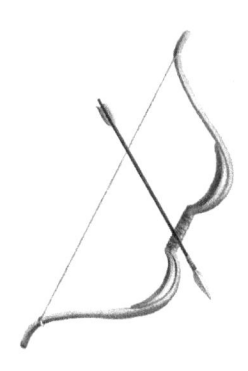

CHAPTER 10

Anasa and Shuriah slowly made their way through the deadly crevasse. Several more times, the young warrior had to use his body as a stepping-stone to free Anasa.

Shuriah had taken all his weapons with him, but Anasa left his bow and quiver of arrows behind, holding his sword in one hand and his knife in the other as they carefully side-stepped along. When they finally made their way past the eye of the moon and down the second half of the crack in the earth into the freedom of openness, relief from both was so overwhelming that Anasa couldn't help but lift the boy into the air, hugging him tightly.

This was completely out of character for Anasa and truly expressed his gratefulness. He thanked Shuriah over and over and said, "You, my young friend, are not a boy but a courageous man trapped in a young body with a heart big enough to beat for a whole army. Thank you for being willing to obey such orders to save an old man." Shuriah looked away, not wanting to take the credit for that false statement.

When they calmed themselves, enjoying this new freedom of space, able to move and fully breathe, they looked around for the small warriors and King David, but no one was there to greet them in the dark night that was ending. Anasa knelt to look closely for footprints, trying to see which direction they went and shortly got his answer.

"That way." He pointed as he picked up a short warrior's arrow lying on the ground, pointing in the direction its owner had gone.

He stood, giving a small shiver at the night air that was at its coolest. He didn't have his thick, leather battle vest anymore to help keep him warm. As he led the way, he said, "Let's catch up with your army and the king."

Far on the horizon to the east, a faint illumination arose, telling the darkness there was a separation of sky and land.

The last two to escape the eye of the moon carefully but efficiently followed along, frequently finding arrows lying on the ground, pointing in a new direction where their fellow Israelites were heading. They had just climbed over large boulders, planted their feet back onto the ground, and believed they were catching up, but both stopped instantly, feeling there was something wrong. Anasa held up his sword and stepped backward, reaching with his free hand to push Shuriah safely behind him.

After waving his hand back and not touching Shuriah a couple of times, he turned to look for him, only to stop with the tip of a knife softly poking at his throat. Rapidly moving his eyes to focus on who was there, he heard a faint whisper of his name. "Anasa, you and the boy made it just in time."

Recognizing King David's voice and understanding the warning, he turned his head in the direction the king was motioning with his eyes.

David bent down to Shuriah, placed his hand over his mouth, held his body tightly against him, and said, "Quiet, Shuriah. Enemy sentinels are hiding in front of us." He gently let go of him and reached back up to Anasa's shoulder to whisper to him, only to feel soft, sweaty underclothes and not the protective, hard battle vest.

David frowned at Anasa, who replied knowingly, "The boy had to cut it off to extricate me."

David did his best not to make a sound as his body silently tremored with laughter. Anasa shook his head at the king, amused when he himself had thought for sure he was dying a pathetic death after all these years as a soldier under King Saul and now David.

After a moment, the king looked down to see that Anasa still had his sword and knife and said, "Two Philistine sentinels are awake, watching for movement below in the valley while two are sleeping. I have six of the warrior boys set up over there"—he pointed in the dim light above the four enemy soldiers in the rocks—"with arrows ready. Since you showed up, I will sneak in and open the throats of the two men watching. Then you do the same to the two sleeping."

It was a bit odd that the king would plan something like this when there was a much easier, safer, and faster way to kill these men by just showering them with arrows. David knew what was going through the master archer's mind and replied, "The warrior boys are continually training. They need to see different ways of how we handle situations."

Anasa nodded, understanding the six young archers above were only for precaution just in case the situation did not go the way they planned.

David pointed in the direction of the other boys. He wanted Shuriah to go get a good view of what would happen. He then signaled, bumping Anasa with the back of his hand, and held his knife as they began to creep toward the four oblivious enemy soldiers.

When he got close, David looked back at Anasa, getting into position. Anasa nodded that he was ready for his king to make his stealthy move.

Coming in behind the two men sitting on their knees, he looked around the hillside, which was coming into view as the sun brightened the morning sky. All thirty-seven pairs of young eyes anxiously watched David's leopard-like movements as he approached his prey in the wide, open clearing.

David hesitated when he was centered between the Philistines an arm's length behind each of them. He scanned the group, safely watching him, and then raised his left hand for the boys to see that he had picked up a rock along the way. Without wasting any time, he tossed it over the Philistine's head down the hill a short way. The rock clanked against other rocks, catching the attention of both soldiers. As soon as they both stretched out their necks to look at what the noise was below, David leaned forward and plunged his knife so deep into the man's neck on his right that the tip stuck out the other side.

David's arm never stopped moving as it sprung with lightning speed, twisting the knife in the other direction, and impaled the other soldier in the same place in one full motion. The only sound heard was the thumping of the two bodies hitting the ground and faint gurgling from the men trying to breathe. David turned just in time to see Anasa retrieve his knife from the fourth dead Philistine that never knew what happened.

Anasa looked up, giving his king a nod that he was finished. They both looked down the hillside to make sure all was well, and there were no surprise soldiers hiding. Then David turned to all the boys and waved them in.

Once they were all there, David went through the steps they

took to accomplish this task. He reminded them they always need to have a backup plan when possible, which in this situation were the archers watching at the ready on higher ground. Then he talked about having someone who can always cover your back—Anasa in this case. But the biggest lesson he wanted to teach them is to always distract your enemies before you attack them. This deters their focus and concentration, keeping them off guard, one step behind, and always in a weak position. A distraction is a very powerful, if not the most powerful, weapon that can help the weakest soldier or situation to be victorious.

As he looked around at the zealous boys, he caught Shuriah's eyes and said, smiling, "That is how you were victorious, killing the leopard in the training arena this time last year. You threw dirt into its eyes, giving you that very brief moment to distract it before stabbing its throat."

All the boys looked at him, nodding in agreement as Anasa stared, thinking to himself, *So this is the young boy who did that!*

Shuriah looked down at his hand and arms with the permanent scars from the deadly cat's claws and teeth. He remembered how much pain it caused as his thoughts drifted to a similar pain: being whipped on his back by the men in Shechem when he was really young.

Anasa stepped up to the boy, putting his arm around him, and knelt facing the king, "Thank you, my master, for sending this warrior son to save my life in the"—he paused, trying to remember the name—"eye of the moon just as he saved the mighty warrior in the training arena."

David replied with a grin, "I did not send him to you, Anasa. He asked to go find you."

The old soldier's face went blank, not sure how to respond. Now he knew Shuriah had lied but was willing to sacrifice his own life to save him.

The small band of warriors finally made it to Bethlehem through a tiring jogging formation to be able to get to their destination by late morning. They met up with the soldiers David left the day before, the fifty horsemen, and the 2,000 local foot soldiers from around the area who were the first wall of defense against the oncoming Philistines.

A messenger had ridden in shortly after they arrived, notifying everyone that General Joab and 20,000 foot soldiers, five hundred chariots with eight hundred charioteers, and five hundred horsemen would be surrounding Bethlehem by midday. King David took the messenger and some warrior sons to the side so the boys could hear battle conversation firsthand. "Did General Joab instruct which battle formation he was coming into the area with?"

"Yes, my king. He said they will be doing wild dog pack formation."

It humored David because this was Joab's favorite. It was also the most effective against the Philistines' own formations.

"Yes!" one of the older warrior boys exclaimed under his breath; he knew it well because it was his warrior father's favorite.

Once he finished gathering information, David gave instructions to the boys, saying, "Many of your fathers are on their way with General Joab, but we are expecting the Moabites to travel to Jerusalem from the north, so some were ordered to stay behind in Jerusalem just in case we failed in one of these two battles.

"A backup plan!" another boy stated, recalling the talk they just had on the mountain.

"Yes, a backup plan." The king smiled at the quick-wittedness of the young warrior and continued, "Which means"—he looked around to make sure he had their attention—"if your father is not here in this battle, you will not fight and will stay in the back, far from the fighting in the city."

There were several moans of disappointment, and David quickly responded, "But you will probably have one of the most important jobs. If any enemy soldiers make their way into the city"—David clinched his fist, flexed his muscles, and gritted his teeth with a piercing glare—"kill every one of them! Protect the women and children! That is your responsibility!" He eyed them all one by one, making sure they all knew their king did not like Philistines and wanted the people of Israel protected.

The boys understood the order and the importance, which triggered their incomparable obedience and faithfulness to the king of Israel. Without another word, all thirty-seven warrior boys stepped into a formal line-up. In perfect unison, they beat a closed fist intensely across their hearts on their battle vests. The action made a loud, pounding sound, which caught the attention of many of the soldiers standing nearby, as well as the citizens of Bethlehem.

Drawing their swords from their backs in perfect formation, they all pointed them directly to the king and went down to one knee. They held their heads up high and, all at once, boasted as loudly as they could, "For the Lord of heaven's armies!" three times.

It went silent as hundreds of eyes in the area were focused on the perfection of the warrior boys and their commitment to the king and Israel. Pride was flowing through the crowd that had gathered to see this small army.

Then one of the local soldiers standing behind the fifty horsemen commented under his breath, "What are a bunch of boys with toy weapons going to do but get in the way?" Unfortunately for him, the comment reached the king's ears; David's head snapped in his direction, and the man's eyes widened as he realized his mistake.

Without hesitating, David commanded, "Shuriah, kill that man pretending to be a soldier of Israel!" David didn't even realize why he had called out Shuriah's name. In one motion, with lightning speed, Shuriah looked in the direction his king was staring and froze the soldier in place. He dropped his sword, stood up, and swung his bow around as the other hand pulled out an arrow and nocked it. Shuriah pulled back and released as soon as his eyes found their mark.

It happened so fast and with such perfection that when the arrow was sticking out of the soldier's chest centered at his heart, everyone stopped breathing in disbelief.

In a quick, determined march, as though his duty wasn't finished, Shuriah had flung his bow around his body and gone straight to the soldier. Everyone hurriedly moved out of his way. When he got to the man, the soldier groaned, holding onto his chest as he started to collapse. Shuriah pulled out the soldier's full-sized sword from his hip and grasped it tight with both hands. He skillfully spun around in a whirlwind with the sword extended out as the man fell to the ground. In one flash, the long, sharp blade found its mark.

The dead soldier's head bounced on the ground as Shuriah dropped the sword and picked up the head by the hair before it stopped. He marched back to his king, set the head at his feet, and returned to kneeling formation, where he raised his sword back up to his Master, yelling, "For the Lord of heaven's armies!" All the warrior sons mirrored him as they repeated it two more times.

No one moved, thinking if they did, orders would be given for one of these deadly assassins to kill them. A fearful respect hit new heights for these young warriors, especially from the regular soldiers watching.

David knew dramatic situations like this needed to be seen in the public eye, so from the poor to the rich, the anointed authorities of Israel ordained by God would be highly honored by everyone, even if it meant killing one of their own who showed a hint of disrespect.

It was an unfortunate thing David always struggled with, that he, the king, along with these boys, needed to remind the people of who they were and what their place was. The boys' minds and hearts continually needed to be catapulted with inspiration about whom they follow: The God of Israel and its king.

David broke the silence, "Rise, warrior sons. Get food and water in your stomachs and then rest. For soon, Philistine blood will be saturating this dry ground!"

They stood in unison, saying, "Praise to the king of Israel!" Then they turned and walked away as if nothing happened.

The eyes of many were still in awe, as was the messenger at David's side, who was waiting for orders himself. Several of the older women near them heard what the king told the young warriors to do and, in motherly tones, waved them forward, saying, "Come, come, we will feed you, warrior children."

In a blink of an eye, the deadly assassins turned back into boys, giddy they were going to have their fill of food. They bumped and pushed one another playfully, talking about what just happened. David watched the boys walk away, proud of them all. This was supposed to be a simple, annual journey to the Cave of Adullam, but it had turned into a greater training ground, shaping them to become what he intended them to be: the next generation of mighty warriors of Israel.

General Joab, his army, and the king's entourage of servants, guards, and personal caretakers arrived in Bethlehem later in the day. Prior to arriving, Joab had arranged for the army to spread out into wild dog pack formation, which consisted of 20,000 foot soldiers separated into five packs of 4,000. The chariots and horsemen were divided up equally as well.

The King, General Joab, and most of the mighty warriors would be in the middle pack, positioned in the center with two tight packs to their left and two to their right, each distanced apart with one mighty warrior and one commander per pack.

What this did was separate the oncoming enemies, confusing them by dividing and conquering. Most of the mighty warriors and their 4,000 soldiers would go straight down the middle, parting the oncoming army quickly into two as the other four packs did the same, weakening the structure of the opposing enemy and leaving many separated groups without leadership. This ultimately suffocated them internally as the packs of soldiers tore apart the enemy.

In addition, the outer two packs were able to flank the enemy; the opposing soldiers on the ends felt helpless with a high concentration of their enemy coming at them with no protection to their outer side. This caused them to retreat inward into the chaos of many different battles going on at once with no leadership.

That evening, many of the warrior sons were reunited with their warrior fathers. The trip to the Cave of Adullam was the only time the boys were away from their fathers. And their very tight bonds, it was a joyous moment when all the boys excitedly told stories of the days they were apart.

The warrior fathers knew that some of the boys' fathers were not with them, and they would be very saddened. Having seen or been there themselves, they understood that the boys needed special attention, especially right before going to war.

King David first brought the fatherless boys together, comforting them and lifting their spirits. Then he sent them away to spend the short time they had before the battle started with their friends' warrior fathers.

Shuriah and Uriah's reunion was an epic moment for them both. Not until they saw each other did they fully realize how much they missed each other. But more than that, it wasn't until Uriah hoisted his son up into the air, put him down, and knelt to his height that they completely understood the depth of love they had for each other.

"Father, I have so much to tell you!" Shuriah could hardly control himself as his face glowed with excitement.

"I know you do! It's always exciting to go into the Cave of Adullam. Every time I spend time there, I seem to grow stronger as a servant of the God of Israel—understanding myself and Him more—"

Shuriah cut him off, "No, Father. There's much more that has happened...I killed a Philistine soldier!" he said, knowing Uriah would be so proud of him.

Uriah stood, taken aback, shifting his whole demeanor. He looked down at his son with concern; Shuriah had been placed in a position of danger without him. He paused, glaring around for the king for an explanation. Uriah didn't see him, but Anasa happened to be walking by, adorned with a new leather battle vest, shield, bow, and quiver full of arrows. He noticed Shuriah with his warrior father and finally put the relationship together.

"You need to be very proud of him, Uriah. He saved my life!" he stated, smiling and patting Shuriah's shoulder.

Uriah wasn't taking this news well since he wasn't able to be there for his son when he needed him. He stepped up close to Anasa with a hard expression, trying to control himself. He asked firmly, "And why did he have to save your life?"

"The king and I separated from the main group of soldiers to keep the boys safe through the...." He looked to Shuriah, forgetting the name again.

"The eye of the moon!" Shuriah exclaimed again with excitement.

"You went through there without me?" Uriah's blood was now beginning to boil. Going through the eye of the moon was a secret place that only the mighty warriors of David knew about. They would use it for a special ceremony when it was time for a warrior boy to become a man or when someone traveling needed to stay hidden—as opposed to crossing a very open area on the top of the mountain in which you could be seen from a far distance.

Trying to calm down, knowing King David was keeping the boys safe and out of sight, Uriah asked, "How did my son save your life? Did he kill the Philistine for you?"

Without thinking, Anasa said, "No, I got stuck and would've died a slow death if the group went on without me, but Shuriah came back for me and figured out how to rescue me by using his body as a stepping-stone."

The visual picture of this man stepping on his son overwhelmed Uriah, though Anasa still didn't see the ugly picture from a father's perspective. He looked at Shuriah and finished with a smile, "And he wasn't ordered by the king to come back for me; he volunteered."

Shuriah saw his father dangerously make a fist, hidden at his side, as his knuckles began to turn white. He knew his father was growing in anger and moved between the two men, ready to save Anasa's life one more time.

Trying not to boast, Uriah responded, "A mighty warrior's job is to serve God and the king. Saving our people, especially a soldier, is our duty, which is a stepping-stone toward greatness—

even if he himself is to be the stepping-stone. For there are no other soldiers besides *us* that are courageous enough, strong enough, and fearless enough to be a mighty warrior."

Uriah inhaled deeply and blew out his building anger as he gazed down at his son, basking in the wisdom spoken, which were basically words repeated to the young warriors during their training. Anasa sensed that what he said angered the Hittite. Understanding that he himself put the boy in danger, he wanted to lighten the atmosphere, so he said, "He did kill two of our soldiers who were disrespectful and stupid if that helps you feel better, Uriah."

Uriah jerked his head back in disbelief, opening his clenched hand and raising both hands in the air. "You did what? Are you hurt anywhere?" He scrutinized the boy, seeing if he had been injured.

Seeing Uriah losing his composure, Anasa gave a faint bow and asked with respect, "Mighty warrior Uriah, may I have a private word with you?"

He took a step to the side as Shuriah had taken a step back to avoid his father, checking him out like he was a defenseless child. "As a father to a father?" Anasa asked with a polite smile.

Uriah nodded, and they moved away from Shuriah. Then Anasa said quietly, "Your son, along with all the others, just went through an unexpected and extremely dangerous situation that could have ended with all their small bodies in tombs today." He paused, making deep eye contact with the powerful man and boldly went on in a harsh tone, letting his age speak wisdom. "Because of their intense training, their passion to serve the Lord of heaven's armies and the king of Israel, and their mighty fathers like you"—he poked Uriah in the chest with every subsequent word—"all thirty-seven boys are alive today!"

He lowered his hand as they studied each other, Anasa increasing in anger as he continued, "Focus on your son right now. Listen to his stories; celebrate his victories and his young life. For tomorrow you might be putting his body in a tomb...as I had to do with my only two sons years ago!"

He paused for a moment, collecting his thoughts as Uriah started to cave inside, doing his best not to show weakness. "Mighty warrior, I know you are a young father of just one year. In that time, I know you must have recognized that Shuriah is not an ordinary mighty warrior's son. That's why you are so concerned for his safety. There is no doubt that he"—Anasa pointed down to Shuriah—"is destined for greatness beyond any mighty warrior I've ever seen. A boy so selfless, giving, smart," pointing to the side of his head, "and has the focus and intensity to follow orders of an experienced and dedicated soldier of many years. But what frightens me"—he tilted his head down slightly, widening his eyes—"is he is a very natural-born killer, the best I have ever seen, and he is only what, ten?"

He put a hand on Uriah's shoulder, somewhat hiding his mouth so no one else could see his words, and whispered, "Love the boy, train the boy, guide the boy, but never smother him with too much discipline, protection, and keeping him from life experiences God allows for him to grow through. If you do...he will only reach *your* potential, walking in the path God has for *you*, Uriah. Don't do that to him because when he becomes a man, I would not want to be at the end of his sword as he fights his way out of *your* life to find *his*. Do you understand what I'm saying?" He looked deeper into the big Hittite's eyes, who suddenly saw the picture drawn for him.

Patting Uriah's shoulder, Anasa ended with, "Let him live to the potential God has for him because," looking from Shuriah back to Uriah, "we both know, Uriah from Hatti, we want him on our side and for him *not* to leave his people to live in a foreign land and become our enemy."

"Hey, you two, why are we so serious?" King David had been looking for Uriah, wanting to congratulate him on the stellar performance of his son. He also wanted to talk with all the mighty warriors to ready themselves for battle.

When the full army arrived, they brought with them David's servants and all the luxuries that came with the crown. He had already bathed and was wearing his brilliant kingly attire with the crown on his head, surrounded by servants and bodyguards.

Uriah and Anasa both bowed as David continued, "Unfortunately, my friend, you missed a very exciting and unexpected last ten days. I witnessed two of your son's kills, although"—he shrugged his shoulders—"unfortunately both were our own soldiers who were"—he searched for a word—"disrespectful." Then he smiled back to Shuriah proudly. "Both were dead before their bodies hit the ground. He even cut a head off with the soldier's own sword while he was still standing." David turned around, pointing to a head that was put up on a long stick a distance away as a reminder of what had taken place earlier.

Uriah leaned to one side, looking past David to Shuriah, who had stepped behind the king, hoping he wasn't in trouble, and gave a friendly grin like everything was all right.

"He even saved this old man's life." The king looked to Anasa and nudged him in the side.

"We were just talking about that, Master," Anasa said. He nodded, gave Uriah a look of confidence, bowed to David, and went on his way.

Uriah and Shuriah followed as David grew serious and started walking, saying, "The priests are preparing for the burnt offering to ask for God's blessing for a great victory. An altar has been built next to my tent, and the Ark of God is in its own tent next to it as well, ready to go forward in battle, so God is with us. Let us all gather there soon, bringing the boys before the sun sets so we can praise the Lord of heaven's armies."

"Oh, and our sentinels have returned; the Philistines have stopped and set up camp less than half a day's march from here...not sure why?" He looked around inquisitively, thinking there was more to the story. Uriah completely understood the look, fully trusting his instincts, strategies, and abilities when it came to war.

David continued after sending Uriah the private message, "We will march the men out before the sun rises, and when it does"—he and Uriah looked up to the sun, shading their eyes—"it will be to our backs!"

Uriah grinned, liking the idea because the sun was always a good distraction before a battle. Then he wondered what the king was truly thinking the Philistines were doing, knowing in their private meeting later, he would be divulging his plans.

After the king and his entourage walked away to stroll through Bethlehem for the evening to mingle with the citizens and see some of his relatives, Uriah stood tall before his son and said with a new perspective on fatherhood, "Shuriah, I am very proud of you, and I want to hear about every move you made since you left my presence, but I must say this to you first. The mighty warriors have been my only family since I left my homeland, Hatti, years ago. I have told you about my dead wife and child and the pain in my chest that I can never get rid of.

"Over the past days with you gone, I realized you *have* taken that pain away for me and replaced it with a joy I haven't felt in a long time. It is hard for me, as you know, not to be an Israelite by blood. But with you as a true Israelite who is now my son, I have never felt so close to someone or to a people with a great purpose than with you in my life.

"Forgive me for my anger earlier. It was not meant for you. And truly it was not anger"—he lowered his voice as he stopped to face the boy straight-on—"but fear."

Shuriah looked to both sides of them, making sure no one heard his mighty warrior father say such a word, and whispered, "Fear?"

"Yes, son. Fear – afraid of an illusion of things that could have happened that never did." He paused, thinking of how to put his next thought, and said, "I'm also very jealous."

"Jealous? What are you jealous about?"

He grinned, slightly embarrassed. "I wanted to be there when you made your first kill."

CHAPTER 11

The half-moon angling low in the night sky was the only thing lighting up the path for Uriah, his son, and twelve well-trained soldiers. They were instructed to go south from Bethlehem in the middle of the night to sneak around the hillsides in the direction from which the king and the warrior sons had come. This was to make sure they were not being flanked, coming around from behind when the battle started in the morning. At the same time, another mighty warrior, Eliam, his warrior son, and a group of twelve soldiers were sent in the other direction going north of Bethlehem to do the same.

It concerned David that the young warriors and his guard ran into so many Philistine sentinels. What the guard told them he saw on a horse in the distance when the young warriors were attacked also concerned David. It further worried him when he thought about the four they killed after going through the eye of the moon.

Before they began, Uriah thoroughly went through anticipated expectations under his command with the twelve soldiers. He then reviewed what they had been training for with Shuriah—how to be a perfect shadow, moving when he moved, stopping, running, and doing all the body motions his father in front of him did. He was to stay a sword's length behind him at all times unless they needed to change up strategies or fight back-to-back.

Uriah himself had to not only retrain how he thought and moved during battle so as not to harm Shuriah but also how to utilize the skills his warrior son had that made them both more effective. He kept in mind that the whole purpose of the warrior son shadowing a warrior father was to train him to be extraordinary at killing while not getting hurt in the process.

The responsibility of the warrior son was to oversee the space between his father and himself, so his father could focus ahead of and beside himself while the boy kept watch behind him. The young warrior would listen carefully past the loud roar of fighting for specific commands, such as positions or maneuvers the father would yell for them to do, which would look like one warrior with four arms and legs.

The weapons of choice the mighty warriors loved their sons to have were bows and arrows and long spears. The boys were always trained not to shoot the man in front of their father but the man just behind that man. This ensured the mighty warrior would never be outmanned with too many coming at him at once.

With the long spears, the boys would keep the enemy at bay, giving the warrior father time to react. The spear was so long that when his father was engaged with his sword or in hand-to-hand combat, the boy would hold the butt of the spear on the ground on his father's side, rotating with the movement of his father while staying behind him. The long spear protruded out in front of his father, facing low in the direction of another enemy soldier coming at him.

The secret was the boy would hold it low, out of direct eyesight, so when the fast, incoming soldier was looking at his father, he would never see the sharp spearhead pointing at his groin or thigh. The oncoming enemy would impale himself with very little effort from the boy. The surprised, injured soldiers would immediately react by jumping back in pain, which innately freed the spearhead themselves. Then the boy would swiftly thrust the spear upward into the throat as the soldier looked down at what inflicted the agonizing pain.

If the warrior father needed the spear, he would yell without looking back, and his son would simply lift the long shaft up into his father's open hand to use. If the spear was gone, the son would use his miniature sword but position himself for snakebite formation, thrusting low but upward at the unexpecting enemy.

After going over many things they had trained together, Uriah took a deep breath, gaining confidence that they were ready to finally go to battle together. He asked his son if he had any questions or was apprehensive about anything. Completely off-subject, Shuriah replied, "Father, I don't think I ever thanked you for sneaking up on me in Shechem and rescuing me. Back then, I could never have dreamed I would be doing what I am right now with a father like you. All I thought about was surviving by finding or stealing food because my stomach was always empty or staying warm at night, hoping not to freeze to death."

Uriah smiled as he replied, "No, son. Thank *you*. For you have become food for my heart, keeping me warm inside."

They knew exactly what the other one was saying as they turned to the other soldiers waiting at the edge of camp to slip out into the night.

They spent the whole night scouring the hillsides but didn't find any sign of Philistines flanking them. They were at the farthest boundary of the nearby wilderness that General Joab wanted them to go to when they took a moment to regroup. Uriah quietly gave instructions of a different route they were going to take back to Bethlehem to join the fighting that would be already in progress by the time they got there.

He turned his head, raising his nose into the air, and stopped talking midsentence as a faint odor came to him. The others all smelled hard into the breeze that suddenly wisped their way. Knowing exactly what the smell was, he whispered ever-so-quietly, leaning into the tight group. "The Lord of heaven's armies has breathed our way, giving us the foul odor of dirty and sweaty Philistines."

He put his finger to his mouth and told the soldiers to lower themselves to the ground and stay put. Hunching over, he slithered in the direction the breeze was blowing, hiding behind anything that would conceal his black silhouette in the darkest part of the night—just before the sun began to reveal its essence from the heavens above.

Shuriah, never leaving his father's back, was soundless, and Uriah caught himself constantly looking back to make sure he was still behind him.

After going a very short distance, Uriah halted, giving Shuriah a hand signal to step up to his side as they crouched low to the ground behind a boulder. Pointing with his finger close to his face, he gestured from his far left to his right, signaling there were enemy soldiers out in front of them. Shuriah first looked straight out and farther away than where his father was pointing. Then his eyes finally caught what he was pointing at, and his ears perked up from snoring sounds flowing sporadically from different directions.

Lifting his head slightly higher and staring downward, they finally came into focus. There, spread throughout the gully below, were bodies lying all over the place. In the dark, he could not count how many, but he sensed there were many more Philistines soldiers than his eyes could see sleeping and waiting for the sun to rouse them to battle.

Uriah needed to know how many there were, so he took a quick count, estimating the number of men sleeping. Once confident he had what they needed, he motioned for them to head back the way they came. As Shuriah turned around, still kneeling in front of his father, he looked up and flinched when he found a man standing only a few steps in front of them.

He looked into the man's face, and the man tilted his head inquisitively at what he thought in the dark was a couple of his soldiers until his eyes widened. His mouth looked like he was about to sound an alarm, but instead of yelling, both hands went to his throat, and Shuriah realized a dagger was sticking out of it. Right away, he knew his father had used a throwing dagger, which was secured low and upside down on his lower back battle vest.

Understanding what to do, Shuriah sprang up to the Philistine's mouth and covered it up with his hands while Uriah grasped both the dying soldier and Shuriah to quietly lower the three of them to the ground.

With a last few rustling and grunting sounds, the soldier died. As Uriah rolled the dead soldier to his stomach, he whispered into Shuriah's ear, "Stay lying down, and pretend to be sleeping."

His father's words were wise. They heard the sliding footsteps of someone approaching them from the crowd of sleeping soldiers. Shuriah had his head lying sideways toward the oncoming footsteps. He squinted his eyes so that no one could see them, but he could still peek through his eyelashes.

A soldier had come over to them when he heard some noise. He hesitated, looking back and forth, but saw nothing out of place. Then he looked at what was behind him, yawned, and moved beside them, facing a bush. He proceeded to lift his battle clothes and relieve himself. After he was finished, he walked back into the sea of bodies and went back to sleep.

After a few more moments, making sure no one else was coming their way, Uriah slowly rose, reaching over to retrieve his dagger from the dead soldier's throat. Then he stepped forward in a cat-like crouch as they both swiftly returned to the twelve who were patiently waiting for them.

On the way back, Uriah whispered to his son because he couldn't get over how silent he was, especially in the dark. "You need to come up with some quiet sound that only I can hear because I can't hear you. I don't even know if you are there and have to look back, taking my concentration off what's in front of us."

Shuriah grinned in the shadow of his father as they made their way, proud of himself for the compliment he knew Uriah had just given him.

Stepping close to the twelve soldiers, Uriah whispered, "There are about a thousand Philistines sleeping right over there, an arrow's distance away from us. We cannot allow them to get any closer to Bethlehem from this direction. They could do a lot of damage while most of our army presses forward in the other direction when the sun rises."

He thought for a moment, coming up with an idea, and said, "We must attack them in the dark. That is our"—he pointed to them all—"greatest defense."

The soldiers looked at him as if he were crazy, and one said, "Thirteen against a thousand?"

Uriah looked at him with a sinister grin. "No, it would be three or four hundred for me, leaving around six hundred for the twelve of you."

The men looked back and forth, very concerned the mighty

warrior was going to make them fight with the odds very much against them. Then he interrupted their fearful thoughts, "But it's not going to come to that. We are each going to kill the same amount as the rest run for their lives from the thousands of Israelite soldiers coming at them." He chuckled at the visual.

Now the faces crinkled up, staring at the mighty warrior as though he were out of his mind, thinking to themselves, *There is no one else around but us. Who are all these Israelites he is talking about?*

Uriah kneeled, used his battle knife as a drawing stick in the dirt, and began to explain the plan as he drew it out. He drew a wide circle and dotted using the tip of his knife many times inside the circle. "Here are the Philistines lying out in the open, sleeping. We are going to quickly make our way to the other side of them here"—he pointed to the other side of the circle making thirteen X marks in a half circle—"getting a little closer than we are now, separating ourselves out wide enough that we have them halfway surrounded. I will whistle once we are in place, and we will shower half our arrows into the blanket of bodies, killing and wounding as many as we can."

"But it's dark, Uriah. We can't aim at specific targets," one soldier pointed out, not yet getting what the plan was.

"The darkness is our distraction and will be our shield as we deceive them. All we have to do is aim high in their direction, and many of our arrows will hit their targets. Shortly thereafter, we will be halfway through our supply of arrows." Looking down at his son, he said, "Shuriah, this is when you will take the ram's horn." Uriah looked around at all the men and asked, "Who has it?"

"I do," one of the soldiers said as he unstrapped it from around his neck and handed it to the boy.

"Shuriah, you will take the ram's horn, starting at the first soldier here." Uriah pointed to the first X, tapping it, and then went around to the last one farthest away. "You will blow as loud as you can. Then I want you to run as fast as you can to the next soldier and blow again, continuing on to the next, and the next until you get to me, the last X here, and blow for the last time."

Looking at the soldiers, he told them, "After he blows the horn, you begin to clank your sword and shield together loudly, continuing until he gets to me. At that point, I will yell, 'For the God of Israel,' as each of you follow, shouting the same thing.

"Once we have cheered, start shooting arrows again into the body of soldiers and stop when you have one left." Uriah looked around with a confident grin, nodding his head.

There was a moment of silence, and the soldiers were all eyes and ears, waiting for further instruction. When Uriah remained silent, one of the soldiers asked, "Then what?"

Uriah peered around, keeping them in suspense a few moments longer, stretched his neck out toward them as though he was going to divulge a secret, and said, "We are going to turn back to Bethlehem and get a big, healthy meal before joining the rest of the army on the front line." He stayed in that position, focusing on each man, none of whom was expecting that answer and did not understand what it meant.

The same man who asked the question spoke up again, "That's it?"

Uriah nodded confidently. "That's it." The soldiers looked at one another with questions. Then he added, "There will be nothing left for us to do because these Philistines will believe we are thousands of Israelites whose God has shown favor and led us here in complete darkness. They will run for their lives after dozens of them are dead or crying in pain from arrows sticking out of their bodies. "Because it's so dark out right now, the illusion of fear will take hold of them, especially coming out of a deep sleep on the cold, hard ground in the late night."

He grew very serious, now speaking through gritted teeth as he grasped two shoulders of men standing next to him. "Do you believe this will happen?"

He waited, and one by one, they reluctantly started to nod their heads. In order to build them up, he continued, "Do you believe the God of Israel led us to these men to conquer them? Did He not breathe our way in the darkness to let us know they were here?"

Now he fully had their attention, reminding them God was with them. "Would God lead us to them for Him to be defeated and for us to die?"

Perking up but in a whisper, Shuriah responded with excitement, "No, Father! He would not!" It had fully come to him; he had just needed to see the broader picture of their situation and of God himself—just as the priests and King David continually taught them the laws of God as part of their daily training.

"No, Uriah, mighty warrior!" one of the soldiers added in the dark. "I will trust you, for you did not become a mighty warrior if you were not great at war, as the Lord of heaven's armies goes before His people to be victorious above all nations."

Uriah appreciated the sentiment more for Shuriah's benefit than anyone else. "Good, but I tell you the truth. You must believe with your whole heart"—he quietly pounded his chest and pointed to his head—"and mind. Because if you don't"—he paused for emphasis—"everything you do in life with your body will eventually be defeated when you get tired or wounded. The mind and heart overcome being tired and look past the wounds. When you fully realize this, you too *will* become a mighty warrior!"

Giving them a last assuring look, he turned to Shuriah, who was now holding the ram's horn, and said, "For this to work with precision, you must blow loud and run fast. Do not use any of your arrows for you will be the only one left with a full quiver.

"When you get to me, position yourself, and watch the God of Israel in action!"

As Uriah said it would happen, it happened. After the showering of arrows, the blasts from the ram's horn, the clanking of their weapons, the yelling of "For the God of Israel," and the final barrage of arrows over the fleeing Philistine soldiers, the thirteen men, and the boy slowly came together. They could hear the thundering of a thousand men running and screaming for their lives up the hillside and over the mountain in the dark.

Once it went quiet after the enemy distanced themselves from the illusion of the powerful Israelite soldiers coming after them, the sun began to open its eye.

The soldiers were silently in awe as Uriah stood there, watching their faces. One of them, overwhelmed and relieved they were not dead, whispered in disbelief, "It worked, it worked!"

They all looked around, quite sure they were alone in the wilderness and eyed Uriah for permission. He understood what they wanted to do, so he grinned and nodded.

The small band of men immediately raised their bows in the air, boasting out a victory cry. Shuriah joined in with the twelve soldiers as they danced around joyfully. As Uriah looked on, he stayed calm, knowing what they were feeling but knew it was too early to rejoice.

"Father, please dance with us!"

Uriah smiled as he pulled the bow over his head and replaced it on his back. "This is a victory of one small battle, son. It is very early to be celebrating the victory of a war."

Hearing those words, the soldiers found themselves quieting down because they realized he was right.

Uriah studied the men as they surrounded him, saying with encouragement, "But we can rejoice in what the Lord of heaven's armies has done here and not on what *you* did here."

The play on words snapped their focus to the truth (without degrading their enthusiasm) as they nodded in agreement about where the glory needed to go. He added, "For the strength of the Lord is *our* power to overcome our enemies…of whom they have not *yet* been completely overcome."

His expression became firmer and impassive. "There are still 15,000 Philistines heading to Bethlehem right now, and the same number of Moabites are on their way to Jerusalem. And that's not counting their chariots, charioteers, and horse soldiers. The war has just begun!"

By the time they arrived back in Bethlehem, General Joab and his large army were already in battle less than a half a day's walk toward Gath. Uriah was informed that the other small group that went to the north of Bethlehem during the night to look for Philistine sentries had not returned, which concerned him.

He ordered his twelve soldiers to eat fast, go restock their quivers, and grab an extra quiver each, including one for him. He also had them each get a ram's horn and a horse from the horse master (again including one for him).

Shortly after being refreshed, stocking their supplies, and getting thirteen horses ready to go, Uriah confronted them, "Our men who went north looking for flanking Philistines haven't returned. This means they are dead, engaged in battle, or in hiding because they are outnumbered."

The energized and excited soldiers from early this morning realized they were in the exact same position, significantly outnumbered—now in broad daylight.

"We cannot allow any number of Philistines to come behind our army or to infiltrate this city. This is where our king was born and must remain unharmed! Do I make myself clear?!"

The small group, having experienced nothing short of a miracle during the night, knew they needed another miracle right now. Uriah began pacing back and forth as though he was a caged animal, talking loudly and not caring who was listening as the soldiers held tight to the horses. "The burnt offering was given up to the Lord of heaven's armies yesterday! The Ark of God is with us here in this place! There will be no fear coming from an Israelite as it's the power of God's might that will conquer anyone in His path!"

Stopping to eye the men who were beginning to erupt with courage, he pointed outward, "He will turn the twelve of you into twelve hundred in the eyes of our enemies!"

He grasped the reins of his horse from one of the soldiers and jumped up, swinging his leg around as Shuriah reached out for his father's hand. Pulling Shuriah up to his backside, he bellowed, "Mount up. Join me in the slaughter of the ones who have defied the God of Israel for generations!"

Not a word was spoken as they all promptly mounted their horses that were also growing in excitement at the loud words, knowing they were about to travel. The horses nervously stepped in place, moving from side to side and jerking their heads up and down.

Everyone had their swords, shields, bows, extra quivers, rams' horns, and other supplies ready as the group felt more powerful sitting high off the ground, feeling the large, muscular animals underneath them. They were now ready to go to war without fear or hesitation.

Uriah controlled his horse, pulling back hard on the reins as it fought him to stay in position. Uriah's and his horse's eyes appeared to be filled with a raging fire, which is the same look many saw from mighty warriors moments before engaging in battle. "Hold on, Shuriah!" he urged.

He loosened up on the horse's reins, digging his heals sharply into the side of the animal as it faced north. It took off with the same intensity that was exploding within its rider as the twelve others burst out of Bethlehem, following their leader and leaving a large cloud of dust behind them in the morning air.

With the horses, they were able to close the distance of where Uriah thought General Joab sent Eliam, the mighty warrior, and his men. Going up a ravine in the middle of a long hillside, they spotted tracks in the dirt that aligned with the group they were looking for.

They all dismounted to give the horses a rest as Uriah handed the reins to one of the soldiers and told them all to keep a watchful eye. He and Shuriah scouted around to see if they could locate where their fellow soldiers might be. He gave them instructions that if they were far up at the top of the hill and needed them to come up to them with the horses, Shuriah would shoot an arrow to their right, hitting the ground next to them. If he wanted them to come without the horses, he would shoot an arrow on their left.

Having full quivers of arrows, the two methodically made their way up, going back and forth to follow the tracks to the top of the hill. Before cresting to see the other side, Uriah informed his son that this was a spot where they could lose their advantage if they were spotted sky-lined on top of the ridge.

Shuriah told him he understood what he was talking about from when he and the other warrior sons were alone, staying low and off the ridge, out of sight, while going back to King David. There was a split second when Uriah wanted to get angry again at not being with him, but he kept his focus on what was going on right now, knowing just over the ridge, swords could be waiting for them.

Uriah belly-crawled, keeping his head low as Shuriah followed his lead. Feeling like they were wide open for everyone to see them, Uriah only wanted to spend a couple of breaths of time in this very vulnerable spot. Ever so carefully, he kept his chin to the ground, pressing forward to see the other side, attempting to blend in with the ground cover and not be silhouetted on the ridge. He examined every detail, first seeing the top of the far hillside. Then he slithered forward to see farther and farther down into another ravine.

He paused, seeing something move in a group of boulders on the far hillside halfway up. Then it disappeared. Scanning for more information, suddenly lifeless bodies of soldiers came into focus scattered all over the place—around the boulders all the way down to the bottom of the ravine. From this distance, he couldn't tell if they were Philistines or Israelites. But he easily saw there were more than twelve. More like two hundred and twelve.

Looking back up to the top of the far hillside, a handful of soldiers began to appear, sneaking around, heading down toward the boulders. As they got closer, one of the soldiers fell to the ground, rolling limply down the hill.

"Arrow got him," Uriah whispered.

Shuriah nodded in agreement. Then his eyes went wide as a large body burst out of the rocks toward the oncoming soldiers. At first, there was one sword swinging, and a long spear could be seen sticking up past the soldier, impaling one of the oncoming men running downhill.

"Eliam!" Uriah exclaimed heavily under his breath.

"Who, Father?"

"That is Eliam, the mighty warrior from behind the rocks. He was leading the other group of soldiers, looking for Philistines that could be flanking Bethlehem."

Uriah turned quickly, still low to the ground, and said, "Get your arrow ready; we need the horses fast!"

When they were out of sight on the ridge, Uriah told him, "Shoot the arrow to their right!" Then he added, "Wait for them here. I'm going to watch what is going on with Eliam and his son." As soon as the soldiers arrived with the horses, Uriah came back down, giving instructions, "We are going to repeat what we did last night, except use horses." He mounted his horse, pulling Shuriah up as he looked at one of the younger soldiers with them and said, "You stay behind and give Shuriah the reins to your horse. It will be for Eliam and his son. Stay behind, keeping a watchful eye all around us.

"Everyone else on this side of the ridge: stay out of sight and spread yourselves out from each other, but this time I will be the middle person. On my signal of blowing the ram's horn, everyone, blow yours at the same time with three long blasts facing the other side of this ridge.

"Then we will take off over the ridge, spread wide, and yell our battle cries. Once at the bottom of the ravine below, six of you"—he pointed them out—"will stop and begin shooting arrows ahead of the rest of us or in the direction where there are Philistines. The other six shoot arrows or engage in fighting if the enemy is present. Your goal is to keep a path cleared for us," Uriah instructed, pointing back to his son on his horse. "We must get this horse to the mighty warrior and his son, who are holding their ground by a group of large boulders halfway up the far hillside. I didn't see any other Israelite, but if you see one alive, get them on your horse. When I turn back with Eliam and his son, we will all ride hard back here. Do you understand?" he rather stated more than asked. Even the horses could feel the tension rise as they began to trot in place, bumping into one another.

All the men nodded to him as he yelled, raising his fist high, "The Lord of heaven's armies will be victorious! Spread out and proudly blow the ram's horn, telling them the God of Israel is angry!"

Uriah watched back and forth, and his small army got into position as an internal power erupted within him, bursting to go out and save his warrior brother. As soon as the outer soldiers got to their post, Uriah raised his ram's horn, as did Shuriah, and blew three times, emptying their lungs each time.

The sound of more than a dozen horns blowing across the ravine at the top of the hillside caught everyone by surprise. The Philistines took a few steps back, looking in all directions to figure out where the daunting and intimidating orchestra of battle music was coming from. After they stopped, it was silent for a moment—almost to the point that they weren't sure if it were real or not until raging yelling struck their ears. Horses appeared all along the top, far ridge, racing as fast as they could directly at them.

"Son, the God of Israel has arrived!" Eliam shouted as he looked down at his wounded boy who had been doing his best to shadow his father with the long spear in one hand and an arrow embedded deep in his opposite shoulder.

CHAPTER 12

As soon as the horses made it to the bottom of the ravine, six of the soldiers dismounted and began to shoot arrows out ahead of the other seven, who were continuing to charge up the hill to the large boulders.

At the same time, as though it was planned, a loud charge of voices came from over the ridge above as the remaining hundreds of Philistine soldiers started piling over and running straight toward Eliam and his son.

Uriah reacted, yelling out to his fellow horsemen, "With the speed of God, get to them and shower arrows!"

He focused on Eliam, who also remained focused, taking the long spear out of his son's hands and twirling it over his head several times, relaying a message to his fellow mighty warrior. Uriah's eyes went wide, and urgency stronger than ever ripped through him. He kicked the horse's ribs hard.

The mass of men was closing in on Eliam, and many of them began to fall down, tripping up others because of the arrows from below that were flying over the seven horsemen, finding their targets. Uriah had to change his strategy since they were going to arrive at the boulders at the same time as the Philistines.

He leaned back and shouted, "Shuriah, let go of the reins of the horse following us! You stay on this horse; Eliam's son is injured! He'll get on with you, and you two go back to the soldier we left on top of the other hill!"

"But, Father—" Shuriah wanted so much to finally engage in battle with his father but was cut off.

"Obey my words!" Uriah said harshly as he stayed focused on what was ahead and how he was going to do this switch. Then he yelled to the soldiers racing in at his side, "Shoot your arrows!" The soldiers did their best to stay balanced, retrieving arrows from over their shoulders to shoot into the hundreds of men charging down.

Shuriah let go of the reins of the horse behind them, but it kept following as Uriah grasped the long spear his son was holding in his other hand and stabbed it into the air.

Eliam saw the return signal and looked back up hill to the men almost to him. With urgency, Eliam yelled to his son behind him as he repositioned the sword in his hand while gripping tightly to his shield, "Run to Uriah now!"

Without thinking or hesitating, the boy reacted to his father's words with only his miniature sword in hand because he was out of arrows. Uriah sat up tall on the horse and threw his spear, passing Eliam's side and hitting a Philistine in the chest so hard he fell backward, causing several behind him to stumble. Uriah jumped off the horse, grasped the wounded boy, and flung him up behind Shuriah as Shuriah slid forward, taking the reins. He twisted the horse around and raced away from the clash of fighting.

Looking ahead down the hill at the six soldiers who had been shooting arrows, they were all now standing with blank faces, watching an impossible situation unfold. Shuriah yelled, "Go to them! The God of Israel is here with us!"

He pulled back hard on the reins, bringing the horse to a stop as dust billowed up around them; they looked from one another and back uphill. This time the wounded boy, Itai, yelled, "Go fight to be a mighty warrior! There are plenty of Philistines that need to be killed!" Itai had blood covering his battle vest that was streaming down his arm and dripping off his fingertips.

Encouraged, the men looked up at Itai with the broken arrow sticking out of his shoulder, giving them that fiery look the mighty warriors always had. "Go, or you will *not* be going home to Jerusalem because our king will cut your bodies into pieces for being cowards, only to be fed to the wild dogs so your bones can never be entombed!"

Reminded of what could be their demise, they all jumped onto their horses and raced uphill into battle. After seeing the men finally take off to fight, Shuriah kicked their horse to continue. He looked back and asked, "Itai, why would they hesitate to go into battle?"

"You will learn most men are cowards, only seeing life through their weakness and understanding—not from the eyes of the Lord of heaven's armies with *His* powerful strength and understanding. We are all weak unless we live and fight in the shadow of the God of Israel! That is why there are so few mighty warriors out of the tens of thousands in our army!" Itai stated proudly as he looked back up at Uriah and his great father, fighting side by side ferociously. Then he prayed to himself, *God, protect them and give them your powers to slay this giant of many.*

When they got to the top of the ridge where the younger soldier was to be waiting, they spun the horse around multiple times, looking for him. Finally, Itai spoke up, pointing, "There! There he is with some others!"

Shuriah followed his finger until his eyes caught sight of what looked like six men running away in the direction of Bethlehem.

"What are they doing?" Shuriah asked, bewildered.

"Running to their grave! We lost track of a handful of our soldiers when we were attacked from all sides, surrounded at the bottom of the ravine." He pointed back to where they came from. "We were killing many with arrows as they ran at us. Then when they got close, our swords and spears were slicing through them, but those cowards running now turned their backs on us and ran away. Then suddenly, all the Philistines stopped and retreated over the hill. When my father and I looked around, all our men except for two were dead or gone."

"Why did they stop fighting and run away when there were just a few of you left?"

"I think they heard or saw you coming from the other side because one of their flagmen came running down the hillside, waving it as fast as he could to give instructions to go over the opposite hill." Shuriah looked out on the horizon as the men disappeared, running away. He told Itai, "Get off! I must go back!"

"No, you must follow orders, Shuriah!"

"Our fathers need help! I have two quivers full of arrows. I will stay out of range of the fighting but will shoot any Philistines I can." Itai swung his leg around, jumping off the horse. When he landed, it jarred his body, causing excruciating pain. "Aahh!" he moaned, bending over and grasping his shoulder. He looked up and said, "Hurry! But when you run out of arrows, come back."

Itai grabbed the reins of the horse that had followed them all the way back to the top of the ridge. Feeling faint, he sat down on the ground, trying not to show weakness, and yelled again, "Hurry!" Shuriah turned his horse and raced as fast as he could back down the hill. Looking far ahead, he decided to fade off to the right and semi-flank the Philistines. At the bottom of the ravine, his horse leaped over many bodies as Shuriah pushed it to go uphill for a bit to get close enough for his shorter arrows to reach the mass of Philistines soldiers who were pushing in on the boulder area to get their turn at the mighty warriors.

Finding a good spot to dismount next to a sturdy, sizeable bush, he quickly wrapped the reins around the branches several times and knelt down, bringing his bow out in front of him. He pulled off his quiver, leaning it against the bush to be able to grab the arrows efficiently.

Trying to stay hidden, he pulled one out and nocked it. Then he aimed into the cluster of bodies, knowing no matter what, he was going to hit someone and hopefully kill them. He let the arrow fly out in front of the two mighty warriors uphill. One of them was swinging a spear out sideways at one man as the other warrior kicked out to the side, breaking the ribs of the Philistine who was running in hard from the opposite direction. Then he stabbed his sword down through his chest.

The arrow hit its mark as an enemy soldier screamed out in pain with the arrow sticking out of his stomach. Then another man unexpectedly was hit, then another and another. Suddenly the attention of many of the Philistines, looking ahead at the men dropping dead or squirming in pain on the ground, turned toward the mysterious source, trying to see where the arrows were silently coming from. All they saw in the distance were dead soldiers all over the place and a lone horse standing near a bush.

Shuriah saw many heads turning his way, so he stopped for a moment, kneeling close to the ground behind the bush. He gazed through the branches, attempting to see where all the Israelite soldiers were in comparison to his and Itai's fathers in the midst of furious fighting and screaming pain.

He thought he counted seven Israelite soldiers still fighting, circled closely together back to back, defending themselves in traditional fashion just below the large boulders. Then above the boulders where the mighty warriors were, it was a completely different scene. To his amazement, all his training suddenly mentally came alive, seeing it in action. The two large warriors looked like they were from the armies of heaven, for they were moving in a smooth, rhythmic, acrobatic motion as though their feet were not touching the ground.

There was a wide circular gap the length of a spear between them; they were centered with their backs to one another, surrounded by the enemy. Each warrior had their strong shields in front of them, blocking arrows and spears flying in, while one held a sword ready to impale anyone who dodged too close. The other was grasping tightly to his long spear near the back end. Its sharp spearhead was swiftly swinging back and forth, ready to slice through throats, eyes, thighs, fingers, or whatever else the tip could touch. Every Philistine warrior bobbed back and forth, in and out of the open circle, attempting to time the deadly dance to get within reach to stab one of these Israelite warriors.

The two were battling in a manner that looked more like an artistic dance than violent fighting, with deadly weapons spinning around and legs leaping in the air, making striking kills with every movement. No motion was wasted; every reaction had a purpose, and their opponents hesitated to engage, not sure how to make their approach. The scene was mystically hypnotizing.

Shuriah finally saw firsthand the many acrobatic movements playing out that the warrior sons and fathers practiced over and over. The Philistine soldiers were beginning to pile up on top of each other, dead.

Then to his surprise, the two jumped on top of the bodies stacking up and leaped as high as they could over the heads of the next men coming at them and into the mass of soldiers, working together again like a desert whirlwind—moving faster than the eye could keep up as blood misted the air with every swipe of a sword or spear.

Shuriah was mesmerized, watching these masters of death. Wanting to join in the slaughter, Shuriah nocked another arrow and began to shoot toward the soldiers again. After shooting a couple more arrows, he suddenly found himself grasped around the middle with his arms held down to his side. He was then lifted into the air, squeezed so hard his lungs were emptied. He heard someone cry, "It's only a boy!"

Shuriah looked at his father, not able to say a word. He strained to reach the lower back of his battle vest with his free hand, where he had daggers hiding upside down. Slowly able to retrieve one, he held it firmly, pointed it toward the man's body, and jerked his head and shoulders as far forward as he could, snapping his head back to plant it in the center of the man's face. As soon as the man's head flinched back, his torso arched forward, and Shuriah was able to stab the dagger in the man's lower stomach.

The soldier dropped him, and Shuriah landed on his feet while the man bent over, screaming in pain. Shuriah had learned a favorite move in training, finding out he was extremely acrobatic himself. He did a backflip, landing on the man's neck so that his head was between Shuriah's legs. Deftly retrieving the second dagger behind his lower back, he raised his hands out to the side, stabbed both daggers deep into the man's ears, and effortlessly pulled them out.

Instantly dead, the body fell forward as Shuriah easily walked off of him. Looking back to see his kill, his eyes caught three more Philistine soldiers standing stiffly a short distance away, stunned at what they just saw this boy do. They looked back and forth between each other, trying to figure out the situation, but

Shuriah was the one to make the first move.

He reached back with a dagger in each hand and threw them at the two men, impaling one deep into a Philistine's thigh while the other bounced off its target; the knife had not completed its rotation, just hitting him with the side of the weapon.

Two soldiers were glaring at the one with the knife sticking out of his leg, but Shuriah had followed the daggers in flight. He pulled his miniature sword out from the sheath on his back, brought it down, and then upward between the legs of the third man, slicing into his manhood. The man dropped his sword, grasping his groin and bending over. Shuriah dropped his own sword, picked up the full-sized Philistine's, and swiftly came down on the back of the man's neck, severing his head.

Shuriah, now in an adrenaline rage, looked up at the soldier whom his knife bounced off and bared his teeth, growling as saliva splattered out. The soldier, unable to move, stared wide-eyed down at this crazy demon-like boy, saying under his breath, "Fire eyes!"

Shuriah didn't hear expressions or see emotion from his enemies as he moved; the intense daily training (six days a week from sun up to sun down for a year now) had perfectly conditioned the ten-year-old to act exactly how the warrior sons and fathers were supposed to—reactive and focused in battle as designed by King David.

They were not to hesitate their movements or stop to think about the situation but purposely respond with wholehearted determination and mental confidence that they *would* kill every enemy within their reach. There was to be no weakness within themselves or outward obstacle that could hold them back from victory because the Lord of heaven's armies was the one doing the fighting, and the mighty warriors were His shadows.

Shuriah spun around low in a crouched position, swinging the heavy sword out with one hand to impale the soldier in the shins as he picked up his dagger on the ground with the other. The soldier jumped in the air, bringing his knees to his chest, saying, "No you don't, boy!"

He didn't realize the fiery-eyed boy had picked up the dagger, and as soon as both of his feet touched back to the ground, Shuriah had already spun around enough that he stabbed the dagger down on top of one of the soldier's feet. Continuing his desert whirlwind, he grasped the sword with both hands, came back around facing his enemy, and sliced the soldier (who was already grasping his foot in pain) in the throat.

Shuriah left the sword in the man's throat but pulled his dagger out of his foot as he pushed off backward, rolling in a ball on the ground to pick up his own sword. Once he had rolled all the way back around to where his own feet touched the ground, he quickly crouched like a lion.

As soon as he stood, he jerked around to locate his next target, only to see the soldier he had impaled was only a few steps away, coming at him with the dagger held high.

Shuriah started to react but heard a familiar, deep voice far behind him yell in desperation, "Shuriah, down!"

Again, reacting without thinking, he dropped prostrate to the ground. With his eyes focused in front of him, the next thing he saw took him by surprise. Both of the soldier's feet left the ground as his body jolted backward, momentarily airborne, and then hit the dirt with a long spear sticking out of his chest.

Recognizing the spear as his father's, he looked back, still lying on the ground. Uriah was a short distance away, running full force at him. But what caught his attention the most was that the other mighty warrior was right behind him, and a herd of Philistines was running after them, trying to catch up with swords and knives held high.

Shuriah whipped around back to the bush where the horse was anxiously walking in place, seized his bow, nocked an arrow, and began to shoot arrows behind the mighty warriors.

After shooting several, Uriah yelled again, saying, "Get on the horse! We are going to outrun them!"

Shuriah slung the bow around his shoulders with his quivers and grabbed his sword as he freed the reins of the horse, pulling himself up on it. He looked back to Uriah, who was getting really close but was waving him to take off.

Obeying, Shuriah kicked the horse and took off across the bottom of the draw, heading up the hillside to the ridge where he left Itai. Halfway up, a horse suddenly bounded over the ridge, racing down the hillside at him. He realized it was Itai on the horse who was waving for him to stop. Shuriah looked back, surprised to find how fast he spread the distance from Uriah and Eliam.

Itai yelled, "Get off and shoot arrows!" as he pointed down the hill.

When he got to Shuriah, he stumbled off, very weak. Pulling himself together, he lifted a full-sized bow that had been left behind by one of the young soldiers who had run away and did his best to pull back on the string to shoot the longer arrow. Shuriah saw how difficult it was for him, so he traded their bows and arrows to make it easier on his wounded friend.

He struggled, pulling back the strong bowstring as he grunted and tightened his lips together but was able to get arrows off, flying high and then down into the large cluster of Philistines running after their fathers. With Itai and him interrupting the Philistine's chase, Uriah and Eliam finally made it to the horses, exhausted from having outrun the enemy. Without words, they all knew what to do; the warrior fathers quickly mounted the horses, pulled their sons on, and took off uphill.

Once at the top of the ridge, they turned around to look at what was left of the battle. Shuriah was the one to ask, "Did any of our soldiers make it?"

Eliam replied, "No, they all perished, honorably fighting for the God of Israel, killing many." It went solemnly quiet as they watched the remaining couple hundred Philistines who had given up the chase walk back down into the draw, knowing they were not going to catch them on horseback uphill.

"Father..." Itai said as he leaned sideways behind his father, falling off the horse. Uriah reached out, catching him, as Eliam reached back to hold him up. Uriah and Shuriah jumped off their horse, and Uriah took Itai from Eliam's hold. He laid him down on the ground and examined the broken arrow in his shoulder. As Eliam got off his horse and knelt next to them, Uriah whispered, "We need to pull it out. It won't go all the way through. It's touching bone."

Eliam's face wrinkled up, knowing how painful it would be, but he knew they had to do it. They maneuvered his battle vest off and removed the soft upper garment. Eliam ripped the cloth garment into long strips to cover the open wound for when the broken arrow and arrowhead were out, anticipating more blood flowing. Uriah looked around on the ground and told Shuriah, pointing, "Son, grab that ram's horn over there, and when I tell you, blow it as loud and as long as you can."

Shuriah nodded as he picked up the horn, not knowing why, and walked back to Itai lying on the ground and breathing heavily. He squirmed, knowing pain far beyond what he has ever experienced was coming. The two mighty warriors hovered over him, holding him down as his father (the older of the warriors) looked into his son's eyes, trying his best not to get emotional, and said, "Do not be afraid, son. It will be over soon, and you can rest for a long time…"

While he was talking, distracting his son, Uriah gently gripped the broken stick of the arrow without Itai knowing it, looked up at Shuriah, and nodded. Shuriah blared the horn as loudly as he could, jarring Itai and frightening him. Before he knew what was happening, Uriah had jerked out the arrow and the arrowhead.

Itai screamed out in agonizing pain but was not heard over the ram's horn (whose purpose Shuriah now understood). The Philistines retreating up the far hillside looked back, hearing the horn but not the young boy screaming in pain. The blast of the horn told them the Israelites were victorious in this small battle. Almost eight hundred Philistine soldiers were either piled up or sprawled out throughout the valley, and only eighteen Israelites were killed.

Itai went limp after the grand shock of pain, and he passed out. Uriah grabbed several cloth strips and attempted to poke them into the open wound. Unable to get them in, he told Shuriah, "Son, you have smaller fingers; use the smallest one to push this down as deep as you can."

Shuriah hesitated at first to do such a thing to a friend but knelt down, dropping the ram's horn, and grabbed the cloth. He wrapped it over his pinky finger, leaned over Itai, glancing at his closed eyes, and whispered, "Sorry, my friend." Then he pressed his finger down in the hole where bright red blood was flowing.

Eliam chimed in, "Slowly bring your finger out, but not all the way. Then push more cloth down, and do it again until no more will fit in."

After he finished the job, Shuriah became queasy and stood

back a few steps as Uriah wrapped long strips of cloth around Itai's armpit and then around his neck several times. Then he wrapped in another direction, covering the wound to make sure the whole bandage was secure.

After the men were done and had laid Itai back flat, they both heard a different sound coming from behind them. They turned just in time to see young Shuriah leaning away from them, vomiting. When he was finished and had wiped his mouth with his leather forearm protector, he looked back at the men staring at him. He blushed, ashamed that he showed weakness.

It was Eliam who said, smiling, "It's all right. It happens to all of us when we have to do things like this to our brother warriors." He turned to Uriah, giving him a wink, and looked back to Shuriah, saying, "Especially when one of us gets our belly skin sliced open, and our stomach and intestines fall out, and we have to push them back in."

Shuriah's eyes went wide, and he quickly spun around and began vomiting again. The two mighty warriors looked at each other and began to laugh out loud. After a little while, they had all recovered from getting tired and sick. Eliam got back onto his horse while Uriah lifted Itai into his arms, carrying this older son in a cradle position. Uriah and Shuriah got back onto their horse, and they slowly went back to Bethlehem.

By the time they arrived in Bethlehem, most of the day had expired. They took Itai directly to the priest for cleansing of his body and for prayer for God to heal him. The bleeding had stopped, but he was very pale from the loss of blood, and he was hot and perspiring all over.

Eliam loved his warrior son that he had taken in five years ago. In about another year, Itai would be sixteen and would be let go to be on his own because he would be considered a full-grown adult by then. He was a very accomplished boy warrior, having killed more than seventy enemy soldiers in one battle over a year ago, while Eliam killed three hundred and twenty in that same fight. He was very good with all weapons, but his favorite was the spear. He had been hurt before, but nothing like this where he had lost so much blood.

Little by little, the main army led by General Joab and King David gradually started to arrive back at their camp outside of Bethlehem. Eliam and Uriah thought earlier about going to the front to meet up with the leaders but decided by the time they got there, the sun would have begun to close its eye, and it would be a waste of time.

So they decided to clean and refresh themselves and re-equip for tomorrow's battle. After they were done, they began the silent process of wandering around Bethlehem with Shuriah's help to find the soldiers who had left them behind earlier in the day. They knew they would be hiding out somewhere or disguising themselves as locals until the thousands of other soldiers returned from fighting on the frontline. Then they would simply blend in with them out of sight and out of mind; they never considered the two mighty warriors and their sons might have made it back alive.

Uriah had put a dirty and torn-up shepherd's robe over Shuriah's battle clothes that also covered his head with the hood. Disguised, Shuriah was the first to spot the young soldier they left on top of the ridge. Taking the lead ahead of the rest, they watched for him to signal that it was indeed one of the cowards.

The soldier disguised himself by covering his military attire with a robe as well. He was waiting for the younger women at one of the wells on the far side of the city to come out and draw water for the evening. As a few young women were showing up, the soldier looked around, making sure he wasn't being watched, and took off the robe, proudly adorning his uniform and weapons.

When the women stepped up to the well, he asked if they would please give him a drink of the cool water. When they did so, he sat down on a large rock next to the watering hole and began to talk to them. After a few introductions, the young Hebrew soldier began boasting of his part in the mighty battle going on with the Philistines.

Shuriah had slowly and inconspicuously made his way to the group around the well, looking like a peasant boy with his hood still covering his head to hide his face. Confirming this was the young soldier, he turned back to the warrior fathers and gave a silent hand signal to wait and not approach yet.

Because it was so fun playing hide and seek, an idea came to him as he turned back around. He asked softly, interrupting the conversation, "Excuse me, sorry to bother you, but could I have a drink of water?"

One of the young women replied kindly, "Of course."

Shuriah drank from the cup she handed him, keeping his face hidden. He handed it back, saying, "Thank you very much. It was a very hot and tiring day in the desert."

"Time to go home, boy," the young soldier said, annoyed he interrupted his moment with the local, unattached women.

"I'm sorry I bothered you. You must be a very important soldier?"

"I am. Now scram."

Determined to get the soldier riled up, Shuriah asked in an upbeat tone, "Did you kill many Philistines today?"

"Of course, I did...." The young soldier stood, puffing out his chest. "When you fight alongside the mighty warriors, there are always bodies scattered all over the battlefield!"

Shuriah enjoyed this masquerade and asked excitedly, "Are you a mighty warrior of King David's?"

All the faces of the young women gazed up at the soldier with more admiration. He looked into their beautiful, dark eyes and stated, "Not yet, but with a few more kills during the battle, I shall soon be one!"

The women exclaimed in awe because they thought they were standing here with this great, handsome soldier, but the dirty shepherd boy took a step closer to him and said, "That's funny because that's what I always say."

The soldier hesitated for a moment; he didn't understand the reply. One of the women reached over, touching the boy's shoulder, and said, "You can be a great warrior as well one of these days, shepherd boy. Remember that our king was one when he was a boy."

Her comment played perfectly into what he was doing as he responded with, "You're right. He told me his story when I sat next to him at his table eating dinner in his palace."

There was complete silence at the absurd comment until he lifted back his hood, exposing his face. The women started giggling at the boy playing a child's game but suddenly stopped when the wide-eyed soldier's face went white with fear, instantly going to his knees in a low bow.

The young women now realized there was something wrong, so they gathered their full buckets and left, not wanting whatever bad thing was about to happen, to happen to them. Shuriah dropped the robe off as he drew his sword from over his shoulder. Uriah and Eliam, still watching from a distance, knew this was their cue to go to him.

CHAPTER 13

By nightfall, when all the soldiers, General Joab, and King David, were back from fighting for the night, Uriah, Eliam, and Shuriah had gathered up all the other culprits from their small battle. But before they brought them to the general for their punishment, all the mighty warriors (including General Joab, their sons, and King David) shared the evening meal together to discuss the day's events.

"We are together once more…" King David began, raising his goblet of wine to the might warriors. "For the God of Israel was our shield, and He gave us His strength and power to battle through the day, killing thousands of our enemies!"

All the men raised their goblets with their king, agreeing with a tame cheer since everyone was very tired.

David got to his feet, walked around to Eliam, and stood behind him. He put his hand on one of the older warrior's shoulders and said, "But there is one of us missing tonight. If you haven't heard, Itai was wounded today by an arrow." Several of the worn-out warriors popped their heads up, unaware something had happened. They looked at their brother with grave concern. "He is with the priest who has brought him to the Ark of God for healing." Pausing to change the atmosphere, he added, "And healing will happen! Just as it has for every one of us when we have been wounded in battle, for the Lord of heaven's armies does not give up on His people!"

All the men quickly stood with more energy to raise Eliam's spirits, whom they knew was very worried and hurting inside for his son; they cheered for victory of healing that was to come for his boy.

"And from what I hear, even though Itai was taken away bleeding during the fighting to a safe place, he went back to rescue his father as did one other warrior son…." The king turned his head until his eyes landed on Uriah and Shuriah. "Both saved their fathers!"

Every head turned to cast a look at the boy. David was extremely proud of him, seeing so much of himself in the young warrior. He was simply exuding admiration.

Eliam stood with everyone as he raised his own goblet. "If I may, Master"—he glanced to David, who nodded that he could interject—"I want to personally *thank* Uriah openly in front of all my warrior brothers. If he had not wisely come to look for me and Itai, there is a good chance I would have lost my son and possibly my own life." He hesitated but, with a grin, added, "I'm not as young as I used to be or as great of a warrior as Jashobeam"—he looked around until he saw him—"who has killed over eight hundred in one battle. At my best when I was younger"—he shrugged—maybe only…four hundred or so."

A commotion of laughter filled the large tent as they all took a drink at the lighthearted joking. When it quieted down, Eliam got very serious. "I owe my brother a debt that I am not sure I can ever pay back." Everyone realized the heart of the older warrior had been pierced deeply by the day's events.

Becoming a mighty warrior was a grand position and accomplishment that usually comes with a cost of a rough and impenetrable exterior. The relationships with the king, each other, and most importantly, with the Lord of heaven's armies were second to none for these warriors. And even though they were strong as iron on the outside, their hearts were as soft as the wool of a newborn lamb. Rarely did anyone, especially people outside their tight alliance, ever see the inside of a warrior's heart…unless the iron exterior had been cracked. Today the family of warriors inside the tent was seeing that crack in Eliam.

He looked directly across the tent and said somberly, "Uriah, I know it has been difficult for you among us over the years because you are a Hittite. I remember when you came into our lives when we were up near Damascus, hunting down some raiders, and you threw your spear, killing the enemy farther and faster than I had ever seen."

There were grunts of approval around the tent as many of the men raised their goblets to Uriah, having seen it firsthand as well.

"And I saw that same man today throw his spear with such force and accuracy that it saved my life and our sons' lives."

Eliam looked down to the ground and back up with a completely different demeanor, slouching as he changed subject midstream. "Even though I've considered you a warrior brother… I have made fun of you for not being a blood Israelite. And you never ever confronted me or any of us for doing so."

The smiles and raised goblets drooped in embarrassment. Shuriah looked around and saw many of the warrior fathers looked guilty for treating a brother warrior, his father, in such a way. Then he stared around at his young friends, and many of their eyes flashed to him and looked away guilty as well for attacking his father through him.

Eliam focused on Uriah, saying, "I will never do that again to you. For you are truly a dedicated warrior brother, willing to sacrifice his own life to save mine and everyone's here." He spread his arms around to everyone. "Which you have done repeatedly in every battle throughout the years. And now, you have a son!" Eliam pointed to Shuriah with a big smile. "Who was trained and taught by all of us, but especially by you, to follow the God of Israel into battle, and without prejudice, to kill our enemies and protect all his brothers without concern for his own safety."

Eliam was building toward something, but no one knew quite what it was; they remained silent to let him concentrate on what he was saying.

"Uriah, you are as much an Israelite as any of us!" He went silent as he stared around the room into regretful eyes. Then as though planned, they all raised their goblets to Uriah, agreeing in their shame that he was their equal.

Now that he got that out of the way, Eliam proceeded with his ultimate intent, looking him in the eyes again. "There is something you need in your life Uriah, and I have it. You have a hole that needs to be refilled since you lost your family many years ago back in Hatti."

Uriah wrinkled his forehead and tilted his head downward at the thought of his painful past. Everyone turned to him, seeing this conversation was getting very serious.

"Yes, my brother. I remember your pain." Eliam nodded with a comforting grin. "Your warrior son, Shuriah, has been a blessing to you, and we can clearly see that. He has renewed purpose for you, and we can see you are a proud father."

Many men smiled and nodded in agreement, witnessing the change in the Hittite's life the past year.

"But you are still not complete, and I have a gift for you to make you complete, my warrior brother. It is a great gift that I have held onto and need to release, but no man has been good enough or has earned it…until now. Uriah, if you would please give me the honor without any payment…." He paused, making sure everyone listening heard the message and the depth of what was happening. "Would you please accept my daughter, Bathsheba, as your wife?"

The silence inside the king's tent was deafening. Everyone knew Eliam's daughter. She was one of the most beautiful young women in Jerusalem. Men have tried, even several of the younger mighty warriors, to earn Bathsheba as a wife. But for Eliam, no one was ever the right man for her until now. And he wasn't asking anything for her because, to him, Uriah fully paid for her by saving Itai's and his life today. Since his eyes were completely opened to the true man that the Hittite was: wise, strong, dedicated, respectful, honorable, and most of all, selfless.

Uriah was taken completely off guard. After his wife was sacrificed with his baby boy in Hatti, he never thought deeply about having another woman. It took him all this time until a year ago to finally adopt a warrior son since becoming a mighty warrior, and that was by the heavy pressure of King David because it was the duty of every mighty warrior to adopt an orphan boy to be trained as a warrior son to continue strengthening the Israelite army.

King David had a joyous expression at the bonding of his mighty warriors and looked back and forth between the two men who had battled together today. All the warrior fathers were eyeing Uriah, waiting for him to accept the incredible gift that each and every one of them would do and give almost anything to have. Bathsheba was a gift of all gifts, and she was always a tease in their minds when she would cook and serve the daily meals in the training arena.

Shuriah remembered the first time he met her this time last year. She was so nice to him, helpful when she served the meals to the other boys with him and helped him clean up after them. She would also hide extra food just for him in the kitchen during his first month when the other boys would grapple over the portions, leaving him little amounts that were left over.

His mind went in many directions. He could see Bathsheba in his father's house and thought, *It would be great to have a female with them, taking care of the cooking and cleaning. How the food would be so much better than the boring stuff Father makes.* Then, a different thought came to him: *Would she be considered my mother?*

As Shuriah was dreaming, Uriah calmly answered Eliam's proposal, "I would be honored to accept this generous gift of yours, Eliam. But I have two requests first." He paused, hoping he was not insulting his brother warrior. "First, may one year pass before this gift is handed to me? Second, this gift must have the willing heart to be handed to me?"

Everyone was stunned as Eliam's eyes vacillated, trying to figure out the reason for such strange requests. Seeing Eliam's questioning expression, Uriah explained, "You cherish your daughter so much that even in her prime age, she is still not with any willing and competent man, even a mighty warrior." Uriah pointed across the room at several warriors who had attempted to gain her as a wife, only to be turned down.

"I need to prepare my heart for her to match your generous outward compliments. For I will not degrade what is very important to you, brother. And in the same way, I want your daughter to have a prepared heart so that you or I will not be despised for what we force upon her."

Uriah paused, looking around the room, knowing the atmosphere was heavy and some of the men might be boiling inside that he, a Hittite, was being given such a coveted gift, and they were willing to pay greatly for her.

With a faint, sideways smile, he added, "For we all know, as men, it would be better to be bit by painful sand flies throughout the day than to have to go home to a resentful and bitter woman."

The tent erupted with laughter as all the men agreed with this rare sense of humor from stoic Uriah.

When they settled down, Uriah added, "Also, I believe everyone here would appreciate"—he looked down at Shuriah, putting his hand on his shoulder—"that I would want this woman coming into my life to fully understand in advance that her role and relationship is not only with me but with my son as well whom I have dedicated my life to raising as my own."

He looked around the tent, eyeing all the warriors and sons who were gaining greater respect for him at how he was looking out first for the new woman and son in his life and not himself.

"You, again," Eliam began, walking around several men to get to stand face to face with Uriah, "have proven yourself worthy of having my daughter as your wife with your selfless wisdom. I also know she will be a very good and needed mother to Shuriah."

He looked down at the brave warrior who had helped today and then back to Uriah. "You have one year to this week, the week when our king"—he nodded over to David—"and a new group of soldiers and our sons return from the Cave of Adullam to marry Bathsheba." He embraced the Hittite and kissed him on both cheeks, signaling the deal was final, and walked back to his spot where King David was standing.

When he sat back down, all the other men followed his lead except the king. With a smile, Eliam added loudly, "I'm getting the better deal." He leaned forward, stretching his head out to look at Uriah past the men beside him who were grabbing more food and wine. They looked at him with a questionable expression, and Eliam continued, "You will be my son-in-law, and I know I will be taken very good care of when I get old because I will be *your* responsibility." Then he laughed out loud.

The warriors sitting in the large circle joined in his humorous but true statement, mouths full and leaning to their sides on pillows as David strolled back to his spot at the head of the group. He sat down, commenting, "That was an unexpected surprise, to say the least. Wasn't it, Uriah?" Lifting his goblet to Eliam, the king nodded with a grin of approval for this wise and gracious gesture.

Uriah also nodded in agreement, but it was Shuriah that verbalized, "Yes, it was, Master. Bathsheba is very nice and a great cook!"

All the men stopped chewing for a second at his naïve comment because he had clearly missed the ultimate point that Bathsheba was a gorgeous, young, virgin woman. They all laughed at his young spirit—even Uriah, Eliam, and King David.

Shuriah's comment reminded David that there was another topic to address. "So, young warrior, besides being gallantly involved in the battle today, I hear you also assisted in capturing a handful of cowards that ran away while you were engaged with the Philistines?"

"Yes, my king."

"If I was to put you in charge of their punishment, what action do you think we should take with them?" the king asked, knowing there was something special about this young warrior, for his mind thought beyond his years, and he saw deeper than most grown men.

Shuriah sat there for a moment and replied, "I would not

waste putting them to death right away when they can be used as human shields going into battle tomorrow."

He looked around the tent, seeing he had caught the attention of everyone and smiled with a crazed expression as he said, "Could you imagine the look on their faces if they were strapped naked to the front of the horses pulling the chariots, screaming for their lives as they approached the Philistine army?" He giggled and added, "Then think about the Philistines' reaction, seeing these men coming at them full force, screaming and wearing nothing with their beards and heads shaved disgracefully, and our king's royal symbol painted on their bodies." He stopped talking and looked around the tent to find startled faces, wondering how such horrifying ideas were coming to a boy with such little battle experience.

King David cleared his throat and rocked his head from side to side. Thinking the young one had gone too far, he replied, "But don't you think doing something of that nature is too much work and is going to extremes instead of being an example to the rest of the soldiers?" Shuriah's thought process had already surpassed the question as he answered, "These men left us"—he pointed to Uriah and Eliam—"behind to die while we were fighting." What is a better reminder to all soldiers running forward in battle than to be watching what their demise would be if they ever turn their backs on their king during battle?"

The boy from Shechem learned quickly. He had been very observant over the past year, figuring out how to hit sensitive spots in certain people in order to gain their admiration through his innocence...and King David was one of those people.

David leaned back, taking a drink of wine as he attempted to look deep into this unique but very curious boy who had, in one year, made more of an impression on him them anybody he had ever met. The impression was positive for the most part, yet there was something about this warrior son that uncandidly pricked a tiny hole of concerned fear in him just as it did with the rest of the mighty warriors. He thought differently and seemed to find himself in places or situations where he was able to quench his thirst for fighting or killing someone.

King David raised his hand to get the attention of one of his servants to come to him. He looked over to his trusted general and asked, "How about it, Joab? Should we do as the warrior son suggested?"

The general raised his goblet in approval, saying, "It's a bit more extreme than just cutting their heads off. But…if it terrorizes the Philistines as the boy dreams it would do, why not. We have nothing to lose." Putting the goblet down and poking a bit of food in his mouth, he added, "Besides, they might not even show up in the morning, for we killed so many of them already."

The wind had begun to blow again after a couple more days of hard and exhausting rowing on the Mediterranean Sea as the fleet was now rapidly skimming the top of the cold, blue water in eagle formation.

The young captain on General Shuriah's ship was continually growing in wisdom and self-confidence as a man and as a leader because of the selfless, purposeful, and experienced instructions and guidance by King Solomon's most powerful soldier that Israel has ever known. Fear of the general turned into deep respect, and the captain was beginning to understand that General Shuriah was truly concerned for everyone under his command. His honest motives as a leader were to support, strengthen, and prepare the fleet for success on this epic journey. "Success is the only option," the general stated over and over as their destiny, and he would not accept fear or failure with anything or anyone.

But the big question that still silently roamed throughout the ships was where they were going and what their mission was. General Shuriah said that he would give that vital information gradually at specific times along the journey.

The sailors on the ships who were acquired in Tyre from King Hiram were more baffled than anyone because of their hidden cargo; it was comprised of many large pieces of a new, unassembled ship that was spread throughout the hulls of their twenty ships, protected by the surrounding twenty-five ships of the Israelites.

They were more than halfway through the first leg of their voyage, heading to the land of Hatti, where they would be spending at least two years traveling back and forth across the country to a high mountain where Noah's Ark was found by Shuriah over a year ago. They would disassemble the ark and assemble the pieces of the ship that King Hiram had made for Solomon to put in its place.

King Solomon, wiser than anyone, saw the greater picture of life and concluded it was no accident for Shuriah to have found the ancient ark. He believed it was completely God's divine intervention to glorify His kingdom at another time in another place. He left the answers and reasons for 'why' to God. Because even for Solomon, God's thoughts and understanding were far beyond his comprehension.

Just before the winds returned, Shuriah had sent for the lead captain of the fleet, whose ship was at the point of their eagle formation. They traveled from ship to ship by small but fast row boats. He had been Shuriah's lead captain over the years when he traveled across the sea and was even on the ship with Shuriah that crashed and sank in the storm over a year ago. That had turned out to be God's first seed that led them to the ark.

In his private quarters, the general informed his ship's older and younger lead captains of their first destination as they sat around in a small circle, leaning against lounging pillows. The older, experienced captain looked concerned as he replied, "General, my thoughts are going in many directions." He looked at the young captain and back to the general. "May I ask our purpose in going to this place?"

Shuriah calmly smiled as he glanced at the young captain, who had a curious look, knowing he was at a disadvantage from what the two older men knew. Then Shuriah peered directly at the lead captain, leaning forward. "Last time we were here, there were only a handful of us with a few weapons. This time…we will arrive with forty-five ships filled with 10,000 soldiers, ninety mighty warriors, their sons, and 5,000 laborers from Tyre, whom we'll turn into soldiers."

"Are we going to war with the Hittites?"

"Only if they want one." The general had that crazed grin he wore when it came to fighting. He loved fighting and especially with the people who killed his warrior father's deceased first wife and baby boy when he was a young man.

"Then why are we going there, and how long do you expect us to stay before we continue on with this epic journey you're talking about?"

As the general sat back against the lounging pillows, his wife's maidservant brought the men goblets of wine to go with the small spread of food in front of them. Slowly taking a drink, he answered, "My old friend, you know very well why we are here. I give you permission to reopen in your mind that which our king and I said would never be discussed and to freely talk about what we discovered when we were here last."

The captain widened his eyes in excitement, but then he narrowed his brows, asking, "And what are we going to do"—he eyed the young captain and looked back, reluctant to divulge any knowledge—"with *it*?"

Seeing the humor in the conversation and its perplexity, Shuriah laughed heartily and said, "Well, you remember what we did, taking a small piece of *it* apart and taking *it* with us?" The older captain nodded, expressionless.

Beaming proudly through his full, grayish-black beard, the general answered, "We are going to take the whole thing apart and bring the pieces to the ships as we replace it with the pieces of a ship similar in size that is currently in pieces in all of King Hiram's ships." There was palpable silence as the captain processed the logistics, workload, disassembly, and reconstruction—not to mention the timeframe it would take to do such a thing. Now that everything was somewhat out in the open, he said, "You're saying we are going to the far, snow- and ice-covered mountain, taking apart the"—he couldn't help himself and glanced again at the ignorant captain, not wanting to divulge specifics—"very special thing, bring it back to the ships, and take one back to put in its place?"

Shuriah just sat there, smiling and nodding his head.

The captain blinked several times, still processing, and asked, "So how long to you anticipate it will take us?"

The general held up his hand, lifting two fingers. "Two years."

"Two years!" the young captain exclaimed, still not knowing what they were talking about. The appalling time frame put the task in front of them into perspective.

The two older men glossed over the comment as the older captain asked, "Do you think we can really do this in that amount of time? That's a huge, old ship." He didn't bother withholding the topic of conversation this time.

"That's our prediction. Plus, that's when we should be receiving the secret destination for its next home."

"We're not taking it back to Jerusalem?"

Shuriah adjusted his position, knowing the next few moments could get heated. He also changed his demeanor, firmly stating, "Absolutely not. That is why this is an epic journey."

"A ship?" the young captain asked, trying to be involved in the conversation.

The other captain, still ignoring him, asked, "So how long do you think we'll be away from Jerusalem after we move this thing to its new home? And I assume we are reassembling it?"

"We are putting it back together. But as to when we will be back to our homeland, I'm not sure since I still don't know where we're taking it." Shuriah looked convincing as he shook his head. His eyes flitted to his wife, Talia, across the room. She was listening to the conversation and knew the truth: they were *never* going back.

This was the ultimate problem Shuriah and King Solomon knew they would have on their hands: a lifetime commitment not just for the mighty warriors (who were already committed to God and their king through life to death) but for the ordinary citizen or soldier who could not all be trusted.

They both knew that in order for Noah's Ark to be secretly positioned somewhere else in the world, no one from the outside world could know where it was, and no one on the inside would be allowed to leave the location once they got there. Knowing this was an epic, lifetime journey, Solomon had all the ships' captains, the captains in his army, and the mighty warriors bring their wives and children that were still too young to leave their mothers.

The wisdom was to protect Noah's Ark in its new, secret location with the strongest, wisest, and most experienced and committed men who were always the leading authorities: captains and mighty warriors. Until further notice, they were expected to birth the next generations to continue guarding the precious, wooden jewel God wanted for the future.

It was only the ninety mighty warriors who knew they were never returning to their homeland. But now, the older ship captain was beginning to think there was more to the story, especially considering they were all allowed to bring their wives. Women never went on ventures out to sea, especially with their children.

"Would one of you please explain what we are talking about?" the young captain asked a little more abruptly.

Shuriah looked at the older captain, nodding his head to answer. The experienced captain thought for a moment, looking at his empty goblet. Then he lifted it up, asking the maid servant, "May I please have some more? This is going to be interesting, to say the least." He rubbed his head with his other hand as she refilled his cup. "Young man, what I am about to tell you will open your mind to a very old and different world—one that is much bigger than you could imagine."

He went on to explain their whole trip last year, from the shipwreck to running from the Hittites across their country to finding Noah's Ark to taking a piece back to their king and keeping it a secret until this moment. After the story, the young captain was overwhelmed. He didn't know what to say or do but did comment, "It sounds like it could be years before we see Jerusalem again."

The older captain replied, "You've already been on other voyages when we go out on trading quests, which usually take us three years. This probably will not be much different." The young captain bit his tongue, looking away and nodding his head. The older captain glanced at Shuriah, giving him a grin and a wink to let him know he knew there was probably more to the story that he personally didn't know about but that he was fully on board and supported everything going on.

The general told the two captains they were not to share any of this until they were on land with all the thousands together, and he would inform them as a whole of their next steps they were to take on this journey.

Shuriah stayed in his cabin for several days after that conversation, getting some necessary rest. He hadn't been feeling well for a couple of days prior and only came out when he had to.

But the bigger issue he's had since the first day of the journey was that his mind was continually in motion and wouldn't stop reflecting back, reliving the story of his childhood. Then at night, when he slept, his dreams felt so real, it was as if he were in the moment, and he would wake up sweating and exhausted from the intense activity that ran rampant behind his closed eyes. Not only that, he would wake up very disoriented, taking some time to realize where he was and that it was just a dream. But these were no ordinary dreams but memories that were beginning to affect him emotionally deep in his chest, hidden from everyone except for his wife.

He knew if these dreams and visions of his past continued, they would eventually lead to the most painful time in his life, and he did not want any part of that experience or memory to rise from its grave. So he attempted to stop his mind from drifting back to his younger years as a warrior son by staying busy with his hands or doing other things, but there was only so much he could do trapped, for the time being, on his ship, sailing across the Mediterranean Sea.

The battle with the Philistines outside of Bethlehem was short-lived in the open arena of the wilderness. The Philistines' plans for splitting up a couple of thousand soldiers to surprise and flank Bethlehem from the north and south were spoiled because of King David's sixth sense, anticipating they could be strategizing such a thing behind their backs. Also, the Israelite army outnumbered the Philistines with soldiers and chariots, and they didn't have warriors like David's mighty warriors.

During their victory celebration, while their long-time enemy was retreating back to their homeland, General Joab had commented to Uriah about Shuriah's suggestion of leading with chariots on the second day of fighting with the cowardly soldiers strapped to the front of the horses: "I watched the front line of the Philistines see the naked cowards with our king's symbol painted on their bodies; it was very effective. The charge hesitated as the men behind them trampled over them, causing the scene to repeat itself several times."

Joab smiled, adding, "Your son's mind isn't ordinary. Sometimes he's…different…and terrifying. You would think he is after revenge or takes strange pleasure in seeing other people's pain or demise. Are you sure he's"—the general pointed to his head, insinuating Shuriah was not mentally normal—"not sick?"

Uriah did not like the comment, but he remained respectful to the highest-ranking officer as he replied, "If he is, I would suggest that we stay on his good side. Would you not, General?"

The question hit its mark, and the general fumbled, nodded, and replied, "I definitely want him on our side. Just think what kind of mighty warrior he'll be when he's grown."

Feeding into Uriah's hand, Uriah answered with a calm but cunning smile, tilting his head. "Yeah…just think…" Then he turned and walked away.

When they arrived in Jerusalem, General Joab continued north to meet up with the other half of the Israelite army fighting the Moabites at the Jordan River. He took half of the soldiers and most of the mighty warriors he had in Bethlehem as well as King David. Eliam and Uriah were told to stay behind with their sons. Itai needed a lot of time to heal, and Shuriah was ordered to take over any duties Itai was in charge of (in Itai's house or at the training arena) since many of the other warrior sons were with their fathers away in battle.

This was a good time for Uriah and Shuriah to spend some quality time together after being apart more than they ever had been—since before the trek to the Cave of Adullam. Even though the remaining army was under continuous alert, which included themselves, they were together nonstop. During times of war, no training was conducted as all attention was focused outside the city walls, not inside.

Shuriah excitedly replayed every moment to his father over the next several days, repeating the highlights that had taken place before the war with the Philistines, especially any moment he had killed someone. After a while, Uriah understood more and more that he needed to have a discussion with his son pertaining to these topics of ending a human life and his infatuation with doing so. It wasn't that it was wrong; he was obviously good at it for his age, but he openly expressed and talked about it with an almost excited and joyful attitude.

Quiet conversations about Shuriah within the city walls were beginning to develop due to his great accomplishments while he was away. It was always reassuring to hear the warriors' sons doing extraordinary things in battles because the other soldiers and citizens of Jerusalem grew in confidence that the next generation of mighty warriors was going to be as strong or stronger and possibly more fearless than their fathers.

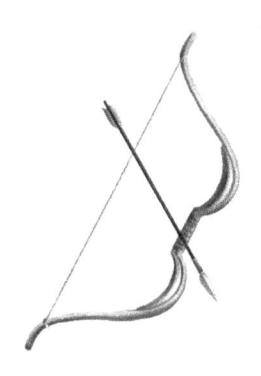

CHAPTER 14

The battle with the Moabites ended similarly to the battle with the Philistines, with the former retreating but taking a while longer.

As the year continued, several other smaller battles with enemies of the Israelites rose up in broad areas around the Dead Sea. King David repeatedly pushed back and defeated all who wanted to harm the chosen people.

During the times of peace, the mighty warriors continued training their sons. One specific thing they would do is travel throughout the region and educate their sons visually on the different areas of their land and where the borders were of different kingdoms surrounding them. They would also visit every city and town under King David's rule, no matter how big or small, studying them in detail and gathering vital information without invading the citizens' privacy.

But the main motive for the mighty warriors to get involved with the Israelite communities outside their home in Jerusalem was to persuade and influence their nation's boys and young men. They hoped to impress upon the next generation to become soldiers by demonstrating their abilities and passion for fighting in extraordinary ways in order to be victorious in every battle. At the same time, they demonstrated their devotion to serving the king of Israel, and their close relationship with the Lord of heaven's armies was seen and heard by their actions and words.

Throughout the year, besides the continuous short-lived fighting, training, and traveling, Bathsheba and Uriah had begun the ritual courtship that would lead up to a marriage.

At first, it was awkward because it was an unexpected situation. Plus, they already knew each other because Bathsheba was one of the cooks and caretakers of the mighty warriors' training facility. But what was most awkward was the difference in age between them. Uriah was in his mid-thirties, and Bathsheba was sixteen, the youngest of Eliam's children.

It didn't take long for the younger Bathsheba to see Uriah in a different light. Normally he was just one of the brutish, mighty warriors, although he *was* a Hittite. Imagining herself as his wife, she began to see qualities in him that significantly set him apart from the other men. Even though he was a man of few words, his body language and gestures were such that she was never intimidated or afraid but rather attracted.

She saw that he was not only a complete gentleman at all times but was an incredible father as well. He was very involved with Shuriah and treated him with more compassion and interest than most fathers she'd ever seen. Furthermore, Shuriah had always been one of her favorite warriors' sons ever since his first day at the training arena a year earlier. He was polite, helpful, and uniquely different from the other boys. He had a big heart for his purpose as a warrior, but at the same time, he was gentle and kind to everyone. He was also never proud or boastful like most of the warrior sons, using their position to intimidate or brag to the common Israelite.

Early on, Uriah made it very clear to Bathsheba that he

would not allow her father to force her to marry him and that she was the one to make that decision. He also told her he would be searching his heart as well to make sure he was making the right decision, first for his son and then for himself.

This comment alone set Uriah apart a great length compared to other men since she knew every man's eyes were on her continually because she was so beautiful. She understood he was looking into the beauty of her heart and not just her body. He wisely and cautiously moved forward, protecting the family he already had, not wanting to be selfish with their possible lifetime relationship.

Shuriah, on the other hand, could hardly control himself about what was possibly going to happen between his father and Bathsheba. He was ecstatic from day one, fully believing it was going to happen. He mirrored Bathsheba's feelings and had always felt a close, friendly connection with her.

As the months went by, the awkwardness dissipated between Uriah and Bathsheba. Everyone was usually together, so Bathsheba and Uriah were only together in the open in sight for all to witness the honest, growing relationship. When they were not seen together, it started looking like an incomplete picture, missing its better half.

When the warriors went to battle or left on training missions for the warrior sons, Bathsheba started feeling empty and alone as she worried about their safety as any wife would do when her man left the security of the city walls of Jerusalem.

Eliam was the one most impressed. His respect for Uriah on how he treated his coveted and prized daughter escalated to a height that was just under King David. Their relationship grew, bonding them closer as a father and son. Even all Eliam's sons were treating Uriah as a blood brother. And for the first time in many, many years, Uriah finally felt part of an actual family—a family structure that had died and was left behind in Hatti. He had taken only his broken, hurting heart and a spear and faded away into the world.

The year came full circle, and King David again took all the warrior sons and four hundred of another group of soldiers to inspire them in the cave of Adullam. The trip was completely different than the previous, returning on time with no battles in sight.

Shortly after their return, Uriah and Bathsheba were married. They had both fallen in love over the past year, and their hearts started beating as one. Bathsheba had become more mature and beautiful, developing into a full-fledged young woman.

King David took extremely good care of his mighty warriors and their families, providing housing and all their daily needs. But Uriah had always been the odd one who was not married, took the longest to adopt an orphan son, and preferred to live more of a solitary life than his peers. His small home was the only warrior home not connected to the palace walls; it was a short distance away and blended in with the rest of the city.

With the anticipation of the marriage and the encouragement of Eliam, Uriah agreed to move into one of the larger warrior homes up against the palace walls. They were filled with every accommodation one could want, including permanent servants to care for the families of the king's valued protectors.

These homes were also closely located to important amenities such as the market place, the palace well, the bath houses for the warriors, and the city's open, ritual cleansing bath for all the women of Jerusalem after they were done with their monthly bleeding. This specific bath was built directly under the upper balcony of the king's private courters.

One of the most important things these homes surrounded was the Ark of the Covenant. It rested in a pristine tent that allowed every warrior to be at its side within a heartbeat if needed.

Ever since the courtship began between Uriah and Bathsheba, Shuriah desperately wanted to call her mother, and now he could. Though when he first started using the term, memories of his real mother flashed in his mind, which he had forgotten or subconsciously suppressed. They were cloudy glimpses in the twelve-year-old's mind that weren't directly of her but of him crying out for her over and over when he was lost in the foreign city of Shechem.

It took a while for Bathsheba to fully accept being called "mother," since Shuriah was only five years younger than her and not related by blood. She understood, though, the need he had to identify her as his mother just as he was calling Uriah "father." They were his only family. And even though he fought as an adult warrior, he still had the heart and mind of a boy with the need to identify someone as family who would guide, discipline, and love him as one of their own.

Life was coming together for the three as they got into a daily routine in their new home. Uriah's heart had been reopened, which opened him up to everyone else in his life. Now he was more of a friendly person, willing to interact and be more social and involved with others—the opposite of who he had been over the years.

Bathsheba was in a moment of life where nothing would bother or upset her. She was a proud wife and in love with a man who had proven himself to be above most men she had ever known.

Her friends constantly and happily bombarded her with assertions that she was so blessed to be married to a mighty warrior. Her working role completely changed; she no longer helped in the training arena since her responsibilities were now with her family in their home, and she was to be kept away from the outside world where she would be surrounded by other men all day long. Besides, since her husband was a mighty warrior, all their financial needs were taken care of, and she didn't need to work outside the home to support herself anymore.

In two years, Shuriah had established himself as one of, if not the, deadliest of all the warrior sons. He was physically remarkable, setting himself apart in many ways. Acrobatically he did things that were at first unthinkable—multiple flips forward and backward, swinging around obstacles, or having the ability to climb rock walls that were straight up with only the tiniest of niches to grasp with his fingertips and toes, maneuvering up and down the tallest of walls.

He demonstrated his new-found abilities one time when he was playing with the other boys, chasing them around the arena, and he climbed up the tall, back city wall and down the other side. Then he ran around the outside to the nearest gate of the city. Once he got back to the arena, instead of crawling through the tunnel where they expected to catch him, he climbed up the arena wall and down, sneaking up on the other boys he was playing with.

What he did not know was that the king saw everything from the palace's back balcony high above them, and he couldn't believe his eyes. Just as many times before, Shuriah envisioned something and just did it, after which he was instructed by the king or the warrior fathers to teach these skills and techniques to everyone, especially the warriors' sons.

Over the next few years, this unique family grew. After the wedding, Bathsheba became pregnant with their first child, a girl. Then another girl was born at the beginning of their third year of marriage. Unexpectedly, Shuriah was in heaven having siblings. He wanted to constantly take care of and play with his new baby sisters. His life was being fulfilled in ways he never dreamed it could.

Uriah continually reminded him that the God of Israel is a faithful God and loves His people. Obedience to the authority over him and to the laws of the Lord of heaven's armies given to Shuriah's chosen people through their ancestor Moses was very precious and important for the success and blessings in his life, the life of his family, and the kingdom of Israel as a whole.

With a reluctant heart, Uriah knew it was important to educate his son on the gods of other nations they continually battled with, which included the one he ran away from in Hatti. He wanted him to understand the evil difference he himself used to live with.

Even though Uriah's blood was not that of the blood of the Israelite ancestors (Abraham, Isaac, and Jacob), Shuriah's did. And he was going to make sure his son followed the laws with passion, persistency, and perfection so he would be blessed throughout his life, which was especially important given their profession in which their life could end at any moment.

It used to bother Uriah that his blood was not the same as the people he lived with, but over the years, he learned to be content and satisfied in the immediate presence and shadow of the chosen people, following the greatest God of all the other gods in the world. Then to be actually in the presence of this God by way of the Ark of the Covenant, living next to it and guarding it, gave him the pinnacle fulfillment he needed to be complete in his gentile mind, body, and soul.

During the past three years of Uriah's marriage, he and Shuriah had to leave Jerusalem three times to go to war in different areas. One was with the Edomites, where they killed 18,000, another with the Amalekites, killing 7,000, and yet another with the Philistines, killing 11,000. With each battle, the Israelites only had a quarter of the fatalities and won.

Twice half the mighty warriors, including Uriah and Shuriah, had to go out into the wilderness to chase down raiding parties of men from different kingdoms who were going into defenseless cities in King David's kingdom and stealing women. It would take a few weeks to track, locate, and eventually eliminate the men. Then it took a few more weeks to return the stolen items and women back where they belonged.

Uriah soon learned how hard it was on his warrior peers and other soldiers to go to war and leave their families behind. It gave him a completely different perspective on life that he had erased from his memory many years ago with his first family.

General Joab called the mighty warriors into the king's palace for a very important meeting with King David over a feast.

As all the warriors arrived with their sons, they were seated at the king's table. They knew every time they received this kind of invitation, it always ended with them going to war—and not ordinary short-lived ones, but a war that needed an immense number of soldiers, supplies, and planning along with precise and extraordinary strategies because it was going to be a long, large, and difficult confrontation with the possibility of losing thousands of valuable soldiers over several months.

After most of the meal had been consumed and all stomachs were full (not just from food but with much wine as well), David stood and walked around the table as he explained why they were there, "Our friends from way up north in Damascus, the Arameans, have decided to confront us again. I believe it has been five years since we were in Damascus, hasn't it?"

One of the warriors who remembered the successful battle spoke up. "I think that was when Uriah finally got his warrior son…in Shechem, right?" The warrior looked at Uriah and Shuriah as Uriah nodded with a smile, answering, "That it was."

"How long have you been with us, Shuriah?" the warrior asked. Shuriah thought back, remembering how the king had treated him the first time they met, and answered, "Our king is right. It has been five years."

"Five years…and how many enemy soldiers have you killed, warrior son? Not including our own people," he jokingly finished.

There was a laugh around the room because everyone knew the stories of him as somewhat of an assassin of those who dishonored the throne. His great abilities on the battlefield as Uriah's perfect shadow, always raising the expectations for warrior sons, had amounted to a rather large number of casualties.

Shuriah did not appreciate being laughed at and answered precisely with a serious expression. "Five hundred and forty-seven enemy soldiers and nine Israelites in five years, and I am only fifteen years old. How many had you killed by the time you were my age?" He pierced the warrior's eyes with his stare as though he was reaching down to the man's soul and strangling it to death. Stunned at the reality of Shuriah's statement, no words came out of the warrior's mouth at the thought of what he was obviously becoming.

No one moved as eyes darted back and forth between one another. Shuriah continued to hold everyone in nervous suspense at his powerful drive toward and success at killing, even though that was their job and what they diligently trained for.

They all were ecstatic and appreciative of his incredible

skills in warfare and that he was on their side. But it was the unpredictability hidden behind his eyes that had them questioning if he was really mentally strong or if one of these days he would go after any one of them like a wild animal if he was crossed or lost control of himself.

Shuriah brought out an eerie and uncomfortable feeling in everyone except his father. Most all the warrior sons were respectfully afraid of him and did not want to be his battle practice partner because he was so good and extremely intimidating, even though he was also one of the nicest and most respectful boys of the bunch.

David broke the tense moment by redirecting the subject back to the topic at hand, although he too was psychologically under the influence of this warrior son but kept it to himself. At the same time, the king valued Shuriah as much as a grown, experienced, mighty warrior in his abilities and dedication to the throne. "As I said, the Arameans have decided to confront us again, but...they are locking arms with the Ammonites."

The men around the room now focused intently on David. "Our spies from both regions have come back with the same report—that they have been getting ready with supplies and training thousands of extra soldiers with the intent of meeting in the city of Rabbah on the Jabbok River, which you know faces the desolate eastern desert.

"From there, they are planning to head west, crossing over the Jordon River in the direction of Jericho, then on to Jerusalem with a vast army of up to 60,000 soldiers, 3,000 chariots, and 4,000 charioteers as 4,000 horses and horsemen lead the way here."

David looked over to General Joab, giving him a nod to take over the conversation. The general stood as the king took his seat in the middle of the long table. Joab paused, choosing his words carefully, and said,

"Obviously, we always attempt to keep all battles as far away from our homeland as we can, which means we will go to them before they begin to leave Rabbah.

"As you all know, the terrain on the east side of Rabbah is a very flat desert with hardly anything to hide behind, so you can be seen from a long distance away unless you're a snake.

"With the river flowing along the city on the west side, it would be difficult to approach them in the water with a large army and horses with the possibility of being swept down the river until we could reach the other side, depending on how high the water is. With it being spring, more than likely, the muddy river will be running high and fast."

Joab strolled around the table, repeating what he always said in meetings like this, "At any time, if any of you have knowledge, wisdom, or different ideas of what we should or shouldn't do, do not hold back, for now is the time to speak."

He looked around, seeing he had everyone's attention, and continued, "We obviously don't want to take our whole army from Jerusalem or our soldiers who live in the outskirt cities going west toward the Philistine territory. That would leave us vulnerable to those barbarians.

"I am planning on gathering 40,000 soldiers, 5,000 chariots, 6,000 charioteers, and 2,000 horses and horsemen to fight in Rabbah. That would leave 25,000 soldiers, 1,000 chariots, 1,500 charioteers, and 2,000 horses and horsemen to stand ready in case our nemesis from the west decides to take advantage of us when we're away. Is everyone in agreement with these numbers?"

There was silence in the room as all the men thought through the proposed numbers and related them to the many wars they've had, knowing their own strength and the strengths and weaknesses of their enemies. Murmuring trickled in agreement with the general and his plan. As he looked around the table, he saw he was validated, so he started to continue. Then an unexpected younger voice was heard, "May I ask questions and give my opinion?"

All the warrior fathers looked first at Uriah and then to Shuriah, who had spoken up. It was very apparent that the sons were never involved in these conversations; they were here only to listen and learn.

The general was taken aback, but he gave him a friendly grin, thinking it was funny that one so young had spoken up. "Sure, Shuriah. I don't see why not?"

The general looked to King David, who gave a silent laugh at the boy's boldness and willingness to be involved in an adult conversation. David lifted both his hands up, signaling approval, at which point Shuriah jumped right in, "I'm not sure why we would go into a war undermanned that *is* happening and leave so many behind for a war that is probably *not* going to happen, which the Philistines probably haven't even considered. If they do go to war with us in our absence, I trust the armies of heaven would go to war on our behalf. Plus, the *walls* of the city will give us the additional protection we would need."

Shuriah was speaking in a confident, matter-of-fact tone, eyeing everyone who was staring at him. "Also, why are we taking so many chariots and charioteers when we possibly have to cross two rivers? We should take 10,000 more soldiers, decrease 3,000 chariots and 3,500 charioteers, and increase our horses and horsemen by 1,500. I believe that would be a better balance for the terrain we have to go through, and it gives us the numbers we would need going against two nations."

Joab's face went stone cold as King David sat back in his

chair and crossed his arms, astonished once more at the boy.

Uriah knew his son was on target with what he said, but he also knew Joab and his pride. He was David's prized general whose strategies were next to none, and almost every time, they came out victorious in battle with fewer soldiers lost than any other military leader.

"I agree with the boy, General!" Eliam proclaimed, hammering his hand on the table and nodding at Shuriah.

In the next couple of breaths, all the other warrior fathers conceded with Shuriah as well after they thought through the geographic dilemmas, logistics, and balance of soldiers with where the priority needed to be.

"General, I think you've been overruled," King David stated proudly, looking at Shuriah.

Maintaining his composure since he knew the boy's suggestion was valid and had the support of the powerful group, Joab attempted to smile, looking at Shuriah and Uriah. "It sure does. So we'll take 50,000 soldiers, 2,000 chariots, 2,500 charioteers, and 3,500 horses and horsemen. That leaves behind 15,000 soldiers, 4,000 chariots, 4,500 charioteers, 500 horses"—Joab changed his expression and tone, making light of the boy's last comment—"and…a wall."

Joab walked around to his chair, sat down, and took a drink of wine. Reorganizing his thoughts to further the conversation, he first wanted to reestablish his superior position, so he asked sarcastically, "So, Shuriah, how would you organize this new number of men, and what would your strategy be to be victorious over 60,000 soldiers?"

Everyone knew what he was doing to put the boy back in his place, especially Uriah, who spoke up to defend him, "General, you are the wise one when it comes to strategizing. You have led us through many battles successfully. Please, you tell us what we need to do."

Joab gave Uriah a look of disapproval for interfering, but David was excited about the idea and wanted to see how far Shuriah's thinking would go. He prompted, "Uriah, it's all right. Let the boy speak if he wants to."

Again, every eye went to Shuriah, waiting for him to answer, but this time he hesitated because he understood the position he had put his father and himself into. He looked to Uriah for guidance, and Uriah nodded with a knowing smile through his large, black beard, letting him know to go ahead and do his best to answer the general's question.

He turned to Joab, who had a smirk on his face, believing he had silenced him. Shuriah did not like General Joab—never had. He wisely kept these thoughts and feelings to himself in respect for the position as his father always taught him. He thought he was a self-centered leader, always walking around and thinking he was better than everybody. He wasn't sure why the king liked him so much, except that he was very good at winning wars.

"We are waiting, Shuriah," Eliam interjected. "What would be your strategy, young warrior?" As one of the oldest mighty warriors, Eliam was not easily intimidated by anyone in the room, including the general. For he, too, saw the man for who he was inside: selfish and arrogant. That's why Eliam wanted to extend some friendly encouragement to his grandson at the moment.

Hearing his grandfather's voice gave Shuriah the confidence he needed in this rare moment during which he had become intimidated and backed into a corner. He slowly stood as he thought about how to answer. He looked around the table at all his young warrior friends and their fathers, who had leaned forward, staying very quiet to make sure they didn't miss a word of what he was going to say.

David's eyes studied the table, seeing the anticipation on his warriors' faces until he got to the general. Joab was staring straight at him, realizing the boy had captivated the attention of everyone as though they were looking to the boy for wise leadership. When their eyes met, the general furrowed his brow in disapproval, but David just smiled back, tilting his head as if to say, *Just go along with it. You are still our great general.*

Shuriah broke the silence as he began, "We need to intercept the Arameans way before they get to Rabbah to form a large army and annihilate them completely. I would send 40,000 of our soldiers, all the chariots, charioteers, horses, and horsemen, and thirty mighty warriors. Once the Arameans are no more, we can march in the direction of Rabbah and pretend we are them. The Ammonites are expecting a large army coming at them from the north and would have their guard down so we can get very close before they know the difference.

"I would send the remaining 10,000 soldiers with the rest of the mighty warriors to the south side of the city. Once they have crossed over the Jordan River, have them march forward only through the wilderness in the cover of darkness, especially once they get to the Jabbok River. When they have crossed over that river in the middle of the night, lie in wait, staying out of sight, which will be easy with no horses or charoites to give them away.

"Once the first part of our army has marched upon Rabbah from the north and engaged in battle, the second group that crossed the Jabbok River from the south would stay hiding for another day or so. Then they would engage in battle on their side of the city while the initial larger group retreats during the night. This would look like they had moved all the way around the city, attacking them from there.

"Then, after another couple days of battling on that side of the city, everyone would engage in fighting both sides of Rabbah at the same time when we will have completely disoriented the Ammonites within their own city walls."

Shuriah sat down, took a drink from his goblet, and contemplated the blank faces and silent eyes staring at him again. The king glanced back to the general, who had turned to him as well now with fire in his expression. Much of what Shuriah had said was already in his plans, but now it would appear to everyone that this was the boy's idea, making him look foolish.

David knew exactly what the general was thinking since they had already had their private strategy meeting, so he knew it was his place to interject as he raised his goblet to Shuriah, turning to him and saying, "Well done, you are a very good student of warfare, Shuriah. You have a keen mind."

Shuriah responded perfectly to settle the tension he could see growing in the general and to release the pressure put on him, "It is easy for us warrior sons," he said, pointing around the table, "to learn when we have a great general to learn from."

David and the rest of the mighty warriors took this opportunity Shuriah just gave them to reestablish the general's pride and control of the meeting by raising their goblets in solute of and admiration for him.

When it quieted down, the king finalized any uncertainty about who came up with the battle plans. "What you presented to the table was almost perfect. So perfect I would think that you, young warrior, were spying on the general's and my private meeting about this war yesterday." The king tilted his head down, giving him a questionable smile. Then he shook it away, raising his goblet again to General Joab.

Everyone knew Shuriah didn't spy on anyone and was an honest boy, but the silent message gave him a sick feeling in his stomach he hadn't felt in a very long time—a feeling that he could not trust anyone just like when he was a small boy back in Shechem. He could remember the feeling even as far back as when he realized his own mother had left him, not knowing she believed it was the best thing for her precious son to survive and that she was prompted by God to do so as well.

Uriah sensed the underlying tension rise in his son, so he grasped Shuriah's leg under the table, firmly holding it to silently tell him not to respond or act out of line.

It worked, and Shuriah was suddenly emptied of all anger and bad thoughts as though his father had sucked it out of him through his hand. Uriah knew his special son very well; they had a connection that very few of the warrior fathers and sons had. Both seemed to understand they were different than the rest. Uriah was a father from an enemy nation, and Shuriah, although an Israelite, was a son whose physical and mental abilities were far past any of his peers, almost equal to an experienced mighty warrior.

They commented frequently to each other that they almost didn't need to talk because they always knew what the other was thinking or going to say. Their connection and bond had become unbreakable. Uriah was an excellent father, and Shuriah was always obedient to him. He never seemed to get out of line like most boys did. It was as if he passed his childhood and went directly to adulthood, always fitting the part.

Shuriah looked at his father, softening his eyes and loosening the tightness in his shoulders. He looked to the king with a genuine heart, saying, "My king, I would never deceive or disrespect you or whoever sits on the throne for Israel because I would *never*"—he narrowed his eyes, looking around at everyone and shaking his head—"want to face the armies of heaven in battle." His response, hitting like an arrow, shot a powerful message directly into every heart, sending tingling sensations around the table that the Lord of heaven's armies ruled over all of them *equally.*

CHAPTER 15

There was something extremely different about this specific war with the Arameans and the Ammonites that no soldiers, mighty warriors, or even General Joab could remember happening before—King David, the mightiest of all the warriors, decided to stay home in Jerusalem.

This was absolutely out of his character and the role of a king. All kings went to war unless they were sick or too old, and he was neither. There was no specific reason he gave as to why he was staying behind except that he was feeling very comfortable that his army would be victorious without him.

By this point in his life, David was distracted—in both his mind and his heart. He was very accomplished in his calling as a king. It had been a long time since Israel had lost a war or had an excessive number of casualties. The kingdom was growing stronger daily in land and wealth. He was highly respected and honored, but at the same time, a very small, quiet pocket of enemies had grown jealous of what this second king of Israel was doing.

"You look ready on the outside, son, with your battle vest, arm and leg guards, and your weapons secured tight and ready,"

Uriah whispered as he reached over to Shuriah, jerking on his thick vest.

"Yes, I'm ready, Father!" he answered quietly as his focused eyes began to smolder with excitement and his teeth gritted anxiously, ready to draw blood from their enemies.

Uriah grasped the handle of his sword forcefully and simply stated, "Good." As he nodded with the same focused eyes, he dropped all expression and asked in a harsh tone, "But where does your power come from, my warrior son, to use your weapons and fight?"

"From the Lord of heaven's armies!" the maturing fifteen-year-old answered as they eyed each other almost nose-to-nose, lying down in a small dugout in the open, covered with grass and shrubs in order to camouflage against what was going to turn into a large battle field in a few moments.

The Arameans were marching five lines wide and 25,000 deep and were two-thirds of the way to Rabbah to meet up with the Ammonites. The 40,000 Israelites had traveled day and night at a quick pace to get to this point and annihilate the Arameans. Then they must turn south to defeat the Ammonites at their own home, ending the battle before it got one step toward Jerusalem.

The area they chose to engage the Arameans was a shallow valley along an ancient roadway going north and south. Off to the side of the road, they both peered through the thin vegetation that was hiding them at ground level as soldiers passed by only a short spear's throw away. Soon, Shuriah was getting impatient as he started to whisper, "Come on. Give the signal…give the signal."

Uriah softly bumped him to tell him to calm down and that the first shower of arrows aimed at the center lines of the marching soldiers would come in at the perfect time. He whispered,

"Never forget the eyes on top of the hill have a better view of the battlefield below than the ones down in the field."

Shuriah, still looking outward, replied quietly, "I know, Father…I'm just tired of waiting."

"Son, have I not told you over and over from the day you first became my student—"

Shuriah interrupted but wasn't rude, "I know, Father…being patient, prepared, determined, and disciplined are the first lessons in becoming a warrior."

"That's right…and if you don't learn and take those skills to heart, it will be even harder on you to become not just a mighty warrior but, more importantly, an honorable and respected man."

"What's the difference between a man and a mighty warrior; aren't they the same thing?" Shuriah twisted his head back to his father in a cramped position with a frown.

Uriah stared dumbfounded at his son of now almost six years, not understanding how he could have missed teaching him the difference between the two titles and positions. Shuriah couldn't hold it in anymore, cracking a smile and said, "Got you, just kidding. I know the difference. You have taught me perfectly to be both at the same time."

Uriah relaxed momentarily, thought deeper about it, and asked, "When did I teach you to be a man?"

Shuriah now changed his demeanor, shocked his father would ask the question, and answered, "Every day you instructed and trained me how to be a mighty warrior for *Israel*. But every day, you also showed me how to be a man for myself and my family."

Thinking he knew where Shuriah was going, he asked, "Every day? How did I do that?"

Without hesitating, he answered blatantly, "By living it, being the man you are—kind, gentle, and giving—but at the same time strong, confident, and always doing the right thing even when it is difficult, or you don't want to do it."

Uriah was surprised his son viewed him in those ways because he didn't feel the words Shuriah used to describe him. He never thought too highly of himself, always sensing he needed to do better and be better at everything. Even being a mighty warrior all these years, he felt he needed to prove himself worthy.

Shuriah's heart sensed something strange as he looked into his father's eyes, seeing that they didn't agree for the first time; Uriah looked stumped at what they were talking about. Shuriah felt overwhelmed as the young one giving instructions and advice. "Father, you have been a man above all men in my life, even above King David. You have demonstrated to me since we first met that man's muscle and how he uses a sword doesn't make you mighty and that a great title of 'mighty warrior' doesn't automatically give you honor or respect.

"What you have shown me is that being a respectful person who honors other people above himself and lives selflessly doesn't have to use muscle to prove he is a man—because he already is one. And if you have a disciplined mind, a gentle heart, and the will to stay in the shadow of God, that's when you are crowned a mighty *man*, and that is who you are, Father. Your crown is much bigger and brighter than King David's to me."

In that moment, Uriah was oblivious to all that was going on around him; he didn't know what to say or think. He never knew his son thought of him that way. For the first time in six years, he wanted to cradle Shuriah up as a baby and cry over him as a proud new father would after a son was born to carry on the family heritage. And if Shuriah carried on what he just said about him, he was relieved of any pressure or responsibility for the future of his son, for Shuriah clearly saw what it meant to be a mighty man for the God of Israel at his young age.

There was an awkward silence as they digested the deep conversation, but at the same time, this joyous moment was elevating their relationship to new heights in the dirty dugout covered with grass and shrubs.

The whisper of hundreds of arrows flying over their heads didn't catch their attention, but the screaming pain from dozens of soldiers marching by did. The second throng of arrows flew by, giving the signal for the hiding army of thousands to spring to life out of the ground as the Armenian soldiers scattered to find cover from any other danger raining down on them.

The shock of the charge took the enemy completely by surprise when the ground suddenly came alive with what looked like horrifying beasts emerging from the depths of the earth. Uriah took the lead in his area and roared to life, completely dissolving the soft-hearted person he was a breath ago, while Shuriah remained invisible to the enemy by following close behind; the Arameans only realized he was there when they were gouged with the long spear in the leg or stomach that came in low from the ground.

Uriah signaled for the spear and grasped downward as Shuriah let go, swung his bow around, and swiftly released arrows behind Uriah toward the enemy, who uselessly scrambled to organize themselves for protection. The volume of noise in the shallow valley became deafening as the clanking of metal swords and shields echoed with screaming and yelling in all directions, making the hair on their backs rise like tingling needles piercing their chests in the chaos of war.

"Take the spear!" Uriah shouted. He didn't have to look down, knowing the shadow behind him would grab it when he let go.

Shuriah opened one hand, seized the spear, and flung his bow back over his head with the other. Out of the corner of his eye, Shuriah saw an Aramean soldier running at them, yelling a battle cry from behind, swinging a sword. He shouted to Uriah, "Twisted monkey!"

Even though Uriah was engaged in a sword fight, he braced his back as his shadow dropped the spear to the ground and ran up his back, pushing off hard near his shoulders to do a high flip. As soon as Uriah felt Shuriah's feet push off, he crouched low to the ground, spun in a flash, and slashed his sword, slicing the knees of the Aramean coming in from behind. Continuing to spin, he did the same thing to the soldier who was in front of him.

Shuriah landed perfectly on two feet directly behind the soldier, who was now leaning away from him in pain. Clutching the two daggers from his lower back, he jumped up on the soldier's back and stabbed him on both sides of his neck. Then he leaped into the air, over Uriah, who was still squatted down, and landed on the ground on both feet again as he embedded the daggers into the neck of the other soldier, who was bowed forward in pain.

As Uriah stood up, he grabbed the spear on the ground, and Shuriah seamlessly put the daggers back into their sheaths. Taking the spear from Uriah, he once again disappeared as his shadow while they continued to fight as one.

The battle with the Arameans went on for days. The Israelite army fought very hard, not allowing even one of their enemies to leave the valley to warn the Ammonites of what had happened to them. General Joab gave direct orders that the valley floor would be the grave of their adversaries and the ring they had formed around the valley would not be broken at any cost. For if it were, it could change the outcome of the whole defensive war they were in to protect their kingdom.

Once they had annihilated this enemy from the far north (having lost 10,000 of their own men), they marched south to Rabbah. On the frontline of the brigade, the men put on clothing from some of the dead Arameans to give an illusion of their identity in order to get as close as they could to the city.

They finally arrived at the outskirts of Rabbah, and several high-ranking Ammonites and a few soldiers intercepted them on horseback to escort their guests to their great city that was fortified with a strong, defensive high wall all around it. The Jabbok River flowed along the west wall, providing life-giving water to the people and to the crops that grew outside the city.

As the Ammonites proudly rode their horses to the head of the oncoming mass of soldiers, a couple of them jolted in their saddles, pulling hard back on their reigns and yelling out to the others; they had recognized the face of a general they had fought many times over the years: General Joab. Before any of the horses turned around, all the men and horses were showered with arrows.

The Ammonites had been preparing for a grand reception for their allies to make an impression and thank them for joining them on the march to Jerusalem to conquer this rival kingdom with a king who seemed to never lose a war. The outside of the main entrance to the gate of the city was lined with large tents and festive decorations for a great feast for the Arameans, that had marched a very long way and would be tired and hungry.

From high on top of the city wall, a loud, deep-sounding gong rang multiple times, echoing out for all to hear inside and outside of the city. Soon rams' horns bellowed as people (mostly women) began running to the large city gate from the outside, leaving the tents, as well as the food, wine, and bedding they had brought out in carts. Fear struck them when they heard that warning gong that signaled they were under attack. The rams' horns were attempts to organize their army to defend the city while all the city gates around the walls were being closed and locked.

Several days prior to their arrival, Joab sent a few sentries ahead of them to collect information on the status of the city and to make contact with the other part of his army, who should have been hiding on the south side of the city by then. They came back stating everything was going as planned. The other part of his army had arrived in their position the day prior, and the Ammonites had no idea the Israelites were coming. To their surprise, they also saw the large banquet outside the city's main gate that had been set up for a lot of food and wine waiting for the arrival of the Arameans, and they were excited to tell their general about it.

With that appealing information, Joab decided to take advantage of an opportunity to strengthen his weary soldiers. In the cover of darkness, he had a handful of men sneak to the festival area and blend in with the locals, acting as though they were helping set up for the army coming from the Damascus region. Then, when their general arrived and the chaos began, they were to steal as much food and wine as they could, anticipating it would all be left behind…which it was. That day, many horse-drawn carts piled high with food burst out of the tents, and more carts filled with wine skins followed behind. There was enough food and wine to fill every Israelite belly and have plenty left over.

General Joab ordered his army to retreat and begin erecting two different camps, knowing this battle would take a long time with a protective wall around the Ammonites. His camp would be farther away from the battlefield, while the other was much closer but at a safe distance. He instructed them to spread their tents out from one another and light many fires. Visually, it would be intimidating for their adversaries to think there were twice as many of them than there actually were.

After being gone from Jerusalem for almost two months now, the Israelite army was surprisingly refreshed and invigorated the following day from the hefty meal they stole from the Ammonites. The general gave very strict orders that a minimal amount of wine was to be consumed—only enough to finish the meal.

The strategies for this next confrontation were completely different. Attacking a city with a reinforced wall was much different than the normal, open-field battles that took place in most wars. The Ammonites had a very secure wall around the city of Rabbah and had the advantage of a river flowing beside its west wall, where they had access to water. Being next to the river, this large community had an abundance of river boats that could be used against their enemies who would not bring boats across long distances.

Before the sun began to rise the following day, the Ammonites had quietly let thousands of their soldiers out through a small, hidden access to the side of the main gate and lined up several bodies deep. Each one was equipped with long spears, and they stood tall all along the width of their city wall, facing the Israelites as they held shields up to their chests and swords at their sides. Lining the top of the wall were hundreds of archers ready to release an avalanche of arrows onto the crowd of hated Israelites. They would be the first to engage in contact with the Israelites, who were well known for having a God that went with them into every battle.

The Israelite army went into one of their abnormal frontline formations to confuse their adversaries in this "jagged teeth" formation. Instead of a straight line, handfuls of men spearheaded the way forward while the ones beside them dropped back, looking like the teeth of a saw blade from a bird's eye view. In this formation, the forward groups would engage in battle momentarily and then drop back as the groups on each side of them charged forward, appearing to engage the enemy from each side. This continuous movement of confusing fighting forward, then to the sides, and then forward again caused the enemy to lose the direction they should be going as they crashed into one another, hindering their effectiveness.

The sun had risen to the point that everyone could see clearly, so the tension began to rise, each waiting for the other to make the first move. The main gate slowly opened just enough that a horse and its rider could get through one at a time as three made their way. Then the gate closed and locked behind them. They continued out between the two lines of armies and stopped halfway. General Joab knew they wanted to talk before engaging, so he kicked his horse forward with two soldiers following on each side of him.

Once the horses were a short distance from each other in the middle of the battlefield, the Ammonite commander spoke first, "Why has Israel come to make war on our people?"

"Why have *we* come to make war on you, Commander?" General Joab asked, insulted.

The commander only nodded his head, holding his ground that they have intruded on them.

Adjusting himself on his saddle, Joab looked past the three men as though they were not there and continued, "That's not what the Arameans said when we slaughtered every one of them who were planning to head here to join you for an obvious celebration...." He pointed out toward all the tents. "Both your nations planned to meet up with the Philistines in Jerusalem to attempt to overtake Israel."

The two men beside the commander looked at each other with concern, but the commander replied calmly, "There must be some misunderstanding, General Joab. We were only setting up for a wedding because the king of the Arameans was sending one of his daughters as a new bride for our king."

It went silent as Joab focused on the commander, narrowing his eyes. "You do know who I am, Commander?"

With sarcasm, he answered, "Of course, King David's shield to hide behind. Where is your king, by the way? Our men didn't see him last night when they made their way through your camp. Is he sick? Or just being cowardly?"

Again, silence shot like daggers in all directions. After a few deep breaths, Joab reached behind him for something tied to his saddle. He brought it forward and tossed it to the ground, saying, "Give this back to the only soldier we let live to bring you a message of fear, which I see in your eyes." He had thrown a severed arm of one of the spies who had tried to infiltrate the camp.

All three Ammonites looked down at the severed, bloody arm, realizing they had been completely outwitted. Joab added, "As for King David, he didn't want to get the stench of *pig* on his robe and crown and told me to devour you and the Arameans so our countryside would continue to have fresh air."

Without any more conversation, the Arameans turned their horses to the city and trotted back. When they got to their army lined up and standing at attention, the commander speared his sword into the air, pointing at someone high up on the city wall. Instantly the loud gong rang again, echoing into the city and out to the countryside, and could be heard from a far distance. The pounding of the gong was different than the day before when the enemy arrived. It was in a specific rhythm, sending a message. The deep, gonging sound was easily heard by the Israelites when General Joab returned to his army. Suddenly screams of pain erupted within his own 30,000 soldiers who had been standing at the ready to charge forward.

It took a moment to realize what was happening; some of his men dropped to their knees or flinched around in agony with arrows sticking out of their backs. Joab looked back up to the high wall at the Ammonite archers, but they hadn't moved or shot any arrows. He then heard several rams' horns from the backside of his army and understood what was happening: the Ammonites were attacking them from behind.

During the cover of night, the Ammonites used the west side gate that dropped down into the Jabbok River and sent several thousand men out on boats, quietly floating passed the sleeping Israelites to come up secretly behind them and take them by surprise.

The instant reaction of the much larger Israelite army was to back up for safety, moving toward the city to get out of reach of the incoming arrows. Their own archers could not react to defend because they were up at the frontline as per usual. As the movement of the mass of soldiers backed up closer to the middle of the battlefield, dozens of flaming arrows were seen flying out from the high city wall, landing short of General Joab and his frontline.

Suddenly, fire flared up high when the flaming arrows sank into the ground. The fire raced out to each side of the battlefield, trapping the Israelite army between the wall of fire and the shower of arrows that were continually coming down from their backside. The Ammonites already had a shallow, camouflaged trench of highly flammable liquid soaked into the ground as a safety precaution just in case the Arameans had a change of heart and wanted to attack them when they arrived.

General Joab shouted out orders for the flagmen to use their rams' horns to signal instructions to change the direction of their charge and split up into wild dog formation, shielding themselves in turtle shell formation to block the incoming arrows. Once the

25,000 systematically split up into large groups, another signal was given to run back at the ones who had snuck up behind them to attack.

It was a short-lived battle as the Ammonites chased their sly enemy back to the river and escaped on their boats, dramatically outnumbered. But they had accomplished their mission: to take out some Israelites and cause confusion. As the last boat got out of their reach, General Joab called a halt to the battle. They were now farther away from the city, so he called in his leading captains and mighty warriors to reorganize their plans, letting the second half of the first day expire and preparing for a much longer war.

It had been several weeks since the army of the chosen people of God arrived in Rabbah. It was an easy battle with the Ammonites even though they played many tricks and had unusual strategies against Joab and his army, who were split up on the north and south side of the city. The mighty warriors and their sons had been fighting hard with different strategies of their own, taking this opportunity to teach their warrior sons to put the many things they had been training into play.

Most of the Ammonite army had been destroyed, but they still had a grand advantage with the high wall around the city. However, both nations knew that if Israel stayed persistent and kept a healthy number of soldiers alive, sooner or later, the city of Rabbah would be conquered. A messenger from Jerusalem arrived by horseback late one evening in the Israelite camp with a message for General Joab. He was escorted to the general's tent, and after Joab read the message, he quickly called for Uriah.

Uriah and Shuriah arrived at the general's tent, and Joab's assistant read the letter from King David: "General Joab, I pray all is going well with the battle against the Ammonites. I understand from your messenger that you conquered the Aramean army several weeks ago. I need you to temporarily relieve Uriah of duty and have him and him alone, without his warrior son, come back to Jerusalem. There are things I need to discuss with him. Then I will have him return a few days later."

Joab and Uriah did not understand why the king wanted Uriah to return to Jerusalem; it was a strange order, especially when there were older mighty warriors who could go back that had more experience and were pure-blooded Hebrews. An ugly darkness whispered in Joab's ears, alarming him, *The king doesn't trust you. Why is he going to the Hittite with private information and not you?*

Uriah was concerned as well but for other reasons. "But, General, we"—he pointed to Shuriah—"are one of the four mighty warriors in charge of protecting the Ark of the Covenant at the frontline."

"Orders are orders, Uriah."

Fighting to stay calm but not wanting to leave his son or mighty warrior brothers behind, Uriah asked, "Do you know what he wants?"

"You have as much information as I do. Collect your belongings, and take a fresh horse. It should take you no more than a few days on horseback to get to our king."

After Shuriah and Uriah left General Joab's tent, they went back to theirs, and Uriah packed up the items he would need. There was an emotional silence; neither knew what to think of the situation. Finally, Uriah spoke up, "Son, you will stay here in camp away from the battle."

"But, Father, I—"

Uriah flashed his eyes to Shuriah. "What did the general say?"

Shuriah drooped his head, responding, "Orders are orders...."

"And we will obey the orders of our superiors, and I'm your superior. You will not leave camp unless the general or another mighty warrior needs you. Do you understand?" He turned directly to his son, giving him a stern expression.

Without hesitating, Shuriah said, "Yes, Father. I understand. What am I to do while I wait for you to come back?"

They walked out of the tent, and Uriah pointed around the area. "There is more than enough to do. Help the armorers with sharpening swords or making more weapons. Assist the horsemen with the horses. Help the cooks prepare food. There is plenty to do during a war, not just the fighting."

"But I'm a mighty warrior's son. We don't do those things."

Uriah paused; the statement struck a sour spot, and he answered, nodding, "This is a great thing for me to leave you by yourself. Your prideful attitude is a weakness that has slithered its way in and needs to be taken out so your heart can be strengthened. And for that"—he gave his son a confident grin—"you will not help the armorers, the horsemen, or the cooks. Shuriah, you must be humbled before you can move forward to grow into a mighty warrior."

"Then what do you want me to do?"

"You will help the keepers of the camp. You will keep the water barrels full. You will clean up after everyone, make new toilet areas, and cover the full ones up. You will help with the wounded soldiers and so on."

The look on Shuriah's face was priceless, telling him this was definitely an area that needed growth. Uriah turned and marched his way through the crowded camp toward the temporary horse corrals. It took a moment for Shuriah to catch up. Clearing his mind of his new duties, he became surprisingly emotional about being apart from his father, even for a young man of fifteen years.

They walked without saying anything, and after a horse was prepared, and Uriah got on it to leave, he looked down at his son and said with a rare smile, "Make me proud. I want to hear General Joab say you were the best camp keeper he has ever seen."

"I will give it my all, Father!" Shuriah responded in a positive tone, trying not to let anyone around see that a saddened, empty hole was opening within his chest. Uriah nodded, confident that he would do just that. He turned the horse and left the camp and his son to a war that was currently an uphill battle.

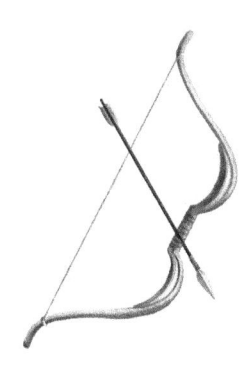

CHAPTER 16

Several days later, Uriah arrived in Jerusalem, dismounting from his tired horse at the base of the palace steps as a servant took the reins. When his feet hit the ground, he looked in the direction of his home connected to the side of the palace near the extraordinary tent where the Ark of God rests when it's within the city walls.

Taking a deep breath, longing to be with his beautiful wife Bathsheba, Uriah knew it was not the responsible or honorable thing to do firstly because the king called for him, so the king would be the first one he saw when he arrived. Secondly, all the mighty warriors had taken an oath created by King David that any time they were at war, they would not relax or be intimate with their wives as long as there was even one of them still away fighting. This created a bond in that all would be suffering one way or another, sharing in their focus on war.

When he got to the top of the stairs, two palace guards holding long spears presented themselves to Uriah with a bow of respect for the mighty warrior who had just come from an ongoing war. He was still dirty and sweaty, wearing his blood-stained battle attire with his long, black hair and strong, black beard needing a thorough cleaning and combing.

One guard greeted him, "Uriah, the king is waiting for you on his private balcony. He told us when you arrive to have you wash and put on fresh clothing before going to him. Please come with us."

They turned and led Uriah into the palace to a bathing room. Servants in the bathing room helped him take off his battle clothes and assisted him in washing his body and hair. When they were done, they adorned him with fresh battle clothes that were exactly the same as what he had taken off, except clean. Once his sword was secured to his back along with the lower daggers and his battle knife was on his hip, the servants attached his clean, metal forearm guards and shin guards to his legs over the crisscrossing straps that secured his leather footwear.

When Uriah walked out of the bathing room, the two guards were waiting to escort him to the king. They walked silently through the long hallway and up a staircase to the entrance of the private balcony. Two more guards were at the entrance, and when the three arrived, the two guards bowed to Uriah. One of the balcony guards said, "Welcome home, mighty warrior. The king is waiting for you. Please come with us."

Uriah left the two original guards who took the other two guards' position at the entrance as he followed them to King David, who was relaxing on some pillows next to a low table with a scroll open in his hands, reading.

David looked up, saying, "Ah, Uriah!" with a little too much enthusiasm for a king. He stood and grasped Uriah, greeting him with a hug and a kiss on both cheeks and then stepped back. "You look refreshed from the long ride with clean clothes." Looking him up and down, he added, "It doesn't appear you've been wounded."

Uriah bowed. "No, Master. I have been blessed along with most of the mighty warriors. Hezro is the only one who has been severely stabbed with a knife to his lower side, but the priest said he will live; it will just take time to heal. A few others have minor cuts and bruises, but all in all, the competition for the most kills still prevails." Uriah tilted his head back slightly, giving David a smile through his thick beard.

David laughed and calmed down, saying, "That is what I like to hear: honest competition to grow one another. I shall send up extra prayers and have the priests make a sacrifice for Hezro of Carmel to be fully healed."

David turned and pointed to pillows on the floor across the table from where he was lying down. "Please sit, my friend. Let's refresh the insides of your body now that the outside is taken care of." As soon as he said that, servants who were prepared for Uriah's arrival brought in several trays of delicacies and a large goblet filled with wine.

Uriah walked over to his spot and waited to sit until his king sat down first. As he took his seat, he had to control himself from gulping down all the food, for he had not eaten a full meal in several days.

"How is the battle going?" David asked, changing his tone to concern.

Uriah swallowed what was in his mouth and answered, "It's taking longer than expected to conquer Rabbah. The Ammonites are strong fighters, but we've taken the lives of the majority of the army from what we can tell from the outside of the high walls, which incidentally are what is hindering us from finishing these people off. Every time we get close, they have a new trick up their tunic that hinders or stops us from getting through one of the six entrances and holes the soldiers are working on."

The king adjusted himself and said with a sorrowful expression, "The general told me we lost 10,000 against the Arameans. Is that accurate?"

Uriah reluctantly lowered his head before lifting it to say, "Yes, Master. Even though we took them by surprise while they were marching to Rabbah, they gave us a good fight."

Uriah took a deep drink of wine and pointed across the table, adding, "We need our king there with us. You help the power of God flow through our veins. Why did you not come with us this time, if I may ask, Master?" He cocked his head, truly bewildered why David had stayed behind, especially since he was the greatest war hero Israel had ever had.

"I'm not sure, Uriah." David looked away at first as though he was thinking about something else. "But I can say I have been preoccupied with many governing issues that seem to constantly need my attention. What I can tell you is that I will never do this again, no matter what political things are going on." He leaned over the table, slapped his hand down, and said, "I'm missing out on all the fun! Wars put a thrill in my life and give us great stories, not this…." He turned around as he gestured, pointing to everything the eye could see.

They continued having casual conversations about the war for a little while until Uriah had his fill of food. Then David said, "I have taken too much of your time this evening, my friend. You have got to be very tired. Go home, relax, and be with your wife. We can continue our conversation tomorrow."

Uriah froze, shocked at what his king just told him to do. He had a strange sensation in his chest that something wasn't right. He asked himself, *Why did he call me away from the war? And now he asked me to do something I took an oath against ever doing in order to honor and respect my fellow warriors by not being with our wives in a time of war.*

Acting casually so as *not* to offend his king and confront him, he replied, "I shall sleep well tonight, safely inside the walls surrounding Jerusalem that keep our enemies on the outside."

David was inscrutable, secretly hiding paranoia, but he nodded his head in agreement. His mind and heart were swirling with anxiety as a dark, slithering voice whispered in his ear, "*Did you hear what he said, 'Our enemies are on the outside of the wall. But you, you are on the inside.'*"

David felt sick but played it off as he stood and started walking to the entrance, saying, "I agree, Uriah. Now go; it's been a long time since you have been home. I will call for you in the morning."

Uriah stood, stretching out his sore and tired back, and straightened out his clothing and weapons. Then he walked right up to him and bowed, saying, "Thank you, my king, for the bath and the meal. I shall see you in the morning." Then he walked to the entrance where the two guards were waiting to escort him out of the palace once again.

When they got back to the entrance, the two guards stopped, letting Uriah continue out to the wide platform before he got to the stairs that led out to the open city. One of the guards said, "It is good to see you again. Will you be here long, or are you returning to the war?"

Uriah hesitated, not knowing the answer. He still wondered why he was called home at all. He looked out over the city and then toward his home, answering, "I'm not sure. The king will have that answer for me tomorrow." As he looked back to the guards at the entrance, he noticed an open spot along the wall and asked, "Is there anything that goes there?"

Both guards followed to where his finger was pointing, and one answered, "One of the extra night guards stands there when these doors are closed."

"That will be my bed for the night."

The guards were stunned and asked why. He replied, "I want to be as close to the king as I can while I'm here since we are at war and do not know what spies have infiltrated our city."

"Uriah, you can sleep in the palace outside the king's sleeping quarters if you are that concerned. I know the lead guard and our king would be happy if you did that. But everything should be okay. We have tripled the guards around and inside the palace when you and the rest of the mighty warriors left months ago."

Uriah contemplated the idea for a moment. Looking down at the ground, he made a decision. "No, this looks like a good spot to keep an eye on you and the other guards to make sure you are not plotting anything against our king while we are away."

The two guards balked in shock at the accusation out of nowhere, and one of them sputtered, "Uriah, we would never…we are all loyal to King David—"

Uriah boldly stepped forward, narrowing his eyes as they both took a step backward, and he said, "I know. I was just checking your honesty by your reaction." Then he winked, cracking a half smile as he raised a hand to slap one of them on the side of the shoulder. He drew his sword from over his shoulder with his other hand, stepped to the side of the entrance doors, and sat down, leaning against the palace wall. As he looked up and placed the sword across his lap, he added, "If you wouldn't mind, could I get a blanket?"

The guards stared at him in disbelief that he was really going to sleep on the hard surface at the palace entrance. At their astonishment, he repeated, "So are you going to get me a blanket?"

One of the guards walked into the palace to get a blanket just in time to bump into another guard that was hurriedly heading out the entrance. The guard coming out asked, "Has Uriah gone home yet?"

The other guards looked at one another, then turned, gazing down to the ground and pointed. The new guard followed their fingers to see Uriah looking up at him.

The guard bowed and asked, concerned, "Are you all right, mighty warrior?"

Uriah nodded, giving him a questionable grin. Understanding the look, the guard fumbled over his words, trying to comprehend what was going on. He reached out, saying, "I am delivering a gift to you from our king."

He held out a small piece of a soft, snow-white lamb's skin folded over something. Reaching up, Uriah asked, "A gift for what?"

"He did not say. He only told me to deliver this to you and tell you he appreciates you being one of his mighty warriors."

Uriah took the lamb's skin, opened it up, and stared down for a moment. He lifted the item up for all to see, wondering if a joke was being played on him. "And what is this?"

"It is extremely special to the king. He said it is the stone that he killed Goliath with when he conquered the Philistines as a boy. The king has held onto it all these years to remind him that the Lord of heaven's armies will conquer all the giants in our paths as long as we stay in the shadow of the God of Israel."

Uriah wrinkled his forehead, examining the stone as visions went through his head of the great story that had been told over and over in this foreign land he had called home for many, many years now.

He looked up to the guard delivering the gift and asked, "Does King David give gifts like this all the time?"

The guard shook his head, saying, "I've never delivered other gifts from him before, but I'm not sure."

One of the other guards commented, "That is a prized gift. My father was a soldier when young David stepped into the open field, calling Goliath, and I watched the whole thing—even David cutting Goliath's head off with his own sword. He was barely able to pick it up. Then he knelt down to pick up the head and dug the rock out with his sheepherder's knife."

All the guards grunted in agreement, familiar with the details of the story. Uriah raised his eyebrows, saying, "Huh...." Turning the smooth stone around in his fingers, still wondering why it was given to him, he thought, *As a Hittite, I should be the last of all the mighty warriors to receive a gift with such a grand story and meaning for Israel.*

He looked up at the deliverer of the gift and said, "I will give him my appreciation in the morning." He put it back on the lamb's skin, wrapped it up, and set it aside on the ground. Then he looked expectantly to the guard who was going to get him a blanket. The guard stood there for a moment, forgetting what he was doing until he said, "Oh yes, I'll be right back, Master."

The evening went on as the extra night guards came on duty, surprised and yet excited that a mighty warrior was there with them to guard the palace (even though he was sleeping). When morning came, Uriah went to the guards' quarters outside the palace and had a meal with them. While he was there, he told stories about the war, and they all hung onto every word of the exciting fighting happening far away. They yearned to one day be able to become a mighty warrior themselves, but if they were only protecting the palace and weren't able to go to war, odds were they would never be like Uriah, able to tell these great stories.

After a while, a guard on duty came into the room, approached Uriah, and bowed, saying, "The king is asking for your presence."

Standing up and adjusting himself, the mighty warrior said openly, "Thank you for the hot meal." Then he himself bowed to all the guards around him and finished, "Most of all, thank you for being the mighty guards of the palace who protect our king! It is an extremely important and very dangerous job. Thank you again."

He gave the men exactly what they needed to be proud of what they do and encouraged them to be the best they could be, especially when the mighty warriors were away from Jerusalem. The guard, who had called for Uriah, escorted him to King David, who was waiting for him in the main courtroom as he sat on his throne, going over things with elders and priests.

When they entered, David sent away the elders, priests, and palace guards to be alone with the mighty warrior. When Uriah approached the steps to the throne, he went to a knee and bowed, waiting to be called upon, indicating it was all right to come closer. "Uriah!" David announced loudly. With that unexpected, joyful tone (out of character for the king), he spread his arms wide and stood to greet him.

Uriah stepped up to David, who gave him an awkward hug. Then he stepped back and said, "What is this I hear that you did not go to your home and relax like I told you? But instead, you slept at the front entrance of the palace on the ground?"

Uriah gave a slight bow, acknowledging that what was said was true.

"But why didn't you go home last night after being gone for so long?" David asked, surprised.

Uriah had prepared his reply for the question he knew would be coming. "The Ark of the Covenant, which I was protecting, and the armies of Israel are living in tents as General Joab and my master's warriors and soldiers are camping outside in the open fields. How could I go home to drink wine, have dinner with my wife, and then sleep with her? We have all sworn an oath we would never do such a thing."

David knew every word spoken was the honorable and respectable truth. Now at a major disadvantage, with colors of disgrace and shame creeping into his face, David was silent for a moment as he backed away. He returned to his throne, thinking about how he could respond and rebound from such unbecoming behavior of a trustworthy king.

Uriah went back to his knee, bowing his head, and said, "Master, my words disgraced you and the throne. Please forgive—" David raised his hand, stopping his faithful warrior, and said, "Stand, my friend. You haven't disgraced me. I have done it to myself." He paused to think of what to say next; the invitation of having Uriah here certainly wasn't going in the direction he was hoping.

Uriah stood, spread his arms out, and asked innocently, "Master, why am I here?"

David was ready, answering, "This is the first war I have not been involved in since I was anointed king. I wanted to know how the war was going by someone I knew I could trust to tell me the truth and not minimize it to appear better than it is."

"I am honored you have that much faith in me. And I assure you, everything I have told you is as accurate as I know." Uriah changed his demeanor and said, "Master, thank you for the very special gift. I am very honored by it." He bowed again.

"You're welcome, Uriah. You are very deserving of it. Keep it safe."

"I will."

They talked for a while longer about other events going on in the war. Then David dismissed the mighty warrior by saying, "Stay in Jerusalem for the rest of the day, and tomorrow you may return to the battle. I will expect you this evening for dinner. One of the guards will call for you when I am ready."

Uriah bowed very low, thanking David for allowing him to spend time with him. He turned and was escorted out of the palace with the guards who were at the entrance of the courtroom.

He spent the remainder of the day doing various things, all concerned with the safety and security of the city. He looked over the training arena to make sure everything was in order and in its place. Then he went to all the guard stations at all the gates and on top of the walls around the city. He also met with many soldiers who had stayed behind, giving them encouragement and hopeful information about the war and everyone coming home victorious soon.

Uriah did everything he could to keep his mind off his wife and physically didn't even get close to his house so he wouldn't be tempted and Bathsheba wouldn't see he had returned. When the evening came, a guard found him to bring him back to the palace to have one last dinner with the king before heading back to the war. David had invited many of the higher-ranking authorities from around the city to join them. It was a festive dinner with music and beautiful dancers entertaining the large group of men. Much drinking purposely took place this night; David had ordered the servants to keep the guests' goblets filled with wine, especially Uriah's.

After the dinner and entertainment were over and most of the guests (including Uriah) had too much to drink, they were escorted out of the palace and directed to go home. Even though Uriah was greatly influenced by the wine, he never lost sight of the oath he took with his warrior brothers, so he didn't go home to be with his wife. He went back to the same spot he slept last night and had no problem falling asleep and staying asleep all night.

David inquired with his guards early the next morning if Uriah went home after he left the dinner party. When they told him he slept at the palace entrance again, he got very angry, went to his private study area, and wrote a letter to General Joab. Then he called for Uriah. They met in the courtroom again for David to give Uriah multiple instructions for General Joab. He gave him the letter he had written earlier that was sealed with a wax stamp, stating this was for General Joab's eyes only.

Their parting did not have that joyful tone the king had been expressing the last couple of days; it was that of stern, high authority speaking down to the common man, not even a mighty warrior. It confused Uriah again as to what he was doing here. It made no sense and appeared to be a complete waste of his time as it put the Ark of God and the Israelite army in harm's way with one less warrior to assist in overtaking their enemy.

Three days later, he arrived back at the battle at Rabbah. As normal practice, he went directly to Joab to inform him of his arrival and to deliver the information King David had given him in the private letter.

They spoke for a while in Joab's tent as he attempted to find out why Uriah was called to the king. Uriah was direct in telling him every detail, even sleeping outside of the palace entrance for two nights. He confessed he still wasn't sure why he was called to Jerusalem instead of anyone else since one of the normal, high-ranking soldiers could have gone back to deliver the message he gave to the king.

After Joab was completely informed and Uriah was brought up to speed with where they were in the battle, he kindly told Uriah he was glad to have him back and dismissed him. Uriah left and went to his tent to find Shuriah. It took a while, but he finally found him where the armory was set up. Shuriah was working diligently on making arrow shafts with the armorers. He enjoyed working with wood more than metal and had a large stack of straightened and smooth sticks that were ready to have arrowheads and fletchings attached.

Uriah quietly walked up to the side of his son, who was sitting with others on a long log with a fire in front of them, and commented in a disguised voice, "Boy, I need a hundred more arrows and two more deep holes dug so the soldiers can relieve themselves before the sun sets."

Shuriah suspended his knife mid-stroke of shaving the shaft smooth and turned around to confront whoever was telling him what to do. When he looked up and saw his father, his arrogance morphed into a boyish exuberance, exclaiming, "Father, you're back!" He lunged forward, giving him a hug.

Uriah wholeheartedly absorbed the affection of his son, whom he loved very much, but the setting of other soldiers around and the fact that Shuriah was almost a sixteen-year-old man made the situation a bit uncomfortable. Shuriah realized this as well and tried to play it off, letting go of his father. He stepped back and put his knife away in its sheath on his hip, saying in a casual tone, "How are things in Jerusalem?"

"Everything is in order, and the king sends his blessings."

"How is Mother?"

Pausing as he took note of how many armors and soldiers were listening, he stated, "Son, during times of war, all warriors have taken an oath that if the army is in battle, they will not go home to be with their wives."

"So you didn't even see her?" he asked, straining his head back in surprise.

"No."

One of General Joab's guards quickly came up to Uriah and bowed. "Uriah, the general requests that you and your warrior son meet with him immediately."

"I was just with him."

"Yes, but he said he has new information for you pertaining to the battle."

"What is it?"

The guard had a blank face and shrugged his shoulders, saying, "I don't know, but he did say it was very important."

Uriah looked down at Shuriah. He saw Shuriah wasn't fully equipped with all his weapons, so he looked back to the guard and said, "We will be there shortly."

The guard bowed, turned, and went back to Joab's tent.

Excitement brewed in Shuriah. Raising his voice, he asked, "What do you think it is? Have the Ammonites come out of hiding behind the wall to fight us like men?"

"I'm not sure, son." Uriah put a hand on Shuriah's shoulder, looked down at him, and said, "Let's maintain a clear mind and a calm body when we hear what the general has to say."

They went to their tent to straighten their attire and fasten their weapons. When they approached Joab's tent, Uriah got an eerie feeling. He peered around the camp, but nothing was out of the ordinary. He looked forward as the guards at the front door of the tent pulled back the entrance flaps to let them in, and it was as if a cloud of heavy, black breath was coming from within the tent.

As a father's natural reaction, he grasped Shuriah by the arm and covertly pulled him to stand behind him while he himself acted as a shield. Shuriah glanced at his father, not understanding what he was doing, but maintained obedience, following his father's commands without questioning him, especially in front of the general and his guards.

They stepped into the tent, and Joab said, "Ah, Uriah, I apologize for having you come back here so soon, but new information just came in from the frontline that needs immediate action."

Uriah relaxed a bit. Then he asked with concern, "What is it? Is the Ark of the Covenant secure?"

"I believe it is, but at the frontline near the main gate of the city—" He paused and did a slight double take that would make one wonder if he was trying to think of something to say. He continued, "I need you to relieve the captain. He is not empowering his soldiers with courage and is missing out on a grand and important opportunity. We have been fighting very hard to take the main gate as it weakens. You are fresh and can lead a group of soldiers to take the Ammonites by surprise by rushing the gate at this time of day."

Uriah cocked his head, unsure what to think of this sudden and foolish reaction from the intelligent leader. "General, the captain is a very capable soldier to carry out any orders. Plus, it is the latter part of the day, and the soldiers are tired. If this area has become so weak, we can regroup, come up with diversions, and plan for an early attack before sunrise to take the remaining Ammonites by surprise then. Especially if we focus all our men and power on this weak spot—like the tip of a sword, piercing our way through before the enemy knows what happened when they were asleep."

Joab responded firmly, "You are refreshed and fully strengthened from your trip away. You will energize the tired soldiers and give them confidence to listen and follow you, a mighty warrior. We can finally get this war over with, possibly by the end of the day, with such a bold move."

Out of place, Shuriah spoke up, stepping from behind his father. "Why would you put men in that kind of danger, especially in the daylight where their archers on top of the walls can easily find"—he pointed to his chest and then his father's—"their targets—us?"

Joab looked down at Shuriah, ignored his input, and looked at Uriah, saying, "You have your orders. Gather a handful of fresh soldiers, and go to the front to relieve the captain. Organize the ones there and take the main gate. Here is a private letter to give him from me, giving him these new orders.

"You'll know what to do when you're there, Uriah. I trust you. Give me this opportunity to tell the king of your heroic and talented efforts to bring this war to an end."

Uriah stood there with a blank face, not understanding what was going on. This is not how they do battle, reckless and taking chances where they know many men will die for no reason—possibly even himself or Shuriah. Mighty warriors go into battle outnumbered all the time, but not at the bottom of strong, tall city walls where the regular soldiers are trained to get through rock walls and wooden gates with strategies to avoid getting hurt.

Taking a step back, Uriah bowed to the general and said, "For the Lord of heaven's armies." He turned and began to walk out of the tent.

Shuriah stood there in disbelief. He knew what was being ordered was wrong. It went against everything he was trained for to be a mighty warrior. *We are to value our soldiers more than winning a battle. We are only to take chances when there is no other way out of a situation. Besides, there is no rush in a war when you know the enemy has limited resources and can be starved out of their stronghold sooner or later.*

"Shuriah, at my side!" his father demanded, looking back to

find Shuriah staring at the general.

Shuriah turned around and walked to his father, following him out of the tent. He glanced back just in time to see a faint smile flash on Joab's face.

CHAPTER 17

The mighty warrior and his son walked silently to their tent to prepare to go into a preposterous situation. With every step, it got heavier and harder to move forward as their heads swirled in bewilderment. Just before they got to their tent, they heard, "Uriah, you're back!"

They turned to see Eliam and a couple of other mighty warriors and their warrior sons making their way across the camp. "How is everything at home? What did our master want?" Eliam asked joyfully, stepping up to greet them. He reached out, clanking their metal forearm guards together.

Without much expression, Uriah calmly replied, "All is well in Jerusalem. Our master only asked how the war was progressing."

The three other warriors looked at one another, confused at Uriah's demeanor. They looked to Shuriah, who was definitely not in his usual, energetic mood.

"What is going on here, you two? Shuriah, you couldn't wait for your father to return. You were making us crazy."

Anger began to bubble up, and Shuriah responded, "The general told us to go to the frontline and take the main gate right now with a handful of soldiers and relieve the captain who is up there!"

"He told you what? Is this true, brother?"

Uriah looked into the eyes of his father-in-law, nodding. Eliam looked to the other warriors and said, "No, you're not. That is ludicrous. Those soldiers up there are doing everything they can not to be shot with arrows or have boiling tar or large stones come crushing down on them. It isn't the right time to rush in and take the gate yet. In a week or two, as we chip away at them or starve them out is when we will have the advantage, not now!" Eliam flailed his arms around, outraged.

One of the other warriors said jokingly, "What did you do, sleep with one of the king's concubines when you were there?"

Eliam swiftly drew his knife, putting it up to the warrior's throat as the warriors' sons giggled at the comment. With his head tilted back, the warrior stretched his neck, wanting to avoid leaning forward into the sharp knife. "I'm just kidding, old man."

Uriah said softly, "I slept on the steps next to the palace entrance every night with the night guards. But it was strange…" He shook his head. "King David wanted me to go home every night and be with my wife.…"

There was silence, and the warriors stared at one another in disbelief. Then Eliam lowered his knife, putting it back into his sheath, and said in disbelief, "No he didn't.…"

Again, Uriah nodded without saying a word. The other warriors grimaced with many questions flashing through their minds about what was going on here.

"I must go." With one hand, Uriah patted Eliam on the shoulder and turned to his tent.

"You're not going without us and any other mighty warrior

who's not out there killing Ammonites somewhere right now." Eliam stormed off to the general's tent.

When Uriah and Shuriah had gotten fully equipped for battle and had gathered twenty soldiers to join them at the frontline to attempt to take the main gate, Eliam and other mighty warriors in camp who heard what Uriah and Shuriah were ordered to do came to meet up with them.

With no enthusiasm and a bit of awkwardness, Eliam tried not to be disrespectful to Joab as he said disgustingly, "Uriah, we are being ordered not to join you. You will be the only warrior on the frontline except for the four who are guarding the Ark of the Covenant up there and can't leave their post no matter what happens, which you already know since you are one of those guards sometimes."

He looked up to the heavens as the sun was getting lower in the sky. "You do not have much time to accomplish your task." He put a hand on each of Uriah's shoulders, adding, "We have been through many battles that appeared to be impossible to win…only to end up slaying those giants in victory because we fight in the shadow of the Lord of heaven's armies!" he erupted, lifting both fisted hands into the air as all the other warriors joined in giving them an encouraging send-off to build energy in this dreary moment.

"We will not sleep until you and Shuriah return tonight, my brother." This time he grabbed his shoulders and kissed both of his cheeks and did the same with Shuriah, saying to him, "Fight like you have never fought before, young warrior!" He turned to the group of mighty warriors behind him and looked back, adding solemnly, "We know the Lord purposely has you here with us…to one day be the greatest of us all." All the warriors gave him a personal cheer, acknowledging this to be true; even the warriors' sons had begun to shout his name.

One of the soldiers who was going with them brought fresh horses, handed Uriah and Shuriah the reins, and gave them a bow before he joined the other soldiers going with their new leader to the front. Something Eliam said about giants reminded him of something. He handed his reins to Shuriah and went back into their tent, getting out the lamb's skin that had the gift David gave him.

He examined it closely, thinking of what his king had said about the stone and its history, and thought of Eliam's words again: "slaying those giants." Putting the picture together, he decided to take it to battle with them. He wasn't sure why but thought, *Does this rock give King David good fortune? But with the God of Israel, there is no such thing as luck?* He shook his head and thought clearly, *No, it is a true reminder that the Lord of heaven's armies is the destroyer of our enemies even when we are outnumbered or the situation looks hopeless because the God of Israel is our hope in all things when we are in His shadow.*

Uriah looked down at his battle attire, trying to figure out where to put it so it would not get lost. Then an idea came to him. He pulled around his quiver from his back, pulled out all the arrows, and dropped it to the bottom. He put the arrows back and thought, *It will be safe there*, and then went back outside.

As Uriah, Shuriah, and the twenty soldiers left the camp, Joab stepped out of his tent just in time to see all their backs as they galloped away and thought to himself, *Why would our king send him to the frontline like this? What did he do or...?* He lifted an eyebrow questioningly, *What did you do, David, that you want to have him possibly killed like this?* The feeling he had earlier, that Shuriah would finally be put in his place as a boy and that he wouldn't be able to humiliate him anymore, faded as memories of brotherhood and fighting hard side by side with the Hittite for years came to mind. He wondered how it could possibly come to an end with these outrageous orders, which were in the private letter sent back with Uriah, who unknowingly delivered his own death sentence.

It took a short time to get to the camp of the frontline soldiers, where the majority of the remaining army was on the northern side of the city. On horseback, they carefully weaved their way through the dirty camp that had tents scattered all over with temporary walls of rocks stacked upon each other here and there for protection just in case they were suddenly charged by the Ammonites. The smell was awful. Men could be heard crying out in pain off and on because they had been injured or were dying. They had been in the same area for weeks, and the conditions were continually getting worse.

Off to one side, downwind from the camp, was where the bodies of dead soldiers were piled up, smoldering. A slow rise of smoke never stopped as the bodies turned to ash, reminding the soldiers still alive that if they died, this was where they would end up. On the opposite side of camp was a large pile that continued to grow as well of all the things that were gathered and stripped from the dead soldiers, such as weapons and clothing. This also included everything of value that was on an Ammonite. If a soldier was in need of another piece of battle attire or a weapon, they would first search through this pile, and if they didn't find what they needed, then they would go to the armor or clothing master for a new one.

Finally getting to the tent they were looking for, Uriah dismounted, and Shuriah did the same. Uriah told his group of soldiers to stay on their horses, for they were leaving shortly. Two guards at the entrance of the tent bowed to the mighty warrior as Uriah asked, "Where is the captain?"

One guard answered, "He just got back from the frontline and is washing up and getting a meal."

"Go get him, and tell him I am here with a special order to carry out right now from General Joab. There is no time to waste." Uriah was back to his normal self that everyone was used to: intimidating, to the point, and with little emotion.

On the ride in, Uriah had reorganized his thoughts and refreshed his attitude, accepting what his superior wanted them to do. With the stone on his mind hidden in his quiver, it helped to calm his spirit and regain confidence in himself and in God. He rehearsed over and over in his head a vision of a shepherd boy younger than Shuriah with no military training who boldly stepped out in front of a giant soldier and an army of thousands. That boy had killed the giant with one simple, smooth stone— not with the deadly weapons he himself was an expert in using.

Fighting close to the walls of cities and overtaking the gates were only for the ordinary soldiers trained in making large apparatuses for ramming gates and using tall ladders to break through or tear away at walls. That made this a very difficult situation for everyone, especially since every mighty warrior's responsibility, training, and purposes were for direct hand-to-hand combat and guarding the Ark of God, the palace, and the king of Israel while creating and carrying out secret warfare strategies.

The captain was escorted back to his tent, where Uriah and the other soldiers were waiting. He bowed to the warrior and asked, "Why do I have the pleasure of having a mighty warrior here?"

Uriah paused, for what was about to come out of his mouth sounded truly ridiculous in his head, but he said it anyways. "Captain, I am ordered to relieve you of duty and to take the main gate right now! Here are your new orders from the general." Uriah gave him the letter, but he didn't read it right away. He was completely taken aback.

The captain and all of his other soldiers looked stone cold.

Then the captain smirked as though a joke was being played on him. He laughed out loud and said, "Okay, Uriah, this will be the first time I have ever heard you trying to be funny about something. What is really going on here?"

They stood silently as Shuriah stepped out from his father's shadow, answering, "This is an order from General Joab, Captain. There is nothing funny about it."

"But why? We are making our typical progress. In only about four or five more days, we should have a hole in the wall going all the way through. By then, their gate should have collapsed or easily broken through with a few more days of ramming it. That is when the mighty warriors do what you do best: destroy armies on the inside."

Shuriah started to respond, but his father held out his hand to keep him quiet as he said, "Orders are orders, Captain. So tell me quickly, what is the status up on the frontline? We are to move out now, and I will add twenty more of your rested soldiers with me," he said, pointing back to the twenty who came with him from the general's main camp.

The captain looked up at them and back down, saying, "Uriah, this is putting everyone, including you and your son, in great harm's way. This is a process that takes time. It's not a situation that we can do differently to just make happen. Storming the main gate, especially right now," looking behind him to the city wall and pointing out, "is doing nothing but helping the Ammonites have clear targets to shoot at."

Uriah inhaled deeply, beginning to grow in anger himself. He replied, "Captain, our superior gave an order, and I will carry it out no matter how difficult or impossible it appears. We go forward in the name of the Lord of heaven's armies. Our Lord will have His way! Do you understand? Now tell me what I need to know so we can get up there!"

The captain shook his head still in disbelief and informed them how he left everything earlier. He explained the destruction of the wall and what the soldiers were doing to create the hole in it, having already broken through the first outer layer. Then he mentioned that the main gate was getting very weak as well since they had set it on fire multiple times and rammed it to the point that it looked like it should collapse on its own very soon.

"How many soldiers are up there right now?" Uriah asked. "There are always 2,000 who maintain a ready position just in case the Ammonites suddenly burst out of their stronghold. Then a thousand are continually working back and forth from the wall and gate to get through, dodging and staying out of reach of arrows and everything else tossed down from the top of the wall."

"Is your ram together and ready to use?"

"Yes, it is. That's what I had the men freshly prepare for tomorrow before I left them."

Uriah thought for a moment, his eyes going back and forth, and looked out toward the city wall. Seeing the position he was in, the captain inconspicuously came to his mental rescue by saying, "If I were you with these strong, fresh soldiers you brought and the ones you're taking from here, I would work the log ram hard and fierce!" the captain asserted, raising his hand in a hard fist through gritted teeth. It gave the mighty warrior, who was out of his element, the courage he needed.

"Have the soldiers who are already up there group together and give a loud diversion by first charging the large hole in the wall, which is some distance away from the gate. It should give you enough time to ram the main gate, possibly putting a hole in it as well or helping it collapse. Then have the army leave the hole and join you to roar through the gate and accomplish this order the general gave you." He was trying his best to be optimistic.

He stepped up close to Uriah, eyed him firmly, and whispered, "I'm not sure why you are being ordered to relieved me of duty, but I am *not* relieved of this war! My men and I are behind you, mighty warrior, watching and waiting." He nodded his head that his words were true and that he would have his back if things went wrong on the frontline. He added, "I might not have killed 300 in one battle with my own hands, but I have killed tens of thousands in my career with my men!" The older captain bowed low as his men around him went to one knee to the mighty warrior. Then he turned and went into his tent to read the private letter with the orders Uriah had given him from the general.

Once inside, the captain opened the letter privately and read it. When he finished reading, he dropped the letter in shock. Every part of who he was as a soldier and an Israelite evaporated instantly. He wanted to hide away somewhere and never be found.

"Father, why are we not going to help Uriah and Shuriah?" Itai asked, very distraught that his friend who had saved his life years ago was going alone to the frontline. They were sitting in their tent having a meal, and Eliam had not said a word, brewing over and over in his head about the absurd situation regarding his warrior brother and son-in-law.

Eliam had had enough. He stood, throwing down the food in his hands, and angrily answered, "We are! Get yourself ready!" Eliam pushed back the flap of his tent and forcefully marched out to tell his brother warriors that he was leaving to be with Uriah no matter what General Joab said.

When he got outside, he looked up and saw, coming from all directions, all the other mighty warriors and their sons working their way to his tent on horseback, fully battle-ready with fierce faces of war. He absorbed the moment, more energized than he had been in a long time. He extended both arms, clenched his fists, raised his head to the ski, and roared, "Ahh, for the Lord of heaven's armies!"

All the horses surrounding his tent came to a halt as the loud and proud men raised their swords repeatedly and shouted, "For the Lord of heaven's armies!"

Eliam went into his tent and shortly coming back out with Itai, now both fully dressed for battle. A soldier had come to their tent with horses, handing them the reins and looking directly into Eliam's eyes. Quietly, he gave Eliam a message, "All the soldiers are behind the mighty warriors...."

Eliam nodded, understanding the brotherhood was not just with the mighty warriors but the whole Israelite army. He and Itai took the reins and mounted the horses. The warriors looked around at one another, knowing they were disobeying a direct order from the general. All the horses began to get anxious, tossing their heads up and down while nervously walking in place and sensing something big was happening. The men nodded to one another without any words to say but knew they were doing the right thing.

All at once, they bellowed their battle cry, raising their voices purposely for all to hear, and Eliam turned his horse that was leading the way toward the frontline camp with all the mighty warriors following. The ground shook and rumbled, heavy with the horses' hooves.

General Joab stepped out of his tent with two guards, one on each side, and heard the familiar echo of warriors going to war. His chest went hollow, and his head swirled with worry at carrying out the baffling instructions from the king.

Even though soldiers were walking around the camp, it was suddenly empty of its extraordinary power because the mighty shields and swords of his army were gone. He was not only emotionally weak but now felt helpless with no mighty warrior in sight. Fear struck him as daunting words rang within him, *What have you done, general? You have no one to protect you. You will be the one to blame.*

Uriah, Shuriah, and the forty soldiers they brought to the front met up with the commander who was left in charge in the captain's absence. They informed him of their orders, and the commander brought them up to speed with where they were now. Uriah took what the captain had suggested seriously on how to attack the strong wall but enhanced it with his own strategies of distraction.

Before moving forward to where he and Shuriah were going to attack, he held tightly to the mighty warriors' first rules of engaging in battle: always utilize a distraction to divert the enemy and confuse them about what was going on. The Israelite army had used a very important distraction to kill a large majority of the Ammonites after the first day of confusion when they themselves were attacked from behind. Then they were surrounded by a huge field of fire.

The part of the army with General Joab and most of the mighty warriors had attacked the northern side of Rabbah at the front main gate. The other part of the Israelite army that had secretly snuck in days early stayed hidden on the southern side of the city. They waited to attack until after the northern army had the Ammonites' full attention on the opposite side of the city. Then they caught their enemy off guard a couple of days later and were able to sneak into the city, killing many until they were stopped and pushed back to the other side of the protective wall.

This diversion caused the people to continually go back and forth within the city, tiring themselves out and costing them many of their soldiers' lives. This helped the Israelites to tear at the reinforced wall, which gave the Israelites the advantage of the battle by weakening the Ammonites' numbers, eventually starving them out.

But with this new order that came from General Joab, something that was supposed to end up being very easy just got very difficult and dangerous. So far, everyone who heard these orders could not understand them or did not want to believe something so stupid was instructed, especially to a mighty warrior.

Uriah had a short, private meeting with the commander, explaining the strategy he had for the attack. The commander was greatly encouraged by what the mighty warrior wanted to do, so he moved forward with new enthusiasm and gathered 2,000 of his men (who were standing back in a protective position, waiting for the enemy to charge out of the city for direct hand-to-hand combat) and another thousand who were working to destroy the wall and main gate.

His orders were to have the combined large numbers of men work their way past the hole in the wall and march toward the east gate of the city. He wanted all the soldiers to space themselves apart from each other to appear as if there were two to three times as many Israelites. Then Uriah told them to drag their feet to create a huge dust storm around them so that from the top of the high wall, the Ammonites, looking down, couldn't see clearly what was happening, which would get their attention in suspense and fear.

Uriah then added that every fifth soldier of the 3,000 would carry a torch, which would tell the enemy that their intentions were to fight throughout the night and to set fire to the next gate they came to. All the while, the plan was to continuously chant, "The God of Israel kills all giants against Him. The Ammonites will be dead when the sun rises tomorrow."

As this diversion magnificently took form, the majority of

the Ammonite soldiers and civilians on the wall and those running along behind it began to move in pace with the roaring dust storm that was growing with glowing flames like the deadly eyes of a leviathan, staring them down.

As the Israelite army made their way around to the east wall, Uriah took a private moment with Shuriah and respectively approached the Ark of God that was always securely placed at the front of every battle just out of reach of harm's way but close enough that the enemy could clearly see the brilliant gold, which held the presence of the God of Israel. Every nation in this part of the world knew how powerful the God of the Israelites was, and when the ark was in the battle with them, His power and faithfulness always led to victory for them and death and destruction for the enemy.

With the Ark of the Covenant at the frontlines where the battles rage and where pain, suffering, and death occur, its visual presence always gives encouragement as well—reminding the Israelite soldiers that God is with them, and His power gives them the strength to conquer whoever they are fighting.

Uriah and Shuriah went to their knees, bowing their faces to the ground at the base of the ark that barely fit in its small, decorative tent with its entrance flaps wide open, facing the city. Four mighty warriors and their sons were standing at attention on the outside of the tent, each at their own corner, looking outward for anyone wanting to harm the ark.

Uriah was in one of these guard positions when he was called to go to King David more than a week earlier. After giving their petition to God for protection, they rose, and Uriah informed his brother warriors of his orders from General Joab. At first, the warriors were amused that Uriah was joking with them, believing he had come back to relieve one of them. When he didn't reciprocate the banter, and they saw the heavy expressions from the father and son, it went silent.

Understanding the shock going through the warriors' minds, Uriah said, "All is well. The power of the Lord of heaven's armies is with us." He nodded to each brother warrior just as Shuriah nodded to each warrior son. Then they left them empty-handed, nonresponsive, and overwhelmed in disbelief.

The two got on their horses, and with the forty fresh soldiers, they reluctantly rode away, taking their time to the newly made, battering log ram near the main gate. They did not want to appear as if they were in a hurry, sneaking in on the enemy, or had the intention of attacking in case anyone on top of the wall was watching them.

Every soldier had a feeling of dread as though they were going to their own execution, except for Uriah and Shuriah. Over time, through intense training and countless experiences, they had seen again and again that when faced with the impossible, the Lord of heaven's armies shows up, uses them as a vessel, and makes the impossible possible. It was not only in their minds but in their blood as well that fear and failure were *not* options.

The vision of young David came back to Uriah clearer than ever, seeing the enemy in front of him as he bent down in a stream to pick up stones for his sling… Uriah and the others dismounted the horses at the log ram, which was just out of reach of arrows shot from the high wall. Uriah looked up at the towering wall of Rabbah and the burnt and damaged main gate. 'The giant' was intimidating but injured. *We will take this city today!* he thought confidently to himself as he inhaled, clenching his fists, standing straight up, and pulling his shoulders back. *Lord of Israel, empower us to conquer these heathens who are against you and your chosen people!*

Then, he looked to Shuriah, who was watching him. He knew what could be going through his mind, so he asked silently, *Lord, protect Shuriah, whom we all know is to be the greatest warrior of us all, even your anointed King David.*

Uriah maintained his intimidating physical stature as he turned to the waiting soldiers who were showing signs of weakness. He walked up a breath away from every face, piercing their eyes with a look of raging fire, which was natural for every mighty warrior going into battle.

Some stepped back, and others welcomed the aggressive stare, hoping that his fearlessness would leap onto them and take control. When he got to the last man, he gritted his teeth and looked at them all, crying out, "We are blessed to be called into this battle here and now! We do *not* focus on the battle as we fight, for that will defeat us!" He paused, looking around until he found his son. "We focus on the one we *serve* during the fight!" He pointed to the sky and screamed again, scaring some who flinched. "Victory…is the only thing the Lord of heaven's armies knows! Defeat is for everyone else!

"Some might die today, and some might live. But either way, will victory come because we are doing this because General Joab ordered it? No! We are doing this to be obedient to the leaders God puts in our paths for the progress of His kingdom first and foremost! Not the kingdom of man and what man understands."

All the men standing beside the ramming log were beginning to act like their horses just before taking off, anxiously swaying back and forth, bobbing their heads up and down as they kicked the ground, ready to explode into battle.

"Are you ready to be a sword for the Lord of heaven's armies? And pierce it deep into the Ammonites' throats?!" He had stepped up to the log that was chopped to a point and pounded it several times with the side of his fist. As though they were reading each other's minds, they all took off their large shields that were strapped to their backs. Raising them over their heads, they all roared out a battle cry.

Now energized and mentally prepared to go to battle, all forty-two of them evenly surrounded the large and heavy ramming log that was approximately forty feet long and almost four feet in diameter. There were niches carved out horizontally on the upper side of the log from one end to the other, so Uriah ordered them to secure their shields there, where they would hang out over their heads, protecting them from things coming from above.

Next, he commanded them to grab ahold of the cross-lifting beams that were evenly dispersed and stuck out several feet on each side. Once they all had a good grip, he counted down, and they lifted it up at the same time.

Straining under the weight, they all took a deep breath as they looked forward to the main gate down the road, where short, medium-width logs were spread out on the ground perpendicular to the ramming log for it to rest on. Once the ram was set on those, the soldiers would easily be able to push it, rolling it along the top of the shorter logs to gain speed and momentum to hit the wooded gate with power.

The command was given for everyone to move forward to the rolling logs. They shuffled their feet, trying to get to them as fast as possible while dodging old, damaged, and burnt-up rams and boulders that had been dropped from the high wall. With every step, they were trying to peek outside the protection of their shields (secured horizontally above their heads) to the top of the wall to see if anyone was watching or if anything was being thrown or poured down upon them.

Not seeing anything or anyone kept their spirits up and helped to propel them forward to begin this unsettling order so late in the day with so few men and no backup archers sending arrows high above them to keep the enemy at bay.

Once they got to the rolling logs, they set the ram down, gasping for breath. They stayed quiet and hidden under the cover of their shields as Uriah whispered, "We have them by surprise. We will only get a handful of times to ram this gate open wide enough to get inside until they return from following our diversion army."

One of the soldiers behind him asked, "Get inside? I thought we were only breaking the gate down, not going inside to fight?!"

Uriah turned back, answering loud enough for all to hear his full plan. He didn't want to give it until now when they were committed to the battle at hand. "It is obvious we are very few compared to what is behind that gate. If we just spend our time ramming this wall until the whole thing is down, we will be here for days without accomplishing what General Joab ordered me to do: to take the main gate today. If we can make a hole big enough for all of us to get in, we can unlock it, open it, and destroy it from the inside.

"So when all the soldiers I sent to the east gate arrive as I planned, they will be able to rush in with torches already lit to burn the city down inside."

They all digested this part of the plan that only the captain, commander, Shuriah, and he had known about, and it made sense under the circumstances. Then another soldier asked, "Why didn't you tell us the whole plan in the first place?"

Shuriah nudged his father, asking if he could answer. Uriah nodded, and Shuriah spoke up commandingly, "How much stronger have you become just now in the shadow of the God of Israel because you *had* to move forward in faith rather than through the understanding and hope in man and what you see? We only become extraordinary mighty warriors when we confront our giants, faithfully throw a small stone, and let God do the conquering for us just as our great king did when he was younger than I am now."

Uriah was caught off guard that his son would bring up such a topic, not having said a word to him that the king had given him that very stone.

CHAPTER 18

Eliam and the rest of the mighty warriors and their sons arrived at the frontline camp. They slowed their horses to a walk after running them hard to get to Uriah as fast as they could. The horses' nostrils flared wide with every breath as the sides of their bodies expanded and contracted heavily under the legs of their riders.

The powerful group wandered through the camp that appeared to be quieter and emptier than usual, stopping at the Ark of the Covenant. The four warriors standing guard were not surprised that the rest of their brothers showed up, and one blurted out with great concern, "What took you so long? We cannot leave the ark. You're probably too late!" He pointed to the top of a wall back toward the main gate of the city a fair distance away.

The warriors on the horses saw what the four on the ground were hopelessly watching: hundreds of Ammonite soldiers running along the top of the wall almost to the gate where a tiny group of men was bunched up against the battering ram that went back and forth, hitting the gate. Before they could respond, the ground beneath the horses' hooves seemed to be rumbling, but it wasn't from them. A thundering echo of battle cries could be heard as the frontline army of 3,000 ran in step but lagging behind as they paralleled the Ammonites.

All eyes went back to the main gate as the ramming stopped. The warriors on horseback stared in disbelief at the small group of men who were moments from being overtaken without the protection of a barrage of arrows darkening the sky that could have been flying up to the top of the wall.

Looking closer to where Uriah and Shuriah were, the front part of the large, ramming log had disappeared into the gate along with most of the men. Eliam roared out, "He's going in to unlock the gate from the inside!"

Without saying another word, he kicked and whipped his horse hard and rapidly took off, with the rest of the warriors and warriors' sons following closely behind to come to their aid. They raced forward, passing the thousands of men who were trampling the ground to create a dust storm and holding torches that blazed like flaming eyes through the thick air with colors of red, orange, and yellow.

The moment was intense as all the warriors watched the scene unfold with the wind in their faces, wondering what was going on inside the gate. It felt like it took forever to get close enough to start hurling arrows in attempts to stop the Ammonites and get them to back away. Leaping to the ground and swirling their bows around to the front, they simultaneously pulled back and began letting go of arrows over and over. You could hear screams as many hit their marks, and some of the Ammonites dropped forward, falling off the wall, momentarily airborne, only to have their bodies slam into the ground.

The army behind them arrived, and hundreds of archers joined the mighty warriors. Then a most unexpected sound rang out; Eliam looked to his side to see the captain racing his horse as fast as he could along the front of his men and blasting a ram's horn signaling to retreat. All the army and warriors in the Ammonite land were shocked, standing still, and completely confused at what was going on. After the captain successfully stopped the barrage of arrows that were shot in attempt to rescue those inside the gate, he fearfully eyed the mighty warriors. Turning back, he rode along the front of the 3,000 men, blowing the ram's horn again for them to go back to camp.

Before the army turned to walk away, every eye focused back on the battering ram and where it had penetrated the gate, waiting to see if their men were going to open it or burst out in retreat. As everyone held their breath, the faint sounds of a battle could be heard just inside the damaged entrance. Within moments, a roar of cheers erupted from the soldiers who had lagged in marching away, and everyone saw one side of the gate begin to open. As it moved, it was finally falling apart after weeks of being attacked and burned. Then it stopped abruptly; the tone of the voices coming out of the hole shifted as a soldier pried his body out of the opening…then another and another. All of a sudden, arrows and boulders were sent down on the men coming out of the gate.

"Warriors, protect our men!" Eliam shouted as he locked eyes with the captain riding away, insinuating, *I am going to kill you for doing what you did.*

A few dozen arrows were released several more times, but it was nothing compared to what hundreds and hundreds of arrows could have done; they would have darkened the sky and rained down on the mass of soldiers on the wall and on the other side of it. The men continued to pile out of the opening. Some barely made it to the outside before dropping dead as the soldier behind him stepped on him to get away.

Everyone watched, horrified, as soldiers were failing to make it past the end of the battering ram because they were being besieged by arrows from above. Finally, the last two out of the city were the only ones they were waiting for. Everyone believed they would get away safely. Shuriah was holding a shield in one hand to block everything coming at him while he did his best to hold up Uriah, who was stumbling forward with blood pouring down his body from stab wounds and arrows sticking out all over him.

Under the shield's protection, Shuriah looked up to where he could take his father, but there was no place to go. He happened to look farther ahead only to see thousands of his own soldiers walking away. Then his eyes caught sight of a different and smaller-looking group on horses. Focusing on them, his eyes went wide as he recognized who they were. He yelled in agonizing horror, "Mighty warriors…help!"

He stumbled over debris, getting just past the log ram. With the weight of Uriah, they both collapsed to the ground. Uriah grasped Shuriah's arm, and with all the strength he had left, he rolled himself on top of Shuriah to protect him. Holding back the pain as blood dripped from his mouth, drenching his beard, he said in choppy, slurred words, "Son…stay here until help arrives or when it gets dark. I cannot protect you more than this…"

"No, Father, let me up! I will get you help! I saw the other mighty warriors. They have come to help us!"

"Listen…listen to me, Shuriah." Shuriah tried to squirm away, but his father held him tightly. When Shuriah settled down, Uriah's eyes were heavy, and he did his best to get his words out. "My son, take my quiver…there is a very special and powerful gift at the bottom that the king gave me when I was home. I want you…to have it."

Not wanting to believe what was happening, Shuriah wrestled again and blurted out of years of deep, hidden pain from his childhood, "Don't you leave me like my mother did!"

Uriah understood the confusing pain his son was going through, so he responded softly, penetrating the intense emotions, "Through my own pains in life…I have learned you will *never* be alone, son. All the mighty warriors will be your fathers now." He grimaced in agony and added, "The Lord of heaven's armies is the Father of all…who will *never* leave you. He was with me through my early sufferings. Then…then He gave me you…and a beautiful new wife and more children."

Uriah attempted to smile and added, "The God of Israel will always have *hope*…waiting for you…as He did for me…."

"Father, please don't talk like this!" begged Shuriah, thinking of anything he could say that would keep his father alive. "You can't die in *defeat*! You're a mighty warrior!"

Uriah did his best to lift his head up high and away from Shuriah so he could look directly in his eyes. He replied with blood still dripping off his lips and nose, "This is *not* a death of defeat, son. This is a death of victory. For I have been obedient…to all authority God put in front of me. I'm…I'm dying an honorable and respectable death…as I have lived and fought in the shadow of God…serving the Lord of heaven's armies. The enemy…may have killed…a warrior in this battle. But the Lord always wins the war… remember that, my beloved son."

As his body deflated, Uriah whispered, "Take care of your sisters…and your stepmother, Bathsheba. Tell them…I love…" His words ended, and so did he, laying his head down on his son's shoulder.

Shuriah lay there in disbelief. It was only moments ago that life made sense and was moving forward in perfect order and harmony as planned. Now suddenly, there was no plan, there was no harmony, and nothing about this made sense. His mind wasn't able to comprehend that his mighty father was dead. *How could this have happened?*

As arrows from above still wisped by, hitting the ground or embedding themselves in the back of the body lying on top of him, a very sour and prickly voice spoke to him with sweet, sweet words. *General Joab, it was he who gave your father the orders that killed him.* "But why…" Shuriah asked out loud.

The proud general who thinks he knows everything has always been after you and your father. Why would he send you two and not any other warriors? Because Uriah was a Hittite, and you were his warrior son who always outwitted the general, which made him look bad.

The words took hold, giving Shuriah a sort of compass, which gave him direction, which, in turn, gave him fuel physically. The empty chasm in his chest was swiftly filling back in. But it wasn't with anything that was there before—but something completely foreign. It was dark and powerful. His teeth were gritting hard, and his jaw muscles flexed. Even though his very large father was on top of him, his lungs inhaled deeply, lifting all the weight on him. He was getting hot as his blood began to boil, working his hands in and out of fists.

He was so focused on his father and himself that he hadn't realized until they got close that the mighty warriors were yelling out to Uriah and him, hoping to find them alive. They were quickly coming to them in turtle shell formation. Arrows were heard dinging off the metal shields that surrounded the large, rounded group.

"Uriah! Shuriah!" Eliam yelled as the group safely made their way to the heap of bodies.

To the side, shields opened perfectly, and two arms reached out to grasp Uriah's arrow-littered body, sliding it into the safety of the shell. "He's dead!" one of the warriors cried out.

"Shuriah, where are you going?" Eliam called. Shuriah had

jumped to his feet as soon as his father's body was off him.

Holding his shield up with one hand to block any arrows coming his way, he looked at his grandfather with a glare none of the warriors had ever seen from the young man (and they had seen many different expressions over the years).

"What are you doing? Get in here!" one of the warriors cried out.

Shuriah finally responded with pure anger and hatred as arrows dotted the ground around him. "I will kill them all. Then—" he roared his last words—"I am going to cut the head off, General Joab!"

He turned, anchoring the shield to his back, and took off running as fast as he could down the west side of the wall toward the river. All the warriors hidden inside the shell stared in disbelief as Shuriah distanced himself from them. "What is he doing?" another asked as they enclosed the round, metal shell made from over thirty shields.

"Not sure…" Eliam responded under his breath, watching his grandson get smaller and smaller. "We need to back away. All the other soldiers are dead." They moved their protected shield back to their horses as they watched the backside of 3,000 soldiers marching away toward their camp.

Suddenly one of the warriors' sons who had stayed back on the horses pointed out and shouted, "Look, he's climbing the wall!" Every warrior and warrior son now knew exactly what Shuriah was doing, for he had played that trick on them many times in the training arena and the wall around Jerusalem.

Eliam ordered the mighty warriors and their sons to spread out wide, single file and parallel to the city wall. They were to ride hard and fast to the east gate, but then he told Itai to follow him as they diverted from the group.

Just before they took off, Itai questioned, "But what about Shuriah?"

"He is on his own now! But we can distract the Ammonites for him so he can make it over the wall and kill as many of those heathens as he can. Let's go!"

The two rode up to several of the soldiers in the massive group walking away, who still had torches in their hands, and grabbed them. Then they took off to catch up to the other warriors. The late distraction progressed just as Eliam ordered as the Ammonites followed them along the top of the wall. They failed to notice that one of the young Israelites had gone the other way and was scaling the high wall only using his fingertips and toes.

The mighty warriors successfully set fire to the east wooden gate and killed some Ammonites soldiers who showed themselves on the wall. They also managed to kill others behind the protection of the wall by silently shooting arrows over it in the last light of the day. When the sun finally disappeared, leaving a dark sky behind, the warriors watched the angry flames on the east gate. A sad and solemn moment consumed them as they all reflected on memories of Uriah, the Hittite.

Once the Ammonites had drenched the fire out with the gate still standing, the mighty warriors decided to go back to General Joab at the main camp and present him with the body of their brother, Uriah. But first, they made a stop at the captain's tent on the frontline to understand why, at the last minute, he came racing in to stop his men from helping Uriah and the soldiers.

It was easy to get the information they wanted; the captain showed them the letter, and everyone saw clearly what happened. The captain was only following orders—orders from the general that, again, made no sense.

When the warriors defiantly left the main camp earlier (going against the general's direct orders), he had ordered extra guards around his tent and stationed all the remaining 5,000 or so fresh soldiers in the camp ready for battle just in case something went wrong when the mighty warriors returned.

On their way into the main camp in the dark, the mighty warriors and their sons had split up to surround the large camp and came in one by one on horseback, targeting the general's tent. They did this just in case the soldiers they left behind had a change of heart about the mighty warriors and decided to follow the orders from the general to have them arrested or had intentions to ambush them for being rebellious.

As they each made their way solemnly through the tents and campfires, it was obvious the soldiers were given orders to act upon their arrival. But as a warrior passed a soldier, the soldier went to one knee and bowed, acknowledging to whom their loyalty really was.

They all arrived at the general's tent at the same time. Large, flaming torches were placed at each corner and on both sides of the entrance of the tent. There was an extra horse with them that had Uriah's body secured to it. Eliam, who was the one holding the reins of that horse, peered at the soldiers standing guard. The guards looked at Eliam, and they all went to a knee and remained in that position until a warrior relieved them.

Joab called to a guard from inside the tent. He didn't realize what was going on outside because everything happened quietly. When he didn't get an answer, he stormed outside, only to be face to face with a large horse staring at him. Looking up over the horse, he got his answer as to why the guards were not responding.

When he looked down at the guards kneeling (who remained kneeling even after he walked out of the tent), the general walked to the side of the horse only to see more mighty warriors and their sons staring at him with no emotion as the flames of the torches around his tent reflected off their faces.

As a strong general, he held his own. He inhaled deeply and stated authoritatively, "You all went against my direct orders not to interfere with the orders I gave to Uriah! What do you have to say for yourselves before I put you all in prison when we get back to Jerusalem?"

There was no response as the men on the horses just glared at him.

"Well, what say you? I am in command here, and I can have you all put to death!"

Eliam slowly got off his horse, walked to the horse behind him with Uriah's lifeless body, and said somberly said to the guards, "You may get up now."

They stood and backed away into their positions around the tent as the general watched closely, noting that he was no longer in charge of his own men.

Eliam stopped at the head of the body, and that's when Joab noticed it. He walked up beside Eliam and asked sarcastically, "What is this?"

Eliam gently uncovered the body that had been blanketed and responded remorsefully, "The work of your hands, general. A mighty warrior is dead."

Joab glowered at the cold face of Uriah, trying to figure out what to say. His head suddenly snapped up, looking around. When he didn't find who he was looking for, he asked in the same sarcastic tone, trying to look unintimidated, "Where is his son, Shuriah? I presume he is dead as well?"

"You presume!" a young male voice yelled from the dark behind all the other horses. Everyone heard the sound of him getting off and walking forward. The general took a step back into a defensive position, believing he spoke too soon about Shuriah being dead.

When Itai came into the light, relief broke across Joab's face, and everyone saw it, including Itai. He stepped up to the general and stated, "You're *relieved*...general"—he swung his arms around to everyone, respectfully acknowledging that Joab was the leader of them all—"that I am *not* Shuriah standing here? But you should be. For I, a warrior son, do not need to inform the general of the Israelite army who its deadliest warrior is."

He paused for a moment, letting the general soak in what he was saying, and continued, "You are the one who killed his father, not the Ammonites. The last words we heard from Shuriah were, 'I will cut the head off General Joab.' And last time we saw him, after his father died in his arms, he was climbing the high wall of Rabbah to kill everyone inside.

"If he is still alive"—Itai shrugged his shoulders, not knowing if he was or not—"we," he said, pointing to the group that had just arrived, "are the only ones who *might*...be able to protect you from getting your head cut off."

The general felt sick to his stomach, and his legs began to wobble. Trying his best not to show any weakness, he held his head high, replying, "Do not patronize me, boy! I am second in command next to King David!"

Itai gave the general a slight nod to acknowledge the general's position and answered with a subtle smile, "I am not patronizing you, General Joab. I am informing you of your possible reality." He turned and disappeared into the dark, getting back onto his horse.

Eliam covered Uriah back up as he asked loudly enough for everyone to hear, "So, General, why did you send Uriah and his son to the frontline and order the captain to have his men retreat and *not* help Uriah and his small group of soldiers?"

Joab was getting extremely frustrated by how things were going and how he was feeling; his mind was quivering, as was his entire body. But the one thing he knew he couldn't answer truthfully was the question Itai just asked. It was a secret order from the king for him and him alone. If anyone ever found out where the original order came from, he himself would be the one executed, not the warriors there on their horses who disobeyed his order.

He finally answered as wisely as he could, "Many times when one is in leadership, the leader himself doesn't understand. Yet he must confidently press forward in what he is doing and have faith in the one he serves."

With that statement, he turned and walked back into his tent. The warriors and soldiers who heard his answer were now the ones thrown off balance, questioning what his statement meant and wondering if he was talking about the God of Israel.

The night had gotten very dark, and it had nothing to do with the night sky. General Joab was in his bed, trying to sleep while four mighty warriors slept inside his tent around him for protection. Outside, four more warriors were standing guard with a dozen regular guards and hundreds of other soldiers who were remaining alert, walking back and forth through the eerie, cold, and quiet camp, watching and waiting for a possible attack from one of their own.

The night went on without anything going wrong or anyone attacking them as all the soldiers and warriors on duty relaxed, and some fell asleep. On the horizon to the east, a faint glow of light struggled to wake up the sun from where it had been hiding all night. A soldier in the middle of camp sitting next to a fire was dreamily watching the distant glow when a shooting star crossed overhead from behind him, high in the sky. As he watched it, it didn't disappear but continued getting closer to the ground. Before he realized what he was looking at, a tent caught fire where the star landed. It wasn't a falling star but a flaming arrow...

As he was beginning to shout an alarm, many more tents were set ablaze as the sky became littered with arrows flying into the camp—one after another. Yelling broke out as some men ran around, attempting to get the fires out, and others grabbed their weapons, searching around to see through the very dim light which way the attack was coming from.

What came next sent everyone running for their lives, trying to get away from an oncoming stampede of about a hundred of their horses tied together in groups. The horses jerked every which way, shrieking in horror. Some attempted to get away from the horse next to it, running, rearing up, falling to the ground, and getting back up. This caused the ropes to get tighter, escalating the mass chaos as they ran frantically, blindly destroying the whole camp.

No one knew what to do as they stared around in disbelief, running and dodging, doing their best to stay away from the beasts that could easily crush them. The mighty warriors were simultaneously thinking through their next steps concerning the general. First, they were to protect his tent from being on fire. They also needed to protect him from the mass hysteria of horses and from the enemy at hand, whom they presumed was Shuriah.

Two warriors inside the general's tent peeked outside to assess the situation, watching for any horses that might be heading toward them, while two others and a few guards attempted to put out a fire on the side of the tent. Once things quieted down inside, the warriors stepped up to the general who was standing next to his bed.

The men looked at him oddly that he was in his sleeping clothes but still had his battle cape wrapped around him. Joab didn't move or say a word as he stood up straight with a grimace of fear, which was very unnatural for him. The warrior closest to him stretched his head forward, focusing through the dim light on something out of place around the general's neck. Realizing what he was seeing, he calmly said, "Shuriah, you do not want to do this."

Everyone in the tent spotted what the warrior saw. Shuriah slowly dropped the cape that he had surrounded Joab and himself with one hand. In his other hand, he had grasped the general tightly around his neck with one of his daggers pressed up against his throat. There was a moment of silence. Then the warrior who had spoken up told a guard in the same calm tone, "Get Eliam and Itai here now."

It wasn't but moments through the loud chaos that was coming to an end as the horses were cut away from one another and the fires were put out when the large flap of the general's tent flew open. Eliam stepped in, not wanting to believe it was true that Shuriah had General Joab by the throat with a knife.

"You did it! And you're alive!" Itai said loudly with pride as he stepped in behind his father, looking at the general who was frozen in fear.

Eliam looked behind him, giving him a glare as Itai replied, "Sorry, Father." Then Ital looked back to his friend and gave him a quick smile and a nod that said, *I am glad you're here. Well done!*

Eliam took a couple of steps forward and to the side to get a clear look at Shuriah. He took it all in and asked, "Son, are you injured?"

Shuriah's eyebrows were pressed together, and the white of

his beady eyes was glowing brighter than usual. Shuriah was composed when he replied, but his teeth glowed with the same brightness because his skin was a very dark, maroon color. "No, I'm not injured. But I am…very hurt…grandfather."

"Then why are you drenched in dried blood?"

Shuriah looked around at everyone in the tent, ending at Itai, and answered emotionless, "I killed them all…."

Eyes went back and forth between the guards and warriors and then to the general whose own eyes were pleading with the men in the hopes that one would boldly step forward and save him.

"And who are these 'all' you speak of?" Eliam asked, not taking his eyes off Shuriah.

He tightened his grip on Joab, causing everyone to flinch, and said, "Every man of age behind the wall. I left only the women, children, and the elderly to live another day."

A guard spoke out of line in disbelief, "That's impossible."

Before anyone took another breath, that guard clutched his neck as the dagger that was just at Joab's neck was now embedded in his own throat. Shuriah had flicked his wrist, sending the sharp dagger on its way as his other hand brought up another from his lower back sheath, putting it to Joab's throat before anyone could react. The guard collapsed, falling forward and hitting the ground hard. No one dared to move.

Talking as though nothing happened, Shuriah said, "Now I need to finish the last thing I told you I was going to do."

Joab babbled, "No, Shuriah, please don't. I had no choice but to send your father and you to the frontline immediately!"

"You had no choice?!" Eliam barked angrily, stepping closer. When he did, Shuriah jerked Joab in front of him, saying, "No closer, Grandfather."

Joab tried to keep his mouth closed, but his lips squirmed back and forth. Then Shuriah let go with his free hand and hit him as hard as he could in the lower back where his kidney was. Joab groaned in pain as Shuriah brought his mouth up to his ear and screamed, "Answer the question!"

The pain in his back and the ringing in his ears dissolved any strength Joab thought he had. Reluctantly his eyes moved across the tent to a table that had a private, decorative box where he kept his valuables. He said defeatedly, "There. It's in there."

Everyone's eyes, including Shuriah's, followed the general's. When they saw what he was pointing at, Eliam said, "Itai, bring the box here."

When Eliam opened it and looked inside, he asked, "What am I looking for, General?"

Joab rocked his head back and forth, attempting one more time not to give in but knew it was useless, so he stated, "I will be executed for this." He slumped his head forward until the knife blade prevented it from going any farther and added, "The letter. Read the letter."

Taking the folded letter out of the box and handing the box back to Itai, Eliam saw the stamp of King David on the outside.

He looked up and said to everyone, "This is from our king."

"Read it!" Shuriah shouted, flexing every muscle in his body and bringing Joab in as close as he could.

Eliam read the letter, and when he finished, he dropped his hands to his sides and looked up in complete disbelief as an overwhelming sadness washed over him. He looked at Joab, whose eyes were now full of tears because he could tell Eliam understood the terrible position he had been put in. Disappointment permeated the tent, and everyone knew something very wrong was written in the letter from the king.

"What did it say?" Shuriah demanded, not wanting the growing softness of the atmosphere to take over his perfect plan to get to the general right from under every mighty warrior's nose and kill him in front of them all.

It appeared Eliam was going to answer, but instead, he ordered to all who could hear him, "Mighty warriors!" He glanced to the ones inside the tent who were all familiar with what he was about to say, including Shuriah, and blurted out a strategic formation, "Cage!"

Cage was a formation the mighty warriors would practice to subdue one of their own if and when one of them went out of control and had intent to harm another warrior or the king. Shuriah understood from Eliam's reaction when reading the letter who had ordered his father to the frontline to be killed. Before Eliam had gotten the words out for him to be caged, Shuriah had leaned into Joab's ear, saying, "You obediently followed orders to kill your own men. You're stronger than I thought."

Then as Eliam was yelling out his order, Shuriah let go of Joab, spun around, and bent down, picking up the large cape. As he bent down, he swiftly lifted one leg up backward, slamming the heel of his foot into Joab's face and knocking him out.

He brought the cape up, twisting around as Joab dropped straight to the floor, flaring the cape out toward everyone and letting go of it in midair. The cape opened wide like the wings of an eagle, blinding everyone who had begun to move forward to cage him in.

CHAPTER 19

After Shuriah had horrifyingly killed his way through the city of Rabbah like the angel of death cloaked in rage, spewing his hatred and revenge by slaying every soldier and eligible male left in Rabbah, he went to the general's camp for one last kill.

In the dark, he mystically made his way around all the soldiers and warriors who were keeping watch for him. One thing he hadn't planned on was running into the body of his dead father, which actually helped him by releasing a cloak of death of sorts that had its talons embedded deeply and powerfully in every pore of his body. At the sight of Uriah's body, he suddenly calmed down and began to think and act more rationally as the rabid animal within him started to disappear. His vision of everything and everyone around him became clearer with every breath, as though his spirit was reentering his body, making him whole again.

He spent a moment with his father, talking in a faint whisper, giving him love and his last respects. As he hugged him for the last time, he noticed Uriah still had his quiver strapped to his back. When Shuriah saw it, he remembered something his father had said during their last moments together. *Take my quiver.*

IN A WARRIOR'S QUIVER

There is a very special and powerful gift at the bottom that the king gave me.

It felt very odd not to know anything about this special gift. He took the quiver from his father's body and tipped it over. The smooth, rounded stone rolled out into his hand. He stared at it for a moment. Looking back into the quiver, he shook it hard upside-down, thinking there was supposed to be something different of great significance that would be made of gold, but there was only this stone.

No one keeps a rock in their quiver, he thought to himself. So, he assumed there had to be something more to the story for it to be so special. And the only one who knew what was special about it was the king.

On the backside of Joab's tent (under which Shuriah had secretly slid during the chaos of the diversions he created with the flaming arrows and stampede of horses), he had a horse himself, quietly waiting, saddled and equipped with all his weapons, shield, and supplies. His plan was to disappear into the wilderness after he cut Joab's head off, never to be seen again. But his plans had changed. He had a diversion, so to speak, going straight to Jerusalem.

Leaving the tent the way he went in, Shuriah jumped on his horse, looking down at Uriah's quiver tied to the side of the saddle with the stone at the bottom of it. *Before I kill the king, I need to find out what's so special about that rock.*

Then he reached out, leaning forward to check half a dozen ropes he had tied to the base of the horse's neck. Confirming they were secure, he smacked the rear end of the horse and kicked its sides. As it bolted forward, the sound like a whip lashed behind them; the center part of the ropes that had been lying on the ground were tied to a corner post of surrounding tents, including Joab's. When the ropes whipped tight, it jarred the horse, but it muscled forward by the prompting of Shuriah's heels to its sides.

In half a breath, the horse was freed when a post from all the tents broke free, collapsing the tents on everyone. They were dragged briefly, tripping anyone who was around before he released the ropes from horse. Once they were free, they took off running—away from the early glow of the morning light toward the river into the darkness, allowing him to distance himself from anyone who might follow.

Shuriah left behind a smoldering camp of confusion with a hundred horses trotting around, trying to calm down as soldiers ran around like ants, attempting to organize the chaos at hand. Soldiers' orders echoed in the distance as Shuriah looked back to see that no one was coming after him.

Making sure he would arrive in Jerusalem ahead of anyone he left behind to warn King David he was coming, Shuriah ran the horse to every town or farmer's house along the way and traded or stole a fresh horse. He arrived in Jerusalem in the middle of the night two days later. During his fast but long ride home, his mind and heart were still at war. He heard his father's voice proudly teaching him how to be an extraordinary warrior and to live honorably and respectfully while learning to stay in the shadow of God because the Lord of heaven's armies was always with them, moving forward in victory.

He saw past visions of training and fighting side by side with his father, the other mighty warriors, and King David, who always had a big heart, encouraging them as he led the way. Then, his thoughts went to the king, specifically when they first met and all the wonderful times they spent together, talking about deep subjects while they practiced new fighting techniques in the training arena behind the palace that he himself seemed to naturally come up with over the years, surprising everyone.

Out of nowhere, these good thoughts suddenly vanished as

the battle appeared in his mind when they entered the main gate of Rabbah. It began like every battle, fighting as mighty warriors fight with extraordinary speed and acrobatic moves. He used the long spear, impaling Ammonites low as his father's sword sliced through bodies with every swing, blocking both arrows and spears hurled at them, swiftly moving their shields all around them.

Gaining advantage inside the gate, he saw his father order the soldiers to unlock and open the badly-damaged gate for the arrival of their 3,000 soldiers so they could charge in and take the city as ordered. Then, in slow motion, he watched the first arrow pass his shield and embed deep into his father's back. The look on his father's face, as he jerked backward at the pain, made him squeeze his eyes closed on his horse, hoping the horror would go away. But it didn't stop as he saw the Ammonite soldier fight through a couple of their soldiers, impaling his father straight in the stomach as he was still arched backward in pain.

Trying to shake the nightmare, a dark, sour voice spoke at that precise moment. *It is you, Shuriah, who killed your father. You didn't block the arrow. He was only following orders, and you were supposed to protect his back while he fought...you failed!*

This vision haunted him as he tried to erase it from his mind. But vengeful words from the evil one held on, twisting his thoughts and keeping him in a cloudy state of mind. In attempts to find relief from his failure, he envisioned slicing the throat of the man who gave the order in the first place to have his innocent and loving father go to the frontline to be purposely killed—and for what?

He had gotten off the horse in the dark and was walking next to it, away from the outer city wall of Jerusalem. He bent slightly so as not to be seen but only to appear to be a horse taking a nightly stroll. Deciding not to go through the main gate and instead using his own way in, he went along the east wall, stopping at Gihon Spring to get his fill of fresh water. He also wanted to thoroughly clean the rest of his body from the dried blood that hadn't completely washed off when he went through the Jabbok River at Rabbah and the Jordan River that flowed into the Dead Sea.

When he sat down in the pool, memories flooded in of his first day in Jerusalem. He and his new father had just been bonded together to become a family after the priest sacrificed a lamb and poured its blood over their heads. Then Uriah brought him to this very pool to clean themselves, and they ended up splashing each other, enjoying a true father and son moment for the first time.

Shuriah didn't realize he had been smiling, reliving the moment, until tears began to fall from his face and reality hit him that his best friend and the only parent he truly ever knew was gone. His heart ached as he poured out the pain he had been holding inside, crying a deep and agonizing cry, shuddering his body to its core.

He got out of the water and leaned up against some rocks to dry off and calm down, but soon fell asleep exhausted. It was the distant call of a rooster that woke Shuriah up very early in the morning. Not knowing where he was for a moment, he turned quickly to each side, looking around. Calming down and feeling physically refreshed, his heart was lightened from the release of pressure last night that had been building from the pain of losing his father.

Then in his head, he could hear the same black echo reminding him of why he was here. *It is time for you to remove the head of the king.* Those vindictive words that were quenching the disaster from several days ago, alongside the joyous contentment that returned last night after his emotional release, suddenly clashed. He felt like vomiting as he whispered, "Lord, what is happening to me?"

The cry for help to the one his father always said in whose shadow to hide for protection started to calm the storm inside him. Peace was taking over. Then more words and direction from the combative, slimy voice that had begun to infiltrate him a couple of days ago asked, *Why call out for Him? Did your God protect your father? Do you still believe your God is actually with you after this tragedy of your father's senseless death?*

This tug-of-war of emotions Shuriah had never felt before three days ago was erupting again as he tried to make sense of where his life was. He laid his head back against the rocks and closed his eyes, holding his hands up to his ears to try to escape from it all. A cool morning breeze whispered across the fresh spring next to him, sending a tingling sensation throughout his body when he suddenly saw his stepmother in his mind's eye as a loving voice said, *Go to Bathsheba.*

Oddly, he ignored the vision and words at first. They were a bitter distraction, taking away from the strong battle of revenge to end the life of the one who took his father away from him.

My son, go to Bathsheba. She does not know her husband is dead. Again, the comforting voice encouraged him, but this time the distraction was sweet and made sense. He pondered as he envisioned himself telling his stepmother the news, causing her to break down in anguish while his three younger siblings attempted to understand why Daddy wasn't coming home.

Shuriah had new direction and felt good about it but didn't know why. Looking around at his situation, he cleaned off any remaining dirt and blood on his battle attire and weapons. He put it all back on, situating it as though he was marching off to war again. Looking to the horse to make sure he had everything before letting it loose, he saw his father's quiver. Taking it off, Shuriah put it around his neck and positioned it next to his.

Finally feeling he was ready, he gave the horse a slap on the backside so it bolted away. He looked up at the wall of Jerusalem and then to the small gate (only big enough for one person) next to the Spring of Gihon and walked to it. He knew there would be guards on the other side, protecting it, especially while they were at war. He contemplated if he should just knock and give his presence away or remain invisible until the moment he whispered in the king's ear, *I have come for your head, my king, and you know why. It's time a new king sits on the throne.*

Unsure why such a thought came to his mind, the ugly voice growled with pleasure, *"It is time, Shuriah—distant relative of King Saul, the first king of Israel. Remember, you were originally named after your great-uncle, Jonathan."*

For a split second, Shuriah pieced together a completely different life picture for himself but knew and felt it to be very wrong—as wrong as his father being killed in the manner it was ordered.

He dismissed the idea, accidentally saying out loud, "There is no way I could or want to be king."

"Who's there?" a guard asked demandingly from the other side of the small, heavily-reinforced door.

Shuriah vanished. He sprinted silently along the wall toward the spot he had often scaled the wall up and down from the training arena. When he got there, he made quick order to the top, knowing exactly where to place his fingers and toes.

Slithering over the top, trying not to be silhouetted by the rising sun, he planned how he was going to make it to his home (that was attached to the side of the palace) without being seen. Knowing where all the guards could clearly see and where they were located, Shuriah was able to sneak to the front door of his home safely.

When he got there, he had a smirk on his face, remembering all the times he and the other warriors' sons would sneak around, hiding, playing games, pulling off tricks on people, especially the guards, and not getting caught. Still very early in the morning, Shuriah put his ear to the door. He didn't expect to hear anyone up this early, so he didn't linger and cautiously gripped the sliding wood handle of the door. Before sliding it open, he heard movement of feet and what sounded like someone choking.

His natural instincts burst forth to help his family, so he eagerly opened the door, stepping in and drawing his battle knife, only to see Bathsheba kneeling over a bucket and vomiting. In a daze, she looked up in the oncoming light, trying to figure out who had barged into the darkness of her home.

"Mother! Are you all right?" Shuriah asked, coming to her aid.

Bathsheba jerked back, raising her arm in defense, still half asleep with an awful feeling and taste of vomit in her mouth. Unable to see clearly, she screamed, "Get out of my house!"

"Mother, it's me—Shuriah. Everything is okay," he said softly, realizing he scared her as he put his knife away.

"Shuriah?" she repeated, drawing back her hair and wiping her mouth on a cloth. "What are you doing here?" Then suddenly, excitement began to blossom in the realization that her family was back. "You're home!"

She dropped the cloth and lunged at him, giving her healthy-built young man a motherly hug. Letting go, she turned to the door; when she didn't see Uriah, she asked with a big smile, "Where's your father?!" She looked at him and then back to the open door. Then she remembered. "I forgot, the ritual meeting with the king and all the mighty warriors when they get back from war. I must have been sleeping hard and didn't hear your entry with the rams' horns coming through the city. Why are you not with them?"

She had the brightest smile. Then without thinking, she turned to a bedroom where the children were sleeping and woke them up. "Girls, wake up! Your father and brother have returned!"

Shuriah was completely out of his element; he didn't know how to handle the situation. He scolded himself silently. *Stupid! What were you thinking coming here? You should have just climbed the back wall of the palace, snuck into the king's sleeping quarters, and slit his throat. Now what are you going to do?*

"Shuriah!" the girls yelled, running out of their room and embracing their big brother they loved so much.

He knelt down, giving them all a hug at the same time. He looked them up and down and said, "Wow, you have all grown! Look at you." He grabbed ahold of them up in his long arms and stood so their heads were higher than their mother's as she walked up to them.

"You're almost as tall as Mom."

He bent down, letting go of them as they admired him with the biggest smiles (missing a few teeth here and there), and that's when it hit him. Suddenly a flood of grief boiled out of him. He felt sick to his stomach, overwhelmed seeing his two young sisters who were now fatherless, and they didn't know it. Right on key, the youngest one asked, "Where's Daddy?"

He glanced up with the wrong facial expression at the wrong time. Bathsheba immediately understood why he wasn't with Uriah at the ritual meeting—because Uriah wasn't there and would never be coming home...

Bathsheba looked away, not wanting to believe what she saw

in the face of her stepson. Trying to maintain her composure, not sure if she was going to be sick again or faint, she prodded the girls back to their room, saying, "Girls…go back to bed. It…it is still early. You can play with your brother later."

They began to whine while Shuriah did his best not to lose it himself. He helped her out, saying, "Listen to your mother. We will play later."

When they were gone, Shuriah and Bathsheba stood for a moment, staring at each other with a mutual understanding that the nightmare of going to war was now a reality. It was Shuriah, still younger at heart, who broke down first and stepped up to her as they hugged hard and for a very long time. He wanted to comfort her but was in desperate need of comforting himself. The pain of what life was going to be like without Uriah melted them to tears, quietly flowing down both of their faces.

After a while, Bathsheba backed away, and they sat down next to each other at the table. They were quiet, each reminiscing as they tried to figure out what they were going to do now. Without realizing it, Bathsheba lowered her hand off the table to hold her lower stomach; she was in a trance, staring across the room. Shuriah noticed her movement and asked in the heavy air, "Mother, are you still feeling sick? Why don't you lay down for a while?"

Bathsheba only moved her eyes to him and bent her head down to look at her inconspicuous, swelled stomach and said without any expression, "I am pregnant."

She looked back up at him to find him trying to process the news in this moment of despair. He thought instantly, *Another child without a father.* Then, he asked in a dull tone, "Did Father know before we left?"

She didn't take her eyes off of him as she replied, layering onto the dread as though she knew she were going to her own execution, "It's not your father's."

Shuriah stared in complete disbelief, thinking he heard her wrong. Tilting his head to the side, he asked calmly, "What did you say?"

"The baby, it's not Uriah's." Again, she didn't move or change her tone. She just stared at him with a blank face.

He blinked a few times like he was waking up as he gasped for air that seemed to have vanished. He shook his head as the sadness of Uriah's death evaporated. He didn't know what to say or do. He was a young, fifteen-year-old man, already emotionally, mentally, and spiritually drained, mourning the death of his father and trying to piece together the tragedy at hand. Now another death blow of a different kind snuck in and stabbed his heart from the backside.

"How...did this...when did this happen?" He shook his head again and escalated, "Why would you do this to Father? Who did you have...?" He stood suddenly, getting a visual of her and another man together, and he violently knocked his chair backward. He exploded with rage as his lungs were now full and ready for war.

In one fluid movement, he grasped his sword from behind his head and came down onto the wooden table, cutting it in half with the crashing sound echoing inside the house. He looked into her eyes as his were flaring with the fire of a mighty warrior going after the enemy.

"Mommy, Mommy, what's happening?" the older sister asked, running out of the bedroom.

Bathsheba looked at her daughter and then into a face of a person she had never seen before. Shuriah looked at his sister, holding the sword with both hands, heaving with anger and baring his teeth. Not intimidated by her older brother, who was always playing and so gentle and kind to her and her sister, she walked up to his side and looked down at the broken table. Pointing, she said, "You killed the table, but the scorpion is still alive."

Her words caught everyone's attention as they followed her finger toward a large, deadly, black scorpion crawling around on the underside of the table. Her innocence and her words overpowered Shuriah like ten strong warriors. He calmly but quickly reached out with the tip of his sword, piercing the God-sent distraction, again directing Shuriah on a new path. He stepped over to the bucket Bathsheba vomited in and dropped the unwanted killer.

"You need to be careful with your sword, brother. You could have hurt Mom. Don't you remember Father always telling you *your weapons are to be played with in the arena*?" In a cocky but fun manner, she walked back to the bedroom.

Shuriah and Bathsheba looked at each other, and that's when Bathsheba became the emotional one who broke down crying, trying to be as quiet as possible.

Shuriah inhaled deeply, thinking of what to do. He put his sword away. Then he wrapped his arm around her and walked his stepmother to her bedroom. He gently laid her down on the bed, sitting next to her as she rolled away from him in shame, saying, "I had no choice, Shuriah."

He sat, digesting what she said. Trying to stay calm, he asked, "Are you saying this man *forced* you to lay with him?"

There was a long pause. Wiping away tears, she answered, "He didn't force me but…I could *not* refuse him."

"I'm not understanding. What do you mean 'you could not refuse him'?"

Still facing away from him, she put her thoughts together and answered, "When someone in authority over you asks or tells you to do something, you do it, correct?"

"Yes, but..." His mind raced back to his father dying in his arms, saying, *This is not a death of defeat. This is a death of victory. I have been obedient to all authority God put in front of me. I'm dying an honorable and respectable death because I have lived and fought in the shadow of God, serving the Lord of heaven's armies. The enemy may have killed a warrior in this battle, but the Lord always wins the war.*

Shuriah had an overwhelming feeling as things were clicking into place in the chaotic picture that started almost two weeks ago when King David called for Uriah to go to Jerusalem without him. Shuriah gently grasped Bathsheba by the shoulder and rolled her over to face him. He had a very questionable expression as though he already had the answer and slowly asked, "Mother... who is this man of authority who put you in the situation you could not say...*no*?" He tilted his head downward at the last word, looking deep into her eyes as his forehead narrowed and his eyes pierced hers, yearning for an answer.

"Shuriah, I can't...I don't know what to do..."

The same soft but powerful voice from earlier gently nudged his pounding heart to beat to a different rhythm of compassion. It took a moment as Bathsheba cried, trying to hide her face, for him to reemerge from the building darkness within him.

Hearing his mother crying, he fully realized the trauma and dilemmas she was going through, forced to betray the man she loved. She already worried about the men in her family at war, and now she had to anticipate Uriah coming home and how he was going to handle her being pregnant.

But now, everything had changed as her worst nightmare came true. She was never going to see Uriah again; she was an adulteress widow with children who would be banished or tortured by everyone when they found out she was pregnant, not by her husband but because she had shamefully committed adultery.

"She is a widow and must be taken care of." The strong and comforting voice breathed through Shuriah as he began to look at life through the eyes of his innocent, pregnant stepmother. He wasn't sure how the words came out of his mouth, but he spoke without thinking. "Mother, you will be taken care of and protected, along with the girls and the baby in your womb."

Her emotions calmed down as she reached out for his hand. They sat there for a while, sifting through their next steps in life, when Bathsheba exposed the complete secret that had plagued her for over two months. "I had just finished my monthly bath in the cleansing pool that all women must go to after our time of bleeding—the one underneath the balcony of the rooftop on the far side of the palace. As I was coming back home, crossing in front of the steps to the main entrance of the palace, a palace servant approached me, saying the king was requesting my presence for dinner.

"I was very flattered at the invitation, thinking maybe all the warriors' wives and officials of the court would be there. That same servant arrived at my door that evening, and we went into the palace through the small entrance on the backside near the training arena." As Shuriah listened raptly, he thought to himself, *I know the entrance. It's the king's private back door for him and his servants.*

"I was escorted through a long tunnel, up a narrow staircase that entered into the back of the king's private living area. We had dinner alone, talking about the war and how all the mighty warriors were gone with most of his army. After we finished dinner," she remorsefully turned her head to the side, "is when I clearly understood his true intentions for me being there."

She held herself back from crying, and Shuriah thought he knew what she would say next. Trying to keep both of them calm, he finished calmly, "And that's when he forced himself on you."

She raised her head. "No, no, he didn't force himself on me. He was a gentleman about it...."

"A gentleman?! Are you kidding me, Bathsheba?!"

"Please, listen," she begged, grabbing his hand again. "Because of his position as ultimate authority, it obligated me to comply with his wishes. He's the king."

"*No*, he abused his authority over you by manipulating you to have sex with him." He hit the side of the bed with his other hand and added, "And the king does not have the *ultimate* authority. The *Lord* of heaven's armies is the ultimate authority! You should've denied him!"

Bathsheba sat up next to him, still holding his hand and searching for hope. She continued, "Do you not think I know that? My heart collapsed the moment I realized what I had done. Now my heart …" She started crying, letting go of his hand and dropping her face into her own hands. "My heart is dying, and my spirit for life…is withering."

He put his hand on top of her head and began to stroke her hair as she leaned into him, slowly letting out all the pent-up pain, worry, regret, and embarrassment that had been strangling her ever since she sent a letter to the king through his personal servant to let him know she was pregnant with his child.

With the full picture, Shuriah asked, "Were there any guards with you and the king from the time his servant came for you to the time the servant brought you back home?"

It seemed like an odd question, but it made her examine her memory of the evening. After walking through it all, she responded, "No, there wasn't a guard at the backdoor or in his living quarters." Shuriah responded under his breath, "That's what I thought. No eyes to see his selfish and defiant act—hiding it from his guards so they would have nothing to inform the king's most trusted people—General Joab and the mighty warriors."

Shuriah spent the rest of the morning there in his home with his family. He and Bathsheba told the girls about Uriah's death in battle and consoled them as they discussed what that meant for them as a family. While soberly sharing a midday meal on the floor (since Shuriah broke the table into two pieces), they heard the blowing of rams' horns coming from far away but getting closer and closer to the palace.

Bathsheba stopped chewing and looked at Shuriah. He didn't react, purposely ignoring it, and continued to eat as he talked with his sisters until the horns ceased (much faster than usual). That's when he glanced up to his stepmother to give her a faint, devious smile that told her, *I have more plans in being here that I haven't shared with you.*

The call from the horns told the people of Jerusalem that the mighty warriors had returned from war, during which time they would normally escort the Ark of the Covenant proudly through the city back to its home, securing it in the decorative tent next to the palace. But this time, the mighty warriors were not escorting the ark into the city but were hurriedly making their way to the palace. The ark was left behind with four mighty warriors and their sons, surrounded by the entire Israelite army of 26,000 who survived the war with the two different nations.

The warriors traveled as fast as they could to Jerusalem after Shuriah left, but he had a lead on them and was obviously much faster by himself. It would take the rest of the army three more weeks to get back after they broke down the camps and traveled carefully with the ark leading the way and General Joab in charge.

"It just struck me. You came home by yourself!" Bathsheba blurted out with a frown. "You came home in front of the Ark of God and left your father's body and the other warriors behind. Why would you do such a thing?"

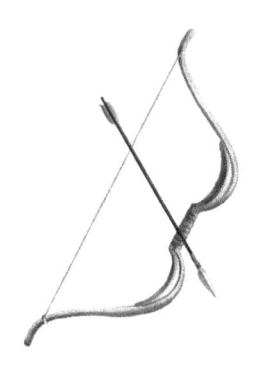

CHAPTER 20

Adjusting his attire and putting all his weapons and metal forearm and shin guards on that he had taken off to relax throughout the morning, Shuriah left his home after giving his sisters a big hug and telling them how much he loved them.

As for Bathsheba, he gave her a hug as well but then held on, whispering instructions into her ear. "Have a friend or neighbor watch the girls. Then go to the palace entrance. When you get there, tell the entrance guards you are there to see the king with the mighty warriors to discuss the death of your husband Uriah, who was just here seven days ago and slept on the outside at the palace entrance with the night guards for two nights."

She snapped her head back wide-eyed, dropping her mouth open in disbelief as he calmly continued looking into her eyes. "The warriors are marching their way directly to the king now with news and *hoping* they're not too late."

She changed her expression and asked, "Too late for what?"

Shuriah put on that devious smile and paused, looking at the girls and back to his stepmother. He whispered just loud enough for her to hear, "Finding him dead with his head cut off." He winked at her, turned, and walked out the door. Before he closed it behind him, he poked his head back in to see Bathsheba still looking at him in shock and said, "Do as I told you. Everything will be fine, Mother. For I serve the *ultimate* one in authority—the Lord of heaven's armies like Father. Remember?" He cocked his head, changing his tone, adding, "You will want to freshen up and put on your best clothes. You will be standing in front of the king here shortly."

As Shuriah walked up the steps to the palace entrance, he eyed the guards who were standing at attention. They saw who was coming and moved into a protective position as one yelled for more guards, and they pointed their long spears forward. Shuriah saw from their obvious reaction that the mighty warriors had spread the news of him and his intentions.

All right, God. What are we going to do now?

He was taken by surprise when he got a silent reply, *Walk in my shadow, for I conquer the giants and have great things coming for everyone.*

As he took his last step up onto the large platform to the entrance doors, the guards ordered, "That is far enough, Shuriah!"

With his hands freely hanging to his sides, he wiggled his fingers, mentally going through all the different ways he could kill them with the weapons he had on him. Taking a deep breath and rocking his head from side to side, he stretched his young shoulders back to loosen his body as much as he could. A loud commotion of more guards came bursting out of the entrance from within the palace and lined up with the others.

He took a slow step toward them and stopped, toying with them as they matched his step going backward. He did it a couple more times until the whole group of guards had squished themselves through the entrance and were standing inside the palace.

As he took one more step onto the palace floor, he asked,

"Guards, are we going to do this all the way down the hallway to the courtroom?"

They looked at one another, asking themselves the same question. One spoke up, asking, "Did you really kill over 2,000 men in one battle?"

The question actually surprised him on many levels, but he answered, "I never stopped to count. I was by myself in the dark, going through the city like the angel of death when our people were slaves in Egypt. The only difference was I was killing grown men... like *you*." He pointed to every one of them, smiling, and finished, "Not baby *boys*."

The men glanced back and forth to one another, getting more nervous as Shuriah crossed his arms, took a deep breath, and asked, "Men, whom do you serve?"

Again, looking at one another, they all replied in mock confidence, "King David!"

"Good answer, but who is the ultimate one in authority over us all whom man serves?" He paused and turned back, pointing to the side of the palace, saying, "Let me give you a hint: He lives over there in that tent."

Their heads followed where he was pointing and turned back to him, answering unanimously, "The Lord of heaven's armies."

"Good. Now, are you going to move out of my way or..." His hand moved to the long battle knife on his hip.

Their eyes again nervously followed his hand. Then they looked at one another, nodded, opened a path for him, and bowed their heads in submission. One answered, "We are no match for a mighty warrior who serves the Lord of heaven's armies."

When the guard called him a mighty warrior, it was the first time he thought of himself that way. *Hmm...a mighty warrior. So, this is how it feels.* Even though he had not moved a muscle, he felt as though his body stood up taller, and his chest was larger than ever before.

Concentrate. Stay in my shadow, Shuriah, the encouraging voice spoke within him as he started down the long, marble floor. Looking back, Shuriah asked, "I assume they are waiting for me in the king's courtroom?"

They all nodded, watching with a glazed look. Approaching the courtroom entrance, the guards' reaction was the same. They got into a defensive posture, and he was getting tired of the delays. "Really?" he asked sarcastically.

They paused, knowing it would be their demise to attempt to fight him. "I serve the Lord of heaven's armies. Do you have a problem with that?"

They were sweet words for a way out of the situation because they weren't ready to release their souls into the heavens, so they stepped back and opened the doors. When they swung open, all was piercingly silent, and all eyes were focused intently on him as everyone slowly repositioned themselves. He peered around, looking at all the warrior fathers and sons staring at him with inquisitive expressions. Then his eyes stopped, and his casual demeanor changed. Lowering his head, he glared across the room, focusing on one person. His fingers wiggled at his side and then turned into rock-hard fists. He inhaled deeply and bellowed the warriors' cry, "For the Lord of heaven's armies!"

Instantly all the warriors and warriors' sons on the main floor and the palace guards around the king on his throne thundered the same battle cry in his direction, shaking the palace walls as they drew their swords and pointed at Shuriah, standing all alone. The guards behind him who had opened the doors quickly retreated and closed the doors.

I am moving forward for My kingdom and My people. Stay in

My shadow, mighty warrior. The new mighty warrior didn't *hear* those words but strangely felt the power and meaning of them permeate his entire body as he stepped forward.

Relaxing his tightened muscles and releasing all the air in his lungs to empty his body of his own strength, Shuriah walked forward. He headed straight toward the king whose throne was behind the blockade of his experienced mighty warriors out front, a line of the warriors' sons, and the palace guards as his last defense. As he got closer, it was Itai who ended the silence, "Shuriah, do not do this!"

Shuriah completely ignored him as Eliam spoke up next. All the warriors started to surround him, ready to protect the king and possibly kill him. "Son, your father's death is inexcusable, but revenge by killing the king will not heal your pain. It will only add to it."

Feeling he was at the right distance (not too close to the steps going up to the throne), he stopped and stared around in a complete circle, eyeing every man whom he always considered a father figure to him. He reached back for his sword with one hand and withdrew the battle knife with his other. Holding them out in one of his deadly and intimidating positions before attacking, several men and many of the sons inhaled between their teeth, readying themselves for the fury that was about to explode.

A moment passed, and tensions peaked. Then Shuriah very slowly bowed his head and kneeled to the ground, facing the king and pointing the tip of his weapons downward, touching the marble floor.

He didn't move in the submissive posture, and one warrior whispered, "A diversion. Do not believe him."

Several others grunted in agreement, and then he surprised them by letting go of the weapons, dropping them to his sides onto the cold marble floor, loudly echoing throughout the hushed courtroom.

It took a moment before the warriors glanced at one another, questioning what he was doing. Then he reached back, grasping his daggers. The warriors' sons saw his hands disappear behind him. Believing they knew what he was doing, they reacted by pressing their bodies together and pulling their shields around from their backs to make a metal wall in front of the king.

When the daggers were out of their sheaths, he let go of them at his back and dropped his shield, adding to the metal clanking sounds. Finally, he withdrew his bow and quiver from over his head and placed them to the side. He stayed knelt on one knee as everyone observed in total confusion. Their only thought was that he was distracting them in some way to get to the king.

"I am here to talk to King David. I have...*questions*," Shuriah stated with his head still bowed, trying not to offend anyone.

David was as confused as all the others, but when he heard his name rebound faintly off the walls in his courtroom, he suddenly felt an unfamiliar fear begin to swell within him. Fighting back the fear, he had had enough of this charade and stood, raising his voice, "Enough! Step aside guards and warriors' sons."

Reluctantly they made an opening as he boldly stepped down the steps, stopping at what he considered a safe distance of a couple of body lengths. He demanded angrily, "How dare you approach my throne like this, Shuriah?!"

Silence reigned as a revived atmosphere of order appeared to have taken charge. Shuriah looked up to his king with a carefree attitude and asked, confused, "Like this? I am kneeling with my head bowed to you. What would you like me to do differently, Master?"

His words were not belligerent or disrespectful but completely innocent, with full submissive intentions. But at the same time, he had wisely shifted the new direction of everyone's perspective. The picture of who was in charge changed again, making everyone in the room, especially the king, look like fools.

Shuriah bowed his head again, staying knelt down, and everyone dropped the tension from their shoulders. They mulled over the situation, trying to come up with a different understanding of why they were all together in the king's courtroom.

"My king, I am here to ask you a question," Shuriah said with his head still bowed.

David looked around at all the warriors now surrounding him; they, too, were in a state of limbo, trying to figure out what Shuriah's intentions were now that he was unarmed. Looking back down at him, David answered, "And what is your question?"

Shuriah lifted his arm up so as not to alarm anyone, leaned back on his heels, and took off the other quiver from his back that was empty. He brought it to his front with a small grin as he scanned the mighty warriors who were waiting for him to be the Shuriah they all knew: unpredictable, boldly courageous, and not scared to do anything.

With the quiver in front of him, he asked, "My king, my father had this in his quiver and said it was a special gift from you." He tipped the quiver over, and the stone rolled out onto the hard floor. It seemed to move in slow motion, making a faint pinging sound as it bounced around. It stopped directly at the feet of the king, and he stood frozen, wide-eyed, for all his most trusted men to plainly see. They had never seen such fear and remorse radiate from their master.

The mighty King David stared at the stone and crumbled to his knees, now the one in complete submission—not to a person but to what the stone represented. That moment the stone delivered a powerful, new message to save him from the greatest battle that takes place (of which he was hopelessly losing)…not the battles with spears and swords, but the battles in hearts that cannot be won with worldly weapons—only by doing one thing.

In a submissive posture, seeing the small rock with which he had killed a giant many years ago, David clearly saw the giant that was in his heart, created by his own doing. There was no way this giant could be defeated by physical force or crafty human diversions, for they had already failed.

Surrender…surrendering was the only way out of this war. The king had deviated from the shadow of God and moved forward on his own, submitting to selfish desires and knowingly breaking laws of man and God. At the same time, he had tied a noose around another's neck, who was completely innocent. He had tried to cover up his sin by killing an obedient and respectful warrior and friend who had nothing to do with his fatal end.

By submitting all of himself (mind, body, and spirit) as a sacrifice to the ones around him and to God, whom he loved so much, David was overwhelmed with a fresh, new sensation of freedom and courage. Visions of impossible situations in his past that had gloriously become possible came to King David. A new king was suddenly emerging as he heard words within him, saying, *I love you and always will, David. Trust in Me, and this giant will be slain. For I, and I alone, win these wars.*

Shortly, tears started rolling down the king's face. Shuriah stood, glancing around at the warriors. He stepped up to his king, kneeling at his side. Shuriah could see that something of great sorrow gripped the king, which meant it gripped the kingdom of Israel as well. Loud enough for all to hear, he said softly, "Master, what is this?"

"It…It is the stone…I killed Goliath with."

Tingling sensations shot through the courtroom, crawling up everyone's backs. They now understood there was much more to this story—a very different and unexpected situation for everyone except for the one with his arm around the king, seemingly consoling him. All eyes were searching for where this was going when suddenly, Shuriah raised his head and smiled at all the warriors.

They gasped, seeing his face and his marvelous diversion to get to King David, now practically with his arm around the king's neck.

No one moved, thinking that if they did, the new mighty warrior could easily kill him instantly. Then, as though perfectly planned, everyone heard a loud knock at the entrance door of the courtroom. A guard opened one of the doors, and everyone looked back and forth between the entrance and Shuriah, waiting to see if he was really going to end the life of the king.

Shuriah looked up to see his beautiful stepmother gently step into the room and pause, looking at all of them. Then her demeanor changed as she crossed the courtroom floor and stopped an arm's length from the emotional king.

Bathsheba studied the scene before walking forward, knowing a woman would not be allowed in the room, especially with the king on his knees and appearing to be crying. She thought she should turn around and leave, but then, God whispered, *Continue. The King of kings will come from your womb.* It was the most magnificent experience she had ever had in her life, and it only lasted for ten unspoken words.

"Bathsheba!" Eliam exclaimed, taking control of the situation. "Daughter, you are not to be here. Leave the king's presence immediately!" He pointed a finger back to the door.

"I don't think so, Grandfather." Shuriah stood, walked to his stepmother's side, looked down at the king, and asked bluntly, "King David, the king of Israel, the anointed one by God, I have one more question for you. Please tell us why you gave this special gift to my father. I presume you gave it to him while he was here seven days ago. I don't believe he had any idea why you gave it to him."

"Shuriah! Enough! You know your place!" Eliam shouted.

David raised his hand to quiet the growing argument and then cleared his face, attempting to compose himself as he looked at the most beautiful woman he had ever seen. Then he made a special hand gesture meant for a servant and said aloud, "Bring me…the sword of swords."

All heads had turned to David and his servant. Everyone knew exactly what sword he was talking about, so they tried to put this new piece of the puzzle together between the stone, Bathsheba being there, and now this magnificent sword. They also wondered what Shuriah was up to; he hadn't done anything yet that would indicate he had any intention of killing the king like he said he was going to.

When two servants arrived, each holding one end of the sword, they bowed, presenting it to the king, who was still kneeling. He shook his head and pointed to Shuriah. The servants bowed, holding out the sword to Shuriah instead. He hesitated and then took ahold of the beastly weapon, straining at first to hold it up.

David looked around to the warriors who assumed he was going to speak, and he confessed in anguish, "I have sinned against Uriah!" He paused as they continued trying to make sense of the drama over the last few days, thinking he was only talking about the order he gave for Uriah to go to the frontline.

The king looked to Shuriah and said, "You are the man of

your home now and a mighty warrior." Shuriah shifted his expression. "Yes, they informed me that you killed more than 2,000 enemies in one battle, which is many, many more than any one of us. You single-handedly ended the war in one night." He paused again and looked at Shuriah, knowing the feeling of a great victory from when he was a boy who did the exact same thing in front of King Saul and the whole Israelite and Philistine armies. Shrugging his shoulders, he said, "But I'm not surprised."

Bathsheba turned her head to Shuriah with wide eyes of wonder, having no idea her stepson had accomplished such an impossible and amazing feat.

"Shuriah, mighty warrior, there is one more enemy you must put to death for me before this war is completely over." His statement confused them all except for Shuriah. The others were starting to murmur, asking who this "other one" was, until the king dropped forward on all fours with his head extended. Shuriah again adorned that wicked smile now that he had the king's permission to kill him (as evidenced by his prostrate posture).

Shuriah was still holding Goliath's giant sword in front of him, pointed upward. As adrenaline rushed through him at the excitement at hand, all the warriors bounded toward him to stop him from cutting off the king's head.

"Stop this madness!" Bathsheba cried out, piercing everyone's ears in her desire to end this nightmare. The high-pitched scream of the only woman in the room slapped the warriors, stopping them in their tracks. Shuriah had never moved a muscle toward David. King David knew this was the moment he needed to fully surrender and confess from his heart as he sat back on his heels and held his head up, saying, "I am the enemy that must be put to death for the crimes I committed against Uriah."

A new word (plural no less), "crimes," engaged different emotions in the battle-worn men who were trying to protect their king. *What did he mean? What did he do?* the men asked themselves, waiting for an explanation. Never in his life had he exposed so much weakness and wanted to disappear as he tipped his head forward, eyeing the floor as his heart ached enough to vomit.

Surrender, letting go of your understanding, and you will be free, David. God's loving voice reached out for him to come all the way back into His safe and powerful shadow.

Taking a deep breath, David leaned back up on his heels and again looked around at all the men who, this time, were staring back with dismal and lost expressions. Meanwhile, his own face had begun to refresh and get brighter as he looked at Shuriah, saying, "Thank you, Shuriah, for wisely bringing me to my knees. I have sinned, as I said, against your father two times. But most of all, I have sinned against the God of Israel by stepping out of His shadow."

He now looked boldly into the beautiful eyes of Bathsheba and explained loudly, "I…seduced Bathsheba to lay with me while you all were at war. Because of my authority over her, she submitted for I am her king. She has no sin in this because I was the one who sinned against God."

No one dared to move or breathe except for Shuriah. They felt that just by blinking, they could be struck down by God for being in the presence of this full, open-hearted confession of the king of Israel, the anointed one of God.

"I then sinned again by murdering Uriah, sending him to the frontline at the main gate, and then ordering the soldiers to draw back and not help him…all because he obediently kept an oath that I created to make us strong and united.

"I called Uriah here so that he would sleep with his wife"—he looked to Bathsheba—"but he never did. He slept both nights at the palace entrance, even when I got him drunk. He was faithful to his king, his brothers of war, his wife, and to himself. But it doesn't stop there. The whole time he was here, what concerned him more than anything else…." David pursed his lips and wrinkled his forehead as tears poured down his face. He tried to control his emotions and continued, "He was worried that he was not at the front, protecting the Ark of the Covenant." A boldness started to erupt within him because of Uriah's actions. "The God of Israel was not only on his mind but was completely in his heart!"

David pounded his chest and yelled angrily, "He wasn't even an Israelite! He…*he* was the faithful one to God, not me!" He reached over, picked up the stone, and lifted it up for all to see, explaining, "I gave Uriah the stone as a gift out of guilt because he was the one who deserved it…not me."

He looked up to Shuriah and said fearlessly, "Shuriah, the leader of the household of Uriah, you may do with me what you want, for my life has now become yours."

The warriors cut into the conversation in a roar of voices that rose up in defiance. They believe Shuriah needed more maturity to make a decision like this, even if he *was* a mighty warrior now. Shuriah took a step forward to the kneeling king, and the warriors immediately went silent, holding their breath and hoping the inevitable wasn't going to happen right there before their eyes.

"Shuriah, please don't," Bathsheba petitioned, stepping up calmly to reach for his arm.

He looked down at her hand and then up to her eyes, giving her a wink to let her know everything was fine. He turned his back to the king and dropped the tip of the sword to the ground making a hard *thud*. He held onto the handle up by his neck and proudly announced, "If I was going to kill you, Master, you would have been dead a day ago." He turned to all the warriors and shook his head; they knew this was true.

Seeing Eliam's face, he stopped and asked him to step over to them. Eliam glanced around at his brothers but complied. Now side by side, Shuriah looked up at Eliam with his large, black, and graying beard and nudged him like he used to when they played games or tricks on each other. He was telling his grandfather to relax; everything would be fine.

Looking back to King David (still on his knees), Shuriah said, "There is one more thing you need to confess to Bathsheba's father and tell him the news."

King David's eyes got big, realizing that Shuriah had talked with Bathsheba and knew the secret that caused all the issues with Uriah. He looked to Eliam, knowing he had a temper himself and that, at his age, he really did not care about holding back his emotions because everyone honored him as an elder.

"What news is this you have for me, Master?" he asked in a deep voice, already having an inkling what the news may be. He looked over to his daughter, who looked away with embarrassment.

One by one, all the warriors came to the same conclusion. Some put their hands to their mouth, trying not to laugh, while others made cautious and wary sounds, knowing Eliam could lose his temper but wouldn't physically harm the king.

David felt like a boy who had to confess to his father for doing a bad thing. Sitting on his heels, he swayed his head back and forth, embarrassed. He raised his hands (one still holding the stone) and lifted his shoulders as he said softly, "Bathsheba is pregnant."

"What? Could you say that louder? I didn't hear you. Remember, I'm an old man." Eliam had lifted a hand to his ear and tilted down toward the king, playing with him.

David nervously shifted and repeated loud enough for everyone to hear, "Bathsheba is pregnant."

The courtroom was silent. Again, no one knew what to do; the king was usually the one to tell them what to do. And if he or General Joab wasn't around, it was usually Eliam who prodded everyone on what to do.

After everyone looked at one another, Shuriah came to the rescue by switching the attention away from the shame of the king, "My father, Uriah, needs to be honorably entombed. For he was a great father"—he turned to Bathsheba with a smile—"and a great husband."

He looked around to all the eyes focused on every word he was saying, eyed the king, and ended by saying, "But ultimately, he was an obedient warrior—proving to his dying words that men are slain in battles, but the God of Israel always wins the wars!" He emphasized the last word, raising Goliath's sword as tears of joy ran down his face.

Without hesitation, the warriors were all thrilled to be relieved of the moment and resounded in agreement. They raised their swords in respect of their fallen warrior brother. David went to stand to join them in celebration, but Shuriah shook his head, indicating that he wasn't finished.

After it quieted down, the new mighty warrior continued confidently, "Master, you said I am now the head of my house. So, my first decision is for my family. After my father is given up to the Lord of heaven's armies, *you*, my king"—he paused, looking up to Eliam and over to Bathsheba—"will be marrying my mother, taking in all my little sisters, and making room for… *this* old man." He was now pointing with both hands at Eliam, who had just realized he was being made fun of. He gave his grandson an intimidating frown. Then he slowly smiled at the idea, looking to the king, who would be his new son-in-law. He studied the highly decorated courtroom and wondered what his area of the palace was going to look like.

A roar of laughter echoed through the courtroom as everyone finally began to recover emotionally and mentally from what could have been one of the most tragic things to have ever happened to Israel. As Shuriah was gallantly parading Goliath's sword around, pointing it up high, he looked down at King David and told him to stand with the stone in his hand.

When he stood up next to Shuriah, he looked around at his other mighty warriors, their sons, and his palace guards. He raised the small stone for everyone to see that God Himself had won another war. Then he yelled in joyful jubilance, "The Lord of heaven's armies will *always* defeat our giants!"

Old General Shuriah and his fleet of forty-five ships had finally arrived at their first destination on the southern shores of Hatti. They were on this epic journey for King Solomon to move Noah's Ark and replace it with a phony replica.

General Shuriah himself had found the ark over a year ago in its icy tomb on Mt. Ararat in northern Hatti. It would take them approximately two years of extreme, hard labor to accomplish this impossible task. They then must stay and wait with the ships for the army of the Queen of Sheba to arrive with instructions on where the ark's final destination will be. They were to move it somewhere deep in the queen's southern lands far away.

As instructed, Shuriah's ship captains gathered all the people on the journey, including wives and their small children, at the base of a high point where he was waiting as he took a position above everyone so they could all hear him speak.

Once people settled down from the excitement of being on dry land after weeks of fighting waves, sporadic weather, and grueling rowing, he had their undivided attention. Anticipation grew among the thousands staring at him. Clearing his throat and inhaling deeply, the highly respected and honored general began his speech.

"Israelites and our loyal allies from Tyre, life takes us down many paths. A few we plan, and we may be able to anticipate the outcome. But as with the wind, most of our lives, we cannot see these paths or know where they are going. We have many surprises along the way—some caused by our own choices, others from the unexpected. Pain and suffering are on some of the paths, and healing and prosperity are on others."

He looked into the anxious eyes of those who were following him on a path to an unknown destiny. Seeking the right words, he continued, "Hope will always be in front of us!

"What you and I"—he pointed to them and then to himself—"must always remember who is the one in *authority* over us during this epic journey and forevermore.

"It will *not* come from our strength and understanding! It will not come from me! And it will not come from our wise King Solomon!" He paused, feeling the golden signature ring that came with Solomon's authority, and continued, "It is the authority of the *only* one who can conquer our giants." He glanced at his mighty warriors and their sons with a fiery excitement beginning to bubble over as he reached high behind his head and pulled out the grandest sword anyone had ever seen.

Raising it powerfully with both hands to the sky, a rumbling emanated from his warriors and the thousands of soldiers who all knew what his next words were going to be. Seeing the sword, they roared at the top of their lungs in this climactic moment in history, "To the Lord of heaven's armies!"

The echo of excitement took a while to simmer down as General Shuriah lowered the heavy sword and said peacefully, reflecting back to his father dying in his arms, "As I said, hope will always be in front of us. But *only* if we stay in the shadow of God."

ABOUT THE AUTHOR

Having a genuine servant's heart to help others grow personally, professionally, and relationally describes D. L. Crager. His plethora of life experiences and mature relationship with Jesus is what inspires him to write incredible novels. He expresses himself emotionally and energetically and encourages people through descriptive word pictures and exciting stories, which ignite his reader's imagination.

All of D. L.'s books are filled with with adventure, mystery, and even a touch of romance here and there. His philosophy is: a book is not considered finished until it makes real-life connections for the readers and gives them a greater understanding of themselves, the world around them, and their personal relationship with God.

He's been asked many times, "Why do you write Christian fiction novels?"

His answer is simple: "There is an overwhelming need in our world today for the type of captivating and entertaining novels I write. Even though they have fictional storylines, the books are astonishing, insightful, and exciting for young teens on up, and for men and women alike."

Without a doubt, D. L. Crager is quickly filling the gap in Christian literature that will be read and talked about for generations.

Milton Keynes UK
Ingram Content Group UK Ltd.
UKHW020625270524
443037UK00020B/619